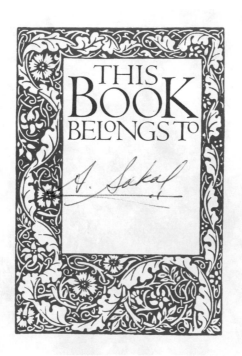

THIS
BOOK
BELONGS TO

# THE
# EROTIC
# IMAGINATION

*[This] is a book to be read only by the sexually mature and psychically balanced. In its psychopathic effects it might prove dangerous in its influence over the neuropathically unstable. To the prurient curiosity of that morbid sexual element, which too extensively abounds in modern social life, its examples and personal histories would prove psychopathic poison.*

*From a review of*
Psychopathia Sexualis
*in* Alienist and Neurologist, *1893*

**IDEOLOGIES OF DESIRE**

**David M. Halperin**
**Series Editor**

# THE
# EROTIC
# IMAGINATION

*French Histories
of Perversity*

**Vernon A. Rosario**

**New York · Oxford**
**Oxford University Press**
**1997**

Oxford University Press

Oxford   New York
Athens   Auckland   Bangkok   Bogotá   Bombay
Buenos Aires   Calcutta   Cape Town   Dar es Salaam
Delhi   Florence   Hong Kong   Istanbul   Karachi
Kuala Lumpur   Madras   Madrid   Melbourne
Mexico City   Nairobi   Paris   Singapore
Taipei   Tokyo   Toronto

and associated companies in
Berlin   Ibadan

Library of Congress Cataloging-in-Publication Data

Rosario, Vernon A.
The erotic imagination : French histories
of perversity / by Vernon A. Rosario
p.  cm.   — (Ideologies of desire)
Includes bibliographical references and index.
ISBN 0–19–510483-8 (cloth)
1.  Erotica—France—History—18th century.
2.  Erotic literature, French.
3.  Sex customs—France—History—18th century.
4.  Hygiene, Sexual—France—History—18th century.
I.  Title.   II.  Series.
HQ463.R545   1997   306.7'0944—DC21   96–29552

Earlier versions of some material have been published:
"Phantastical Pollutions: The Public Threat of Private Vice in France" and "Introduction: The Politics of Solitary
Pleasures," (co-authored with Paula Bennett) in *Solitary Pleasures: The Historical, Literary, and Artistic Discourses of
Autoeroticism*, ed. Paula Bennett and Vernon Rosario (New York: Routledge, 1995). Reprinted by permission of the
publisher.

"Pointy Penises, Fashion Crimes, and Hysterical Mollies: The Pederasts' Inversions," in *Homosexuality in Modern
France*, ed. Jeffrey Merrick and Bryant T. Ragan, Jr. (New York: Oxford University Press, 1996). Reprinted by
permission of Oxford University Press.

"Inversion's Histories/History's Inversions: Novelizing Fin-de-Siècle Homosexuality," in *Science and Homosexualities*,
ed. Vernon Rosario (New York: Routledge, 1997). Reprinted by permission of the publisher.

1 3 5 7 9 8 6 4 2

Printed in the United States of America
on acid-free paper

To A——,
*who fires my imagination*

# CONTENTS

# ACKNOWLEDGMENTS

In the process of writing this book, I have sometimes felt like a mere organic computer accessory inputting a text composed by dozens of teachers, colleagues, students, and friends who have inspired me over the years. This book exists thanks to all of them. I am grateful to Paula Bennett, Allan Brandt, David Halperin, Anne Harrington, Dorothy Porter, and, especially, Robert Nye who all guided me through my research and writing. Many other colleagues provided invaluable comments and insights along the way, including Henry Abelove, Emily Apter, Joel Braslow, Kent Brintnall, Robert Grimm, Sandra Harding, Andrew London, Henry Majewski, Jeffrey Merrick, Peter Redfield, Henry Rubin, Margaret Schabas, Lawrence Schehr, Eve Kosofsky Sedgwick, Thomas Spear, James Steakley, and Sharon Traweek.

I am grateful for many informal, informative conversations and the unflagging support of my friends Garland Allen, Kaila Compton, Irv Cummings, Daniel Delgado, Sandi Dubowski, Harlan Lane, Elizabeth Moodey, Fergus O'Reilly, Frank Philip, Richard Pillard, Micheline and Edward Rice-Maximin, Susan Rosenfeld, Ed Scarcelle, William Summers, Denis Sweet, and Chris Thorman.

I can only collectively thank the numerous scholars in feminist and queer studies whose pioneering work has opened up controversial and socially transforming fields of research. Their brief mention in the endnotes hardly does them justice when every thought I have is inflected by their wisdom and courage.

Kind and knowledgeable librarians at Holmes Hall in the Countway Medical Library, the Bibliothèque Nationale, the Bibliothèque Henri Ey, the Faculté de Médecine de Paris, and the Louise M. Darling Biomedical Library have placed all sorts of precious documents at my fingertips. I am grateful to the administrative staff in the Department of the History of Science at Harvard, the Harvard Medical School—M.I.T. Division of Health Sciences and Technology, and the Department of History at U.C.L.A. who helped me navigate bureaucratic mazes. T. Susan Chang, my editor at Oxford University Press, has been enormously supportive and patient in coaxing me through revisions.

My research and writing were sustained by the following sources: a National Science Foundation Graduate Research Fellowship, a Henri Lurcy Foundation Traveling Fellowship, a Deutscher Akademischer Austauschdienst Fellowship, a SmithKline Beckman Medical Perspectives Fellowship, the Clendening Traveling Fellowship in the History and Philosophy of Medicine, the U.C.L.A. Center for Cultural Studies of Science, Technology, and Medicine, the U.C.L.A. Center for the Study of Women, and the Mellon Fellowship in the Humanities at the University of Pennsylvania. I greatly appreciate their support.

## Note on Translations and Citation System

Unless otherwise noted, all translations are mine. I have rendered foreign-language titles into English. Medical documents are cited by the original year of publication, and well-known literary works are cited by their title.

# THE
# EROTIC
# IMAGINATION

# INTRODUCTION

## *In Quest of Erotism*

> Often eroticism is just a manifestation of illness, exhibited as a
> more or less marked symptom in a syndrome of manic exaltation.
>
> Dr. Joseph Guislain (1852)

**W**hat is the origin of the "erotic"? The question seems unanswerable in the contemporary Euro-American context, where the erotic leaks out of the confines of the imagination and the bedroom to saturate all aspects of everyday life. Titillating images are almost numbingly omnipresent. Could anyone imagine selling alcohol, cigarettes, motorcycles, or perfume without at least a soupçon of eroticism? This ubiquity masks the haziness of the subject matter: What *is* the erotic? A dictionary definition—"of, devoted to, or tending to arouse sexual desire"—fails to capture the erotic or its mechanisms of action, which are as diverse and ambiguous as they are controversial.

From the municipal level to the United States Supreme Court to international courts, some of today's most heated legal battles concern the definition and regulation of the erotic: pornography, censorship of sexually explicit art, sexual harassment, red light district zoning, AIDS education, sex surveys, same-sex marriage, and "indecent" material on the Internet, to mention only a few. Fascination with eroticism shifts quickly from prurient curiosity to politico-moral inquisition as the public scrutinizes transsexuals on the "Oprah!" show, J. Edgar Hoover's alleged homosexuality, Manuel Noriega's pornographic predilections, Saddam Hussein's supposed penchant for transvestitism, or politicians' sexual peccadilloes.[1]

Individuals' erotic desires and the societal erotic imagination are confluent, but their sources are multiple and murky. It would be short-sighted to trace our current obsession with the erotic only as far back as the 1960s "sexual revolution," the Beat Generation, or even Sigmund Freud's sexual analyses of the psyche and of culture.

A hundred years ago, sexuality was already being declared a powerful personal and social drive. Ernest-Armand Dubarry, a journalist and scientific popularizer,[2] penned *The Insane Lovers,* a series of melodramatic novellas. To justify these potboilers, he declared:

> Sexual life occupies such a high position in social life, even national life; it plays such a major part in our thoughts, our acts, and has such great influence on us all, that to neglect this power that leads us, under the pretext of not shocking the ears of rigid prudes, is the height of absurdity and foolishness. (1896b, 8)

While Dubarry insisted on the social importance of discussing sex, he also recognized this as a perilous enterprise. To legitimize his representations of the erotic, he deployed medical protagonists who deliver lengthy, well-documented lectures on "perversions of the sexual instinct." In one introduction, Dubarry borrowed the oft-cited apologia from Ambroise Tardieu's treatise on rape and sodomy: "No physical or moral misery, no wound, however corrupted it be, should frighten those devoted to the science of man; the sacred ministry of the doctor, in obliging him to see all, also permits him to say all."[3] Dubarry warned that to silence his "psychopathological passional novel series" would be tantamount to covering up a political scandal. Science was a "common patrimony," he exclaimed: it should not be "confiscated" by any one group but had to be employed by all for the sake of social education and salvation (7–9).

Dubarry's posturing betrays his awareness of the fact that contemporary medical literature was the only legitimate place for representations of the erotic. But was this medical concern with individual and national sexuality an ancient professional prerogative? Or, to rephrase my opening query: Is there a genetic history of the erotic?

In this book I investigate sexual pleasures: their genesis, history, mechanics, and effects. I argue that all eroticism in the modern Euro-American context is perverse because of the way sexual behavior and fantasy were theorized by physicians since the eighteenth century.[4] My focus is on France not simply be-cause of the enduring allure of steamy French eroticism (for example, heady perfumes, the films *Belle de Jour* and *Last Tango in Paris,* or Ravel's *Bolero.*) The mystique of *l'amour fou* is the product of a French "perversification" of sexuality that arose through the circulation of sensual stories, medical ideas, and literary styles among French physicians, novelists, and sexual "perverts" who populate the pages of post-Revolutionary medical and literary texts.

Victorian doctors and laymen in Britain and America believed France was a pernicious source of erotic literature.[5] Initially, they thought perversity was almost exclusively a French disorder. For example, in praising the transla-tion of Léopolde Deslande's French treatise on masturbation (1835), Dr. Samuel Woodward, superintendent of the Worcester Insane Hospital, never-theless noted: "The opportunities for discovering [masturbation's] extent with females is much greater in France, than in this or perhaps any other country" (1839, 348). In a review of Continental works on "perverted sexual instinct," Drs. Shaw and Ferris of New York observed that "no cases that we are aware of have been published in America" (1883, 185). For these distressed physi-cians, "sexual perversity" was a culturally and temporally variable phenome-non: it had spawned on the Continent and might spread to America. Thus, while physicians deployed biological theories to explain erotic pleasures, these scientific ways of understanding sensuality are also historically and socially contingent.

## Erotic Appetites

The first French use of *érotique*—in the contemporary connotation of *sexual* rather than *amorous*—is surprisingly recent.[6] It only emerged in 1825, not in a licentious novel or sexual treatise, but in the seminal text on gastronomy: *The Physiology of Taste, or Meditation on Transcendental Gastronomy* by the jurist, politician, and gourmand Anthèlme Brillat-Savarin. This eclectic amalgam of anecdotes, recipes, and philosophical musings is an amiable parody of earlier sensualist scientific texts and marks the epitome of a literary fad for "physiolo-gies" of various professions and even marriage.[7]

By Brillat-Savarin's own admission, medicine was his mania and he con-sidered himself an "amateur doctor" (27–34). He cultivated close links with the medical profession and it was his friend Dr. Richerand who convinced Brillat-Savarin to publish his treatise on food. His happiest day, Brillat-Savarin con-fides to us, was when he was mistaken for a great physician while attending

Dr. Hippolyte Cloquet's medical lectures (34).[8] Like Cloquet, Brillat-Savarin was intrigued by the relationship between taste, odors, and emotions. His researches led him to invent an "irrorator": a little, mechanized room deodorizer to boost people's mood (34).

The "erotic" emerges, curiously enough, in his discussion of truffles: the black, dense, spherical fungus with a pungent perfume. "Who says *truffle*," declared Brillat-Savarin, "pronounces a great word that awakens erotic and gourmand memories amongst the sex in skirts, and gourmand and erotic memories amongst the sex with beards" (100). The mysterious and succulent truffle can serve as a metaphor for the erotic imagination itself: "The origin of the truffle is unknown," explained Brillat-Savarin, "one finds it, but we know neither how it is born nor how it grows" (100).

However enigmatic its origins, the truffle—like the erotic imagination—nevertheless has a cultural history. The ancient Romans appreciated the Greek, African, and Libyan truffles, claimed Brillat-Savarin, but the fungus disappeared from all records of human gastronomy after the Latin Decadence. Brillat-Savarin's contemporaries had witnessed its resurrection, and in the 1820s "the glory of the truffle [was] at its apogee" (101). Every fashionable dinner had to have at least one truffled dish. In part this was due to food merchants who, observing the growing popularity of the costly delicacy, had combed the countryside for them and expedited them to the cities. But why had truffles captivated the palate?

Brillat-Savarin believed it was due to the general conviction that truffles "predispose one to genesic pleasures" (102). This word *génésique,* also of his coinage, first appears as the "genesic sense" in his meditation on the senses. He accused philosophers of seriously neglecting or misunderstanding this all-important sixth sense of "physical love, that draws the sexes one to the other, and whose goal is the reproduction of the species" (39). Nevertheless, in the evolution and perfection of the human senses, it was the genesic sense that had "invaded the organs of all the other senses" (40). Since the Renaissance, particularly in France, this "capricious and tyrannical sense" had stimulated romantic love, coquetry, and fashion—the "three great motors of contemporary society" (41).

He even attributed the "genealogy of the sciences" to the human drive to gratify the genesic sense: "In looking more closely, one will see that all the most delicate and ingenious that [the sciences] have to offer is due to desire, hope, and gratitude, which are related to the union of the sexes" (41). As we will see in the Supplement, he was not the last analyst of sexual desire to propose that the erotic drive had spurred science and all of Western civilization.

Fancying himself a man of science, Brillat-Savarin wanted to test the popular belief in the "erotic virtue" of truffles, "to know if the effect is real and the opinion founded in reality" (102). However scabrous and comical such research might be, he was certain that "all truth is worth discovering." But how to research the subject? He turned to women. Only one, however, was thoroughly candid. "I will let her speak," he writes.

His informant recounts a domestic supper in the company of her husband and his friend, Verseuil, a frequent guest and a handsome young man of some wit. The otherwise light meal nevertheless stars a superb truffled fowl. Called away on business, her husband thinks nothing of leaving his wife and Verseuil alone. "At first the conversation revolved around the most inconsequential subjects," she reports, "but soon it took a turn for the more intimate and exciting. Verseuil was successively flattering, expansive, affectionate, caressing, and, seeing that I did nothing except laugh at these amusing proceedings, he became so insistent that I could no longer misinterpret his intentions." Suddenly she comes to her senses and narrowly escapes with her virtue unsoiled by insinuating that his desires will be satisfied another day. Escaping from his clutches, she collapses in her bedroom, exhausted.

Only the following day does she judge her conduct reprehensible. Her pride should have been alerted earlier; she should have silenced Verseuil's first phrases and not lent herself to a "conversation that presaged nothing good. . . . What can I tell you, Monsieur? All of this must have been on account of the truffles; I am truly convinced that they gave me a dangerous persuasion; and although I have not renounced them (which would be far too severe), at least I never eat them without their pleasure being tempered with a bit of distrust" (103). The truffle sparks a double incitement to discourse and to erotism.[9] It stimulates both Verseuil's lascivious conversation and the lady's picaresque confession, which, despite the sober conclusion, has all the flavor of popular licentious literature (and may well be a fiction spun by Brillat-Savarin himself).

Distrusting a woman's confession, however, Brillat-Savarin consulted several men to arrive at the conclusion that the truffle was not a "positive aphrodisiac" (104). Its erotic virtue did not arise from any biochemical action on the genesic sense, but from the situational license afforded "the great word" truffle by the cultural associations between the savory fungus and erotic memories. Even while he claimed his own research concerned *natural physiology,* he also recognized that objects and practices, like words and beliefs, all have *cultural histories:* "In any case, how could words not change when customs and ideas undergo constant modification? If we do the same things as the Ancients, we do not do them in the same manner, and there are entire pages in some French books that could not be translated into Latin or Greek" (37). He would probably be the first to affirm that the sexual "erotic" was not so much a radically new phenomenon as a new expression of altered customs and ideas.

In addition to this nominalist and discursive approach to a cultural history of the erotic imagination, I have taken another cue from Brillat-Savarin: to turn to the erotic confessions of individuals and to "let them speak." As he noted, his contemporaries were quite reticent on the subject of the genesic sense, but one medium insisted that Truth knew no shame: scientific literature. Of course, we must be skeptical of this claim, and of patients' freedom to voice their truth under the glare of the medical examination lamp. Nineteenth-century medicine did, unquestionably, offer an unprecedented platform for the exploration of sexual pleasure. Historian Michel Foucault only fleetingly acknowledged that the confessional *scientia sexualis* might produce a pleasurable *ars erotica* (1976, 96). Here I will be showing how physicians, patients, and novelists coaxed (and even coached) each other to reveal and consolidate the pleasures of the erotic imagination.

## Medical License

Doctors enjoy the professional privilege of inquiring into private matters under the cloak of confidentiality and clinical relevance. To arrive at a diagnosis, a physician extracts a patient's history and tries to match it with a recognized "natural history" of a disease. Health care professionals translate the patient's story into technical language and distill it into a concise "clinical case history," which circulates orally and is recorded in the patient's chart. An unusual case might be transformed into a published study.[10] In telling their story, patients are also struggling to make sense of their illness and suffering.[11] In my clinical experience, the psychiatric interview particularly encourages the most intimate confessions since, given the insights of psychoanalysis, patient and doctor alike intuit that the most hidden or forgotten aspects of experience are also the most significant to psychic pain and healing. While sexual *practices* may be quite relevant to a general medical interview, sexual *fantasies* and other elements of the inner life become explicit only in the psychotherapeutic encounter where, perhaps for the first time, patients are encouraged to verbalize, examine, and explore their erotic imagination.

The first psychiatric patient I interviewed as a medical student was a forty-seven-year-old man with a long history of clinical depression and suicidality.

As I was quietly listening to his story, I was struck by its uncanny correspondence to psychoanalytic models: Oedipal conflicts, narcissistic erotic attachments, the implantation of fetishistic interests in childhood, the mourning over lost ego-introjects, etc. Had Freud simply gotten it right, and was I cleverly interpreting the deeper psychosexual truths to which the patient was oblivious?

Fortunately, I was more skeptical. I realized that this man had gone through decades of psychoanalysis and had generously volunteered to be interviewed by students. Whether consciously or not, he had rehearsed his story many times. It had been transformed into a classic psychiatric history, but he genuinely sensed it as uniquely his own. And it was.

We all fall in love, have sex, choose friends, and fight with them. The affective and erotic activities of our life seem to be directed by personal reasons and emotions, calculation and fancy, yet they are also constrained by the ties of family, class, gender, culture, and nationality, as well as the invisible pulses of our body.[12] I will be focusing on how those extrapersonal forces shape a variety of histories of erotism: individuals' sensual autobiographies, doctors' scientific histories, and fiction writers' *histoires passionelles.* I purposefully set out to blur the boundaries between these narrative genres, or, more accurately, to show how political, rhetorical, and professional conventions establish these boundaries. This is not to deny the personal or the biological. We will see that these two are tightly interwoven into people's stories of their erotic lives.

Nineteenth-century French medical literature is exceptionally rich in erotic memoirs and confessions for reasons that have to do as much with general professional developments as with specific concerns about sexuality. France was preeminent in neurology and psychiatry throughout much of the nineteenth century.[13] Therefore, French doctors also dominated the semiology of the erotic—the interpretation of signs of sexual pathology.

It was an era of medical professionalization and specialization along with the multiplication of new human sciences (such as anthropology, sociology, public hygiene, criminology, and sociology).[14] Thanks to these ancillary medical sciences, the profession claimed expertise in medicolegal issues and social policy, where nosological matters were critical. However, the nosologies (classification systems) of sexual "pathologies" were imprecise until the late nineteenth century.[15] Lacking specific diagnostic labels, earlier doctors instead provided lengthy clinical descriptions, often transcribing their patients' first-person confessions. Doctors could indulge in long case descriptions thanks to the explosion of industrial printing and the proliferation of specialty and regional professional journals that provided new outlets for biomedical publishing. Medical texts therefore could include a variety of documentary materials:

doctors' descriptions of patient histories and physical examinations, police and legal documents, newspaper articles, and patients' testimonial letters, legal confessions, and personal writings.[16]

Out of this complex literary amalgam I will be drawing attention to the so-called patients' own writings about their sexual lives and to the ways in which they used these medical confessions to explore their erotic imaginations. Surrounding these patient histories are the doctors' interpretations. These tell their own professional and sociological stories of the origins, nature, and functions of the erotic. This medical framing gave *érotisme* a strong pathological flavor that diffused beyond the medical journals into the general public.

Medical and lay cultures exchanged information in both directions through numerous means. The erotic medical confessions were liminal narratives, situated in the shady boundary between scientific documents and licentious popular literature. Bold warnings that "sales of this book are strictly limited to doctors and psychologists with a professional interest in sex" probably only boosted "illegitimate" sales. One book reviewer for the *American Journal of Insanity* (1893, 91), for example, questioned the popularity of Richard von Krafft Ebing's encyclopedia of perversities, *Psychopathia Sexualis*:

> How much of its sale has been due to professional interest, how much to the interest of sufferers in what concerns their own cases, and how much to a morbid and prurient curiosity, it would not be easy to determine. Surely, it would be an extraordinary appetite for nastiness that would not be satiated by the records which it contains of the inconceivable depths of degradation into which human beings, often in some respects highly endowed, may be plunged by the vagaries and perversions of the sexual passion.

While "perverts" relied on medical literature for information and titillation, doctors added color to their medical tales by relying on popular novels. Novelists, in turn (especially Realists, Naturalists, and Decadents), utilized medical literature to inform their portrayals of a variety of "degenerate" and "psychopathic" characters. Armand Dubarry, for example, earned quite a reputation and a fortune with his eleven "genesic deviation" novels which came hard on the heels of the popular French translation of *Psychopathia Sexualis* (1895). Dr. Rolet (1907) and other physicians might have condemned "scientific novelists" such as Emile Zola and Dubarry as "scientific dilettantes" feeding the prurient interests of the public, but Dubarry's defense differed little from that of the physicians themselves. Dubarry declared,

The philosopher, the psychologist, the poet, the novelist, the historian, the legislator equally insist upon that which the physician claims as his right; and the duty of these agitators of ideas, these anatomists of the soul, is to initiate the world, for whose benefit they fight, to all that touches or interests it. (1896b, 9)

Can I as a historian claim much more as I search for the medical and cultural roots of the erotic imagination? I will be alternating between the place of the erotic in the soul and in the world. Novelists, doctors, and the individuals they treated will be the primary speakers. In elaborating their personal stories, patients were not only struggling to make sense of their erotic experience, but were providing the material for doctors' "scientific" narratives of erotism in society.

My historical narrative proceeds chronologically with individual chapters on the eighteenth-century concern with masturbation, the early-nineteenth-century construction of erotomania, and the late-nineteenth-century discoveries of homosexuality and fetishism. These four chapters focus on broader issues concerning the emergence of modern eroticism: individualist subjectivity, medicolegal matters, nationalist rivalries, and consumer culture. Each new erotic entity grew out of earlier medical knowledge and social concerns, but also incorporated the professional and social issues of the moment. Therefore, while these erotic phenomena have a pre-nineteenth-century ancestry, it was during the "long nineteenth century" (from the late eighteenth century till World War I) that they emerged as sexually perverse and the objects of focused biomedical attention.

These four "disease" entities are different aspects of a single morbid phenomenon constructed in the nineteenth century: the erotic imagination. The medical "discovery" and manipulation of the erotic imagination was, as Dubarry suggested, of enormous social and political import. He and the physicians of the erotic, however, believed the "genesic drive" to be a biological, natural appetite that had an effect on the health of the nation, but we will see that the vicissitudes of the nation also molded the erotic imagination of individuals and society. Thanks to the legitimacy of medicine, the erotic could fly from the confines of the individual imagination, and "prurience" could become the object of cultural politics.

As we consume a heavy diet of erotic narratives, we—like the lady led astray by truffles—must be vigilant of their pleasures and perils just as the doctors, patients, and novelists were. The imagination, erotic and otherwise, plays a subtle role in the narrative production of all three speakers, as it must inevitably in my own. We would do well to self-reflectively heed Dubarry's disclaimer:

> In the passional oeuvre in which we are engaged, we will utilize not only our personal observations, we will make use of, among other things, the work of alienists, of indubitable facts collected by ourselves, of criminal trials dealing with the task we have set before us, we will try to insure that the imagination serve only as an embroidery to the truth. (1896a, 7–8)

Dubarry pretended that the relationship between imagination, truth, and history was unproblematic. However, in knitting my own passional historical oeuvre, I will be regularly asking: Is there any truth to either the erotic or the historical imaginations, since both involve delicately embroidered narratives of fact, experience, and fantasy? Just as erotic fantasy can become a source of real sexual arousal and pleasure, so too a historical narrative can be made real for individual as well as national pleasure, politics, and pride. I will not be as coy as Dubarry and discount the prurient pleasures of history. On the contrary, I hope my narrative will indeed satisfy an "extraordinary appetite for nastiness" even while examining the historical and political physiology of that appetite. For I presume all my readers are historical paraphiliacs. Although "paraphilia" is the current psychiatric term for the sexual perversions, psychoanalyst Wilhelm Stekel originally defined it simply as the "interest in perversion" (1924, 1:341)—implicating us all in the history of perversity.

# CHAPTER **1**

## Onanists: The Public Threat of Phantastical Pollutions

I had returned from Italy, not quite as I had left for it, but perhaps as no one of my age had returned. I had brought back my innocence, but not my virginity. I had felt the progress of the years; my restless temperament had finally declared itself, and its first quite involuntary eruption had triggered alarms concerning my health that attest to the innocence with which I had lived till then. Soon reassured, I learned that *dangerous supplement that deceives nature,* and preserves youth of my humor from many disorders at the expense of their health, their vigor, and sometimes their life. *That vice which shame and timidity find so convenient, has an even greater attraction for lively imaginations:* it allows them to dispose, so to speak, of the entire female sex at their will, and to make a tempting beauty serve their pleasure without needing to obtain her consent. Seduced by this fatal advantage, I worked at destroying the good constitution that nature had established in me, and which I had allowed sufficient time to mature. Add to this disposition my situation at the time, rooming with a beautiful woman whose image I caressed in the depths of my heart, seeing her constantly throughout the day; in the evenings, surrounded by objects that reminded me of her, sleeping in a bed where I knew she had slept. What stimuli! The reader who pictures all this must already imagine me half-dead.[1]

That dangerous supplement that deceives nature? Titillated readers of Rousseau's *Confessions* in 1782 would have immediately deciphered his peculiar euphemism for masturbation, or the "solitary vice" of "self-pollution." Rather than simply identify this eighteenth-century concept with our current notion of masturbation, let me begin by examining *pollution* historically. Today the term evokes images of smog and toxic waste, but the French word *pollution* only acquired this meaning in the twentieth-century.[2] Diderot and d'Alembert's *Encyclopédie* (1751–1772) provides three definitions of *pollution:* (1) Moral: "the effusion of seed outside the function of marriage"; (2) Medical: a disease of involuntary ejaculation of seed; (3) Jurisprudential: defilement of sacred places (26(2):568–71). The reader is referred to a separate article on *manustupration* for a discussion of the medical ailments of "those abandoning themselves without restraint to that infamous passion and sacrificing themselves to that false Venus" (570), that is, voluntary, manually stimulated ejaculation.

The *Encyclopédie*'s article on *pollution* reflects traditional distinctions between the theologicomoral condemnation of the "spilling of seed" versus medical concerns with seminal discharge or "gonorrhoea" (from the Greek *gonos,* seed, and *rhoia,* flux). The *Encyclopédie*'s entry for *manustupration,* on the other hand, reveals a new medical preoccupation with masturbation which had only arisen in the early eighteenth century. In this chapter I examine the medical and cultural evolution of "onano-phobia" in Francophone Europe. I connect this anxiety to evolving constructions of subjectivity using Rousseau as my principal informant and paradigmatic subject. We can begin by asking: Why did Rousseau believe the "convenient vice" was a threat to health, vigor, and life? We must also wonder, as did Rousseau's contemporaries, why he publicized his lifetime addiction to the "dangerous supplement." Jacques Derrida (1967) examines how Rousseau criticized several overlapping dangerous supplements (things that add as well as make complete): masturbation as a supplement to reproductive coitus, writing as a supplement to speaking, the imagination as a supplement to reality.[3] I further argue that, for Rousseau, eroticism itself is a socially stimulated supplement to "natural" living, and for later nineteenth-century critics, *érotisme* was a supplement that threatened to undermine the very civilization that sex was "naturally" intended to perpetuate.

The confrontation between the "natural" individual and "artificial" society preoccupied Rousseau and many of his contemporaries. I will be teasing out several themes of this Enlightenment conflict. After a brief review of the pre-Enlightenment ecclesiastical teachings on pollutions and the medical treatment of gonorrhœa, I turn to Rousseau and Samuel-Auguste Tissot. A prominent Swiss physician who legitimized the medical treatment of onanism, Tissot shared Rousseau's anxieties about the polluting effects of "civilization." I then focus on critiques of civilization and masturbation as corruptors of the "soft," impressionable nerves of children. Intimately tied to these discussions of the nervous system was an emerging concern for the impressionable imagination and the impact of "literature of the imagination." Perhaps one of the most feared perversions of the imagination was the confusion of pain for pleasure, and I return to Rousseau for his analysis of his own masochism. Finally, I examine the new role of published confessions or autobiographies such as Rousseau's in mediating the tense relationship between the personal and the public. We will see how the revelation of private vice gained its confessor a modicum of public absolution while making "perverse" sexual identities common knowledge. By the nineteenth century, "social hygienists" no longer portrayed these new sexual beings (like the "onaniac") as unfortunate, innocent victims of a corrupt civilization, but as dangerous, even criminal, social pollutants of a country threatened by industrialization, urbanization, foreign conflicts, and stagnating fertility.[4]

## Sins of the Flesh Versus Diseases of Semen

In the Middle Ages, Roman Catholic theologians elaborated doctrine on the mortal sin of *pollution* or *mollicies*.[5] They considered self-pollution a "sin against nature," and they pointed to God's condemnation of Onan. He had spilt his seed on the ground to avoid conceiving an heir by his widowed sister-in-law Tamar as levirate law demanded (Genesis 38:7–10). Biblical scholars debated whether Onan's crime was masturbation or *coitus interruptus,* since Genesis is unclear on this point. Nevertheless, they consistently condemned such voluntary emissions along with fornication, adultery, *mollicies* (softness/effeminacy), sodomy, and bestiality—all classified as forms of unlawful sex.[6] But as far as we can tell, these strictures were only addressed to adults. Furthermore, according to church writings the ills of manustupration (pollution by the hand) were confined to defilement of the soul and mind; they did not suggest that *organic ills* were the wages of self-defilement, nor did they envision lasting psychological damage.

Medieval physicians were generally careful to acknowledge church injunctions against "illicit" sexual acts, but, on the whole, their concern was more with the retention of semen than with its waste—whether voluntary or involuntary. Medical writers since antiquity have proposed theories of seed physiology.[7] Galen, the most influential classical physician, proposed that male and female health was the result of the proper balance between the production and excretion of the precious seminal humor. Although Galen described gonorrhœa (useless, involuntary excretion of seed) as a pathological condition (IV:41vF), he was far more concerned with accumulated seed. This could putrefy in widows, nuns, virgins and other chaste women, producing diseases such as hysteria.[8] Galen's call for humoral, seminal balance was widely echoed by medieval medical authorities. As in the theological texts, medieval medical literature made no mention of childhood masturbation nor did medieval physicians, as far as we know, attach morbid physical or psychological consequences to the act of masturbation.

Renaissance medical texts betray an increasing concern with gonorrhœa, particularly in conjunction with venereal disease and various forms of illicit sexual activity. For example, the highly respected and widely translated Swiss physician Felix Platter described a case of "Gonorrhœa or Running of the Reyns": "[a] young man with pain and heat in the hypochondria [abdomen] and Loyns, and a Gonorrhœa, his seed came forth and he felt it not, like water seven years, it consumed him" (1664, 471). But Platter did not mention manustupration as a cause of gonorrhea in his chapter on "Observations on excretion of seed." Furthermore, he was unperturbed by a patient's admission of voluntary "voiding of seed" (517).

The eccentric, self-styled "Doctor of Physicke" Andrew Boorde did evince a more moralistic attitude toward seminal loss, identifying three kinds of "gomorrea": pollutions against nature, pollutions due to infirmity, pollutions due to imbecility. He was apparently the first to suggest that "gomorrhea" comes from "Sodome and Gomer" which "dyd synke to hell sodenly" for practicing the "gomorrea passio" voluntarily, that is, "to meddle with any brute beast or to pollute hymself wijlfully" (1552, f. 59v.). To the modern reader, Boorde seems to blur a variety of "sinful" sexual acts which today we categorize as distinct behaviors. However, his varieties of "gomorrhea" and even their signification cannot be matched with current sexual practices or terminology.[9] Boorde condemned "voluntary pollution," but as it was traditionally understood: one among many varieties of "unnatural" and illicit "venery" and in itself composed of a number of different kinds of polluting acts. Similarly, Hermann Boerhaave, an influential Dutch physician and philosopher, was far more concerned with seminal discharge (of any variety) than he was with masturbation per se. His description of the symptomatology of excessive seminal loss bears a striking resemblance to the portrait of the terminal onanist sketched in Enlightenment antimasturbation tracts:

> The *Semen* discharged too lavishly, occasions a Weariness, Weakness, Indisposition to Motion, Convulsions, Leanness, Driness, Heats and Pains in the Membranes of the Brain, with a Dulness of the Senses; more especially of the Sight, a *Tabes Dorsalis,* Foolishness, and Disorders of the like kind. (1708, 5:456)

However, we should be wary of clumping Boerhaave with the later anti-onanism campaigners. For Boerhaave, the *causes* for such cachexia or wasting include not only voluntary and nocturnal emissions, but also, in the case of *tabes dorsalis,* the lavish discharge of seed which "most frequently happens to those who are too furious and earlier [*sic*] in their Combats in the Camps of Venus" (i.e., sexual intercourse) (5:456n). Moreover, Boerhaave sets the whole section on excessive discharge of seed in the context of the morbid effects of excessive humoral loss, be it blood, lymphatic juice, bile, urine, or perspiration. To Boerhaave, the lavish discharge of semen was no different from the loss of any other vital fluid in causing a nonspecific "atrophy or wasting of the whole habit for want of nutrition." In summary then, pre-Enlightenment medical texts were concerned with generic "seminal loss" as a source of humoral imbalance. With only two known minor exceptions, humoral theory was not used to defend the theologicomoral condemnation of "self-pollution."[10] Western medical opinion had not singled out onanism as a uniquely pernicious personal and social disease.

This changed radically with the anonymous publication of *Onania; or, the Heinous Sin of Self-Pollution, and All Its Frightful Consequences, in both Sexes, Considered, with Spiritual and Physical Advice to those, who have already injur'd themselves by this abominable Practice* (1710?). *Onania* dramatically reordered Euro-American cultural perceptions of masturbation, transforming it from one of many forms of seminal and excretory loss into a sexual practice potentially fatal to individuals and society alike.[11] Like other broadsides by mountebanks and quacksalvers, *Onania* started as a brief pamphlet and advertisement for nostrums: "Strengthening Tincture" (10 shillings) and "Prolifick Powder" (12 shillings). The author promoted these and total abstinence as the only salvation from the ills of onanism, which included stunted growth, priapism, gonorrhea, cachexia, blindness, phthisis, insanity, countless other disorders, and, ultimately, death. By 1750 *Onania* had appeared in nineteen editions and had sold thirty-eight thousand copies. With each edition, it swelled with new "testimonial" letters from customers rescued from the deadly clutches of onanism.[12] The medicomoral condemnation of solitary vice quickly made its way to Germany via a 1736 translation of *Onania* and to France by mid-century thanks to the translation of another British work, Robert James's *Medicinal Dictionary* and its entry on *mastupratio:* "A vice not decent to name, but provocative of the most deplorable and generally incurable disorders."[13] One of the three translators of James's dictionary was the future *encyclopédiste* Diderot.

By the mid-eighteenth century then, medical and quack literature condemning the disease of self-pollution had reached the French-speaking public, but the notion had probably already penetrated the popular imagination—as evinced by Rousseau's guilty confession of his adolescent discovery of solitary vice in 1728. Physicians, however, lent professional credibility to *Onania*'s moralistic views and the subsequent folk beliefs. Although some historians have dismissed the medical campaign against masturbation as a delusion, a conspiracy, or a form of torture, it is clear from abundant medical literature, as well as clinical records of patients diagnosed as "onanists," that masturbation was considered a serious, even epidemic, disease by eighteenth- and nineteenth-century doctors and public alike.[14] Rather than dismissing the anti-onanism crusade as a historical aberration, we need to examine how the persecution of solitary pleasure was consonant with major social and cultural trends of modernity.[15]

## Tissot and Rousseau Battling Pollution

Onanophobia did not gain full medical legitimacy until the Swiss physician Samuel-Auguste-André-David Tissot published *Onanism, or A Treatise upon the Disorders Produced by Masturbation* (1760). Tissot assured readers that, except for the topic, his work had "nothing in common with the British *Onania*," which he dismissed as "a true chaos" full of "theological and moral trivialities" (18, 41). He instead proposed to describe "the diseases produced by masturbation, and not the crime of masturbation" (17). To this effect, he cited noted medical authorities on the subject of seminal loss, and explained the pathology of onanism by relying on the soundest humoral physiology. For Tissot the ills of masturbation included, nevertheless, most of the disorders listed in *Onania*. To dramatize the chronic decline of the onanist, Tissot described the case of L. D., clockmaker, who abandoned himself to masturbation at the age of seventeen, repeating the act up to three times a day. Within a year the youngster grew weak and feared for his health, but too late:

> The slightest irritation immediately provoked an imperfect erection, this was immediately followed by an evacuation of that liqueur, which every day augmented his weakness. [Orgasm] had become habitual and often seized him with no apparent cause, and in a manner so violent that throughout the duration of the attack, which sometimes lasted fifteen hours and never less than eight, he experienced in the entire posterior neck such violent pains that he did not just cry, but howled. . . . [H]e languished without succor for months. . . . Having learned of his state, I rushed to his side; I found there less a living being than a cadaver lying on straw, thin, pale, filthy, exuding a vile stench, practically incapable of any movement. He frequently lost through his nose a pale, watery blood; spittle ran continuously from his mouth; stricken with diarrhea, he voided his excrements in his bed without noticing it; the flow of semen was continual. . . . The disorders of the mind were no less severe. . . . [A] spectacle whose horror is inconceivable, it was hard to recognize he had once belonged to the human species. . . . He died at the end of a few weeks, in June 1757, edematous throughout his body. (45–46)

As with *Onania,* new editions of Tissot's *Onanism* included plaintive confessions from addicted masturbators. One wrote, "I cannot take . . . two hundred steps without resting; my weakness is extreme; I suffer continual pains throughout my body. . . . *The private part [penis] is more flaccid than a cotton thread, incapable of any erection; while it allows the semen to flow when manually stimulated it never truly ejaculates, and besides this it is shrunken and retracted such that one is scarcely able to visually determine my sex*" (51).[16] These and *Onanism*'s other portraits of masturbatory decline were, if anything, more sensationalistic that the ones in *Onania* thanks to their medical realism. Although he set aside the heavy-handed moralizing of his British counterpart, Tissot was equally convinced of the sinfulness of onanism but reasoned that it "is easier to turn people away from vice through the fear of an immediate ill" than through abstract reasoning (17). Both *Onanism* and *Onania,* therefore, were part of a common trend in the Enlightenment: the secularization and medicalization of morality. Improper acts were analyzed as violations of familial and social rules, and physiological and natural "laws" rather than ecclesiastical doctrines.[17] While *Onania* listed the diseases of masturbation and hinted at humoral pathology to condemn the "sin" of onanism, Tissot deployed the full arsenal of medical rhetoric to the same moral aims: making reproductive sex normative and promoting the regulation of sexuality. In other words, the spiritual and the material aspects of pollution were telescoped: not only was onanism the defilement of the temple of the soul, but also of the temple of Nature—the body. Tissot feared that "civilization," in particular, threatened the salubrity of Nature and the natural body, for he was dedicated to the idea that social forces caused health and illness.

Although Tissot served and was rewarded by the Bern aristocracy, he also had close connections with the *philosophes*.[18] Their radical, democratic politics are evident throughout Tissot's popular self-help books: *Advice to Common People on their Health* (1761), *On the Health of Men of Letters* (1766), *Essay on the Diseases of the Valetudinary* (1770). Tissot complained that the fundamentally sturdier health of peasants was deteriorating due to contact with "civilized" city life when employed as soldiers or domestic servants (1761, 7). He also worried that European populations were declining, in part due to military conscription and emigration to the colonies, but mainly because of bourgeois, urban lifestyles (1761, 1–4). This critique was even sharper in *On the Health of Men of Letters* and *Essay on the Diseases of the Valetudinary* where he suggested a close correlation between class and health. The healthiest were the peasants, followed by artisans, the bourgeois, and finally the sickly *gens du monde*—people from different classes who had no vocation but shared a lifestyle of leisure and indolence. To fight boredom they searched for pleasures, not in the natural satisfaction of labor, but in those "factitious pleasures" that were "opposed to the usage of nature and whose bizarreness is their only merit" (1770, 11). Tissot particularly warned of the ills brought on by the valetudinary and luxurious lifestyles of men of letters who had no occupation but that of their minds (1766, 20–21; 1770, 11).

Relying on current physiological principles, Tissot explained that sedentary life slowed down humoral circulation and produced nervous enfeeblement and visceral congestion (1766, 70–77). He also claimed that the seminal fluid—which some compared to "nervous sap"—was weakened, thus explaining why the sons of geniuses were less gifted than their fathers (1766, 85–86). Since Tissot had relied on identical physiological principles in *Onanism*, it is not surprising that he claimed the nervous exhaustion of the valetudinary was the same as that produced by diseases of "excessive humoral expenditure," most notably, masturbation (1766, 45–66). This association between the exhaustion of men of letters and that of onanists would be strengthened by nineteenth-century physicians who warned that overexertion of the literary or the erotic imaginations caused "softening" (*mollesse*) and effeminacy.

To support his contention that mental work was debilitating, Tissot turned to Rousseau. In his comedy, *Narcisse, or the Lover of Himself,* Rousseau staged the amorous intrigues of an effeminate, conceited, young aristocrat who falls madly in love with a portrait of himself dressed as a woman. Tissot cited the preface, where Rousseau made explicit the play's critique of the effeminizing effects of contemporary, elite culture:

> Study [*le travail de cabinet*] makes men delicate, weakens their temperament; and it is difficult for the soul to maintain its vigor when the body has lost its strength. Study wears out the machine, exhausts the spirits, destroys force, enervates courage; it is thus that one becomes cowardly and pusillanimous, incapable of resisting either sorrows or passions. (*Narcisse,* 966; quoted in Tissot 1766, 41–42)

Appropriately enough, the preface was Rousseau's vehicle for defending his *Discourse on the Sciences and Arts* (1750), the prize-winning response to the question proposed by the Academy of Sciences and Belles Lettres of Dijon: "Has the re-establishment of the sciences and arts contributed to the refinement of manners?" Rousseau's resounding "No!"—suggested and approved by his friend Diderot in 1749—brought him fame and censure. One could say, in turn, that both of Tissot's essays on the health of valetudinary men of letters were Tissot's reply to the hypothetical question: Has the progress of civilization contributed to the refinement of the body? Echoing Rousseau's negative response on the *cultural* state of civilized men, Tissot replied in the negative on their *physical* state.

Given their common skepticism concerning civilization, it is not surprising that great philosophical, political, and personal sympathy existed between the two men. Tissot was quite familiar with his countryman's writings and he exclaimed in reference to Rousseau: "That Genevois is my hero."[19] They first met in June 1762 at Rousseau's home in Yverdun, Bern, and corresponded frequently thereafter.[20] Despite the enormous controversy that erupted over Rousseau's pedagogical text, *Emile,* Tissot remained Rousseau's staunch defender.[21] Rousseau, in turn, admired Tissot, sought his medical advice, and recommended the doctor's services to many notable friends.[22] This is remarkable since Rousseau despised doctors and once described medicine as "an art more pernicious to men than all the ills it pretends to cure" (*Emile,* 269).[23]

Rousseau, however, had no knowledge of Tissot's *Onanism* when he warned educators: "If [your student] once knows that dangerous supplement, he is lost. Thenceforth his body and heart will be enervated, he will carry to the grave the sad effects of that habit, the most mortal one to which a young man can be subjected" (*Emile*, 663). This passage so delighted Tissot that he sent Rousseau copies of *Onanism, Advice to Common People,* and *Inoculation Justified.* In a letter accompanying this gift, Tissot praised Rousseau effusively, and exclaimed:

> You will see, Sir, in the *Advice to Common People* p. 520, that we are almost of one mind regarding this Science [medicine]. . . . [He discusses several points in *Emile* on which they are in agreement.] *Onanism* will prove to you that finally there is a physician who has recognized all the danger of that odious practice you so vigorously attack, and has had the courage to make that danger public knowledge. This book has been banned in Paris. Could there be governments for whom it was important for the ministries to prohibit all assistance that can stop the enfeeblement of the soul or the body?[24]

Rousseau did indeed share many of Tissot's concerns about the insalubrity of cities and the decline of healthy, rural life.[25] Tissot therefore had good reason to feel that his social mission was comparable to that of the literatist-philosopher Rousseau. Not only did they share the same scientific task of observing humanity and diagnosing its ills, they were in similar political trouble for their candor in this task. Tissot portrayed Rousseau and himself as solitary, courageous figures sounding the alarm on the deterioration of health and morality in their time. After all, had not *Emile* and *Onanism* both been condemned as immoral, dangerous tracts when in fact they were important pedagogical texts?

The aging Rousseau thanked Tissot for the books, and wrote that, although he no longer read—especially not medical works—he had immediately read *Onanism* and he regretted not knowing of it earlier. He commiserated with Tissot on the banning of their books.[26] Radical critiques of the institutions of "civilization" and democratic proposals for public hygiene were indeed controversial at the time—particularly when they touched on childhood pedagogy and erotism. So the struggle over the bodies and imaginations of children naturally drew together Rousseau and many doctors concerned with civilization's ill effects on developing brains and the social interventions necessary for mitigating those effects.

## Civilized Corruptions of Soft Nerves

In drawing attention to children, the anti-onanism literature participated in a broader trend in the construction of childhood.[27] Since the flow of semen (male or female) coincided with the changes of puberty, semen was praised as the precious fluid essential to maturation. Doctors believed that the body needed to invest all its energy into its self-construction during childhood and adolescence. This "somatic economy" was vulnerable to the effects of both the "physical" and the "moral" (understood as environmental, behavioral, or psychological factors).[28] Masturbation threatened both of these; therefore, the malleable nerves and imaginations of adolescents required careful management.

The dangers of puberty were vividly portrayed in Rousseau's *Emile, or On Education* (1762)—one of the most influential pedagogical works of the eighteenth century.[29] In this peculiar hybrid of pedagogy, philosophy, moralism, and fantasy, Rousseau recommended that instructors constantly watch over their charge: "Do not leave him alone during the day or the night; at least sleep in his room. Beware of the [sexual] instinct as soon as you are not watching; it is good as long as it acts alone, it is suspect as soon as it mixes with the institutions of mankind" (*Emile*, 663). He emphatically claimed that one of the "most frequent abuses of philosophy in our time" was the belief that the onset of puberty was due to physical and not "moral" causes. His evidence for this was the variation in the age of onset of puberty with the degree of civilization: "Puberty and sexual potency are always earlier in instructed and policed peoples than amongst ignorant and barbaric peoples" (495).

As we have seen, both Rousseau and Tissot blamed "civilization" for polluting the state of "nature" and stimulating the rise of masturbation. Later medical sources echoed Rousseau's pronouncements on the etiological role of civilization in precociously stimulating puberty and inciting children to self-pollution. The *masturbation* entry in the *Dictionary of Medical Sciences* (1819) noted: "The diseases that are the product of the excesses of onanism become more frequent in proportion to the higher degree of civilization achieved by modern societies. This opinion, which is generally adopted by medical observers, seems to rest on numerous and well established facts" (Fournier & Béguin 1819, 101).

In Rousseau's case, it was after leaving his rural Swiss town and during his stay in Italy—the cradle of the Renaissance—that Rousseau lost his "virginity." While a catechumen in a monastery there, he was sexually molested before the altar, and when the molester masturbated, Rousseau reported that for the first time "I saw shooting towards the chimney and falling upon the ground I don't know what sticky, white stuff that turned my stomach" (*Confessions*, 67). Later, back in Switzerland, it was the constant company of a beautiful woman that inflamed his desires. Rousseau's conclusion was that sexuality in general was a supplement of civilization and that in the ideal state of nature chastity would remain undefiled: "For myself, the more I reflect on this important crisis [of puberty] and its proximate or distant causes, the more I am persuaded that a solitary [man] raised in the desert, without books, without instruction, and without women, would die virginal at whatever age he reached" (*Emile*, 663). Rousseau thus evoked the three most frequently mentioned culprits of civilization's epidemic of onanism: women, education, and literature.

Throughout his work, Rousseau vehemently blamed women for the ills of modernity and the "unnatural" state of civilization.[30] It was the combined strategy of female coquetry and sexual reserve that maintained civilized men in a state of desire and dependency (*Emile*, 456).[31] It was only this feminine sexual modesty that prevented the naturally more voracious female from sexually exhausting the male (447). Rousseau especially criticized the "artificious and wicked women" of society (that is, the elite) for enslaving men and denaturing the natural, maternal instincts (713). Rousseau recommended that at the critical time of puberty tutors should "distance [the young men] from big cities, where women's ornamentation and immodesty rushes and frustrates the lessons of Nature. . . . [R]eturn them to their first quarters where country simplicity lets their passions develop less quickly" (517). In Rousseau's eyes, women were fundamentally responsible for bringing on civilization and its discontents. More commonly, medical sources warned of "abominable women" and nannies who use masturbation to pacify infants, or "more infamous yet, engage in simulacra of coitus with little boys" (Fournier & Béguin 1819, 105).

Schools were perhaps even more nefarious than women. Rousseau repeatedly complained of the corrupting effects of education at the time: "It is from the very first years that a senseless education decorates our mind and corrupts our judgment. All around me I see immense institutions where, at great cost, youth are raised to learn all things, except their duty" (*Discours*, 24). Even more to the point, Tissot reported that "a whole school, by this maneuver [onanism], sometimes tried to avoid falling asleep and diverted the tedium of scholastic metaphysical lessons delivered by a drowsy old professor" (1760, 97–98). The problem only became more acute with the advent of public schools. Doctors bemoaned the ironic fact that "it is principally in public establishments, where large numbers of young people of one and the other sex are united, that the habit of masturbation develops with ease. Public education is without a doubt one of the best results of perfected civilization. . . . But by how many grave side effects are those advances compromised?" (Fournier & Béguin 1819, 105). If public schools were the hazardous environment where children learned self-pollution, it was through the imagination that the addiction took hold and through the nervous system that onanopathology crippled its victims.[32]

Rousseau's oft-repeated message was that the genital instinct or sense was excited by a precociously aroused imagination: "As I have said a thousand times, it is by the imagination alone that the senses are awakened" (*Emile*, 662). This observation was given a solid physiological explanation by Dr. Ménuret de Chambaud in the *manstupration* entry of the *Encyclopédie*: "The mind continually absorbed in voluptuous thoughts, constantly directs the animal spirits to the generative organs, which by repeated handling, become more mobile, more obedient to the unruliness of the imagination: the result is almost continual erections, frequent pollutions, & the excessive evacuation of seed" (20(2):991).

The nervous system was viewed in the eighteenth century as an exchange network, linking all other systems in sympathy. As such, it was the principal player in the somatic economy and was considered the most refined product of the progress of civilization. The genital system, usually portrayed as the most primitive or animalistic, was nevertheless supremely important for maturation and reproduction. Together these two systems dominated the developing body: "We can consider, in youth, these two important parts of the organism, the brain and the sexual organs, as two centers that mutually convey the impressions they receive, and that excite one another in the most direct and energetic manner" (Fournier & Béguin 1819, 109). This cerebrogenital axis embodied and materialized two axes of conflict that preoccupied the antimasturbatory literature: civilized versus primitive and intellectual versus sensual.

As in the case of education, the nervous system was caught in the dilemma of civilization. The more refined and civilized nerves became, the more vulnerable they left children to onanism. Therefore, it was a fine line between the production of high genius and of base decadence:

> The excessive development of nervous sensibility, which is the source of so many laudable actions and so many vices; this cause, which, depending on the direction it is given, *bears the most admirable productions of genius, or those shapeless works that attest to the force and deviations of the imagination,* may be the result of a natural disposition of the organs, or the product of early education. [Infancy is remarkable for the dominance of the fully organized nervous system over the rest of the body, which is still relatively underdeveloped.] It is immediately after early childhood, during that period when the faculties of the new being are energetically beginning to develop, that he runs the greatest risk. If then an unhappy accident, or, too frequently, strange handling, reveals to him a new sense, so to speak, the genital organs become a site

for concentrating more or less energetically the forces of life, and the subject, swept away by a deceitful pleasure, abandons himself with furor to a vice that will soon be his perdition, or draws upon him ills even more terrible than death. (Fournier & Béguin 1819, 103; emphasis added)

Childhood was a perilous time of extreme nervous and imaginative impressionability when all forms of stimuli could prematurely excite the genital centers and trigger onanistic addiction. Lascivious talk, romantic novels, and sensual images were especially blamed for igniting the imagination and, by sympathy, inciting the genitals. "One can affirm that this reading of novels, which so easily becomes the object of a veritable passion for young ladies, is today one of the most active causes of their depravation" (106). The *Encyclopédie,* for example, warned that

the truly morbid *nocturnal pollution* is always the effect of immoderate debaucheries of the body and the mind when, not content to indulge without excess in venereal pleasures, one continually feasts the imagination with lascivious, voluptuous images, filthy conversations, libertine and indecent readings; then, dreams, which are often just a representation of the objects that most occupied the mind during the day, replay the same matters; the generative organs (which frequent exercise and an overheated imagination hold in a continual tension) are much more susceptible to lascivious impressions; they obey the slightest misdirection, and the movements destined to the ejaculation of semen, having become almost habitual, are executed without effort. (26(2):570)

We have seen that antimasturbationist doctors were preoccupied with moral and pedagogical issues, particularly the pathological effects of civilization: cities, urbanization, schools, "artificious women," and "unrespectable readings." This last problem, the nervous impact of licentious texts and the somatic effect of their mental representation, haunts the antimasturbatory literature, which arose in conjunction with two other important historical developments of the Enlightenment, the proliferation of "pornographic" literature and the birth of the novel.

## Les Liaisons Dangereuses

Both the middle class and literacy rates rose in France during the eighteenth century. The Enlightenment also witnessed an associated explosion in the publication of "licentious literature" often colored with political and anticlerical overtones.[33] The rise of novels in general and pornographic novels in particular was criticized by eighteenth-century cultural observers as a major pollutant of the imagination. Medical critics also worried that novels and pornography encouraged readers, particularly those with "impressionable brains" (specifically, children and women), to mistake the imaginary for the truth, resulting in unhealthy, unsatisfiable hyperexcitation or "false" pleasure.[34] Rousseau perfectly described this pubescent, literary escape into a solitary, imaginary world:

> I nourished myself on situations that had interested me in my readings, I recalled them, varied, combined, and appropriated them to such a point that I became one of the characters I imagined and I always saw myself in the most agreeable positions according to my taste. . . . This love of imaginary objects and this facility for entertaining myself with them ultimately made me disgusted with all my surroundings and determined that taste for solitude which has persisted since that time. (*Confessions*, 41)

Rousseau's friend, the sensualist *philosophe* Etienne Bonnot de Condillac, authored one of the most influential Enlightenment critiques of the "vices and advantages of the imagination," the *Essay on the Origin of Human Understanding* (1746). Relying on John Locke's associationist psychology, Condillac suggested that the imagination allowed the free linkage (*liaison*) of perceptions, thus producing new ideas that were not derived from nature. These liaisons could either be made voluntarily or accidentally through foreign impressions. The latter were especially tenacious and dangerous because, unlike consciously made liaisons, they were erroneously considered to be natural (1746, 111). This was how permanent prejudices were formed, for example, associating particular character traits with certain facial physiognomies. As an example, Condillac mentioned Descartes's reputed amorous predilection for cross-eyed women. He attributed this unusual passion to the fact that Descartes's first love was cross-eyed. As we will see in chapter 4, Alfred Binet a century later would "diagnose" Descartes for the first time as a "fetishist." Condillac only labeled this erotic preference a dangerous liaison. In the same vein, Condillac criticized novels which, normally harmless, could become substitutes for reality in the hands of sad people or women (who, he believed, had more "tender brains" than men) (120–21).

Condillac's theories of the imagination were enormously important to the alienist (or "mad-doctor") Philippe Pinel in his conception of the pathology and treatment of the *demi-follies*: intermediate mental conditions between sanity and raving lunacy.[35] Condillac had warned that the imagination could easily lead one to dangerous liaisons and tenacious errors. Pinel realized that this very property of the imagination could be exploited to therapeutic benefit if deployed by professionals schooled in the techniques of "moral therapy." Thus, by the second half of the eighteenth century, physicians represented the imagination as a perilous site where irrational, "unnatural" associations might take hold. But it was also a malleable organ for implanting therapeutic ideas.

The erotic imagination, in particular, was theorized in this period as an especially important locus both for dangerous associations and for regulatory control. As we have already seen, licentious and imaginative literature had been specifically blamed for stimulating solitary vice. Rousseau coyly referred to "those dangerous books . . . whose inconvenience is that one can only read them with one hand" (*Confessions*, 40). Conversely, genital excitement was believed to make perverse demands on the imagination:

> Thus the adult man, led by the stimulation of the generative apparatus, performs acts that his conscious will disapproves, and whose extravagance he will deplore once his calm is reestablished. This demonstrates how great is the influence of [these acts] on the deliberations of the ego [*moi*]. We are familiar with the effects of this excessive irritation of the genitals which gives rise to *satyriasis* and *nymphomania*. (Fournier & Béguin 1819, 109)

Fournier and Béguin warned that imaginary excess provoked hypersexualism in both men (satyriasis) and women (nymphomania); however, doctors felt that women were at greater risk because of their greater impressionability. Tissot, for example, had claimed that, although the female seed was less precious and refined than the male, women were more vulnerable to onanistic pathology since, "the nervous system being weaker in them and naturally more predisposed to spasms, the fits are violent" (1760, 91). Tissot therefore devoted a separate chapter to the specific effects of onanism in females. These included hysteria, vapors, incurable jaundice, clitoral scabbing, and a uterine fury that, "depriving them of their modesty and their reason, reduces them to the level of the most lascivious brutes" (62). By this late stage of masturbational addiction and uterine fury, a patient's mind was totally subjugated to her genitals: "The habit of being occupied by a sole idea, makes it impossible to have others: it becomes imperious and reigns despotically" (99). The naturally weaker nerves and receptive imaginations of women would become a recurrent theme in the antimasturbation literature and other texts on erotic disorders. (See Figures 1 and 2.)

Figure 1. A young female onanist. Frontispiece to Dr. Rozier's *Of Secret Habits, or the Ills Produced by Onanism in Women* (1830). (Courtesy of The Boston Medical Library in the Francis A. Countway Library of Medicine, Boston.)

These connections between masturbation, nymphomania or *furor uterinus,* and the imagination were carefully elucidated for the first time in a monograph by the Dutch physician J. D. T. de Bienville in his *Nymphomania, or Treatise on Uterine Fury* (published in Amsterdam in 1771 by the printer of Rousseau's works).[36] Bienville was a medical popularizer and, like Tissot, wrote on the inoculation controversy as well as popular health misconceptions. In *Nymphomania,* Bienville dramatized the female onanist's shameful decline into passional insanity:

> The sensation of pleasure, together with those diverse images the imagination repeats endlessly, soon renders the patient raging and unbridled; finally

*Pag. 26*

Figure 2. An insane onanist. Dr. Rozier describes her sad case history: "A young girl of eight became disquietingly thin; the lower members, such as the thighs, the legs and the feet were agitated by extraordinary movements that were promptly communicated to the upper limbs; it was impossible to use them; the agitation was excessive in the muscles of the face and the eyes. The child could not rest in her bed; it was necessary to strap her into a large armchair." Finally, a savvy doctor suspected that these were the "effects of a bad habit, and he was soon convinced of this. Some advice to the parents, their constant surveillance, the use of cold baths, musk, and camphor procured a radical cure" (1830, 26–27). Unfortunately, she returned to the evil habit at age eleven with even greater intensity than previously. Consequently, she perished within two years from chronic pericarditis. (Courtesy of The Boston Medical Library in the Francis A. Countway Library of Medicine, Boston.)

> transgressing all the limits of modesty without remorse, they betray the frightful secret of their villainous soul through utterances that shock even the most chaste ears with astonishment and horror, and soon their excessive lasciviousness having exhausted all their strength, they cast off the important and glorious yoke of their modesty, and with openly disgraceful impudence they solicit (with a voice as vile as it is criminal) the first comers to reciprocate their insatiable desires. (1771, 39–40)

He flatly blamed the imagination for being the "artisan" of the "fatal rage of Masturbation" (174). More generally, Bienville accused the imagination of being "almost always the principle or mother of most of the passions and their excesses" (157). "Lascivious novels" further fueled the infernal flame of the nymphomaniac's lubricity (34). Bienville argued that the imagination should also be the dominant medium for therapy: "There are cases [of nymphomania] that will admit of a cure by limiting oneself simply to the treatment of the imagination; but there are no cases (or at least, scarcely any) in which physical remedies alone can effect a radical cure" (159).[37]

Bienville reiterated the physiological belief that self-defilers and nymphomaniacs could become trapped within the closed loop of their genitals and imagination, thus becoming sexually deviant and erotically autonomous. Tissot had issued a similar warning: "A symptom common to both sexes and which I place in this section [on women] because it is more frequent in women, is the indifference that this infamous practice leaves for the legitimate pleasures of hymen, even as these desires and forces are not extinguished" (1760, 63). Or worse yet, the shameless, sensually voracious *onaniste* would be driven to evermore "unnatural" stimulation in order to excite her overtaxed genital system. Tissot specifically condemned "clitoridian" pollution by lesbians—"women who love girls with as much ardor as the most passionate men," or those unnaturally clitorally endowed women who "feel they have to erase the arbitrary differences of nature" (65–66).[38] These associations between masturbation and lesbianism were used to great effect in political pornography aimed at discrediting Marie Antoinette as both dissolute and power-hungry: for example, *The Uterine Furies of Marie-Antoinette, Wife of Louis XVI* (1791) and *The Private, Libertine, and Scandalous Life of Marie-Antoinette* (1791), the latter including an engraving of the Queen being masturbated by one of her ladies-in-waiting.[39]

This indifference to the "legitimate pleasures of hymen" (marriage) was not limited to women however. One of the most frequently cited cases of masturbatory indifference to the opposite sex was that of a shepherd, Gabriel Galien, who demonstrated the terrifying extremes of onanistic associations: linking erotic pleasure with physical mutilation. Surgeon François Chopart described how Galien had obsessively begun masturbating at age fifteen. Ejaculation becoming ever more difficult, Gallien began tickling the urethral canal with a stick. His occupation as shepherd gave him the solitude and free time to titillate himself thus, and "this shepherd frequently allowed his sheep to wander." Eventually, the urethral canal became callous and insensitive; in a fit of despair, he pulled a dull knife from his pocket and incised his penis lengthwise. "This incision," Chopart noted, "which in any other man would have produced the sharpest pain, instead procured for him an agreeable sensation and complete ejaculation. . . . Finally, given all the effort of his passion, he managed, perhaps after a thousand instances, to divide his penis in two equal parts" (1792,

322–23). A later medical writer would echo Chopart's comment that Galien had "an insurmountable aversion of women, which is not rare in masturbators" (*Bulletin générale de thérapeutique médicale et chiurgicale* 1837, 322).

Galien's autosadomasochism was a particularly literal form of "self-abuse," but it was just one of a variety of onanistically inspired "unnatural" stimulations and liaisons that increasingly preoccupied nineteenth-century physicians.[40] Once again, however, Rousseau provided the most publicized example of how the "convenient vice" and a "bizarre taste" could induce a youngster to avoid "normal" sexual contacts and imaginatively associate sensual pleasure with "unnatural" acts. The critical passage is the famous spanking scene of the *Confessions*. Rousseau recounts how as a child he had feared being punished by Mlle. Lambercier, his surrogate mother while he was a boarder in her brother's house. To Rousseau's great surprise, he found the first spanking pleasurable and it further endeared him to Mlle. Lambercier: "because I had found in pain, in shame even, a mix of sensuality which left me with more desire than fear of receiving this treatment by that same hand." Alas, the second time the spanking was cut short after Mlle. Lambercier "noticed a certain sign that the punishment was not achieving its aim." Thereafter, they were made to sleep in separate rooms and the young Rousseau was treated as a "big boy." Reminiscing over this outwardly innocuous event, the adult Rousseau concluded:

> Who would have believed that this childhood punishment, received at age eight by the hand of a girl of thirty, would determine my tastes, my desires, my passions, my very self for the rest of my life, and furthermore quite contrary to the sense that naturally should have ensued? At the same moment that my senses were set afire, my desires took a turn that, confined to what I had experienced, they never decided to seek anything else. . . . Long tormented knowing not why, I visually devoured beautiful women; my imagination continually recalling them, only to put them to use in my own fashion as so many demoiselles Lamberciers. . . .
>
> To be at the knees of an imperious mistress, obey her orders, beg her forgiveness, were the sweetest pleasures, and the more my lively imagination inflamed my blood, the more I seemed a transfixed lover. One can imagine that this fashion of making love does not get one very far. . . . Therefore, I have possessed few, but nonetheless I have enjoyed great pleasure in my own fashion; that is, by the imagination. (*Confessions*, 15–17)

In this much analyzed passage, Rousseau attributes his lifelong sexual attraction to "punishment" (what we now would call "masochism") to a commonplace experience of childhood—spanking.[41] The importance of associationist mechanisms stands out in this "psycho-sexual genetic narrative": affection for a maternal figure was transferred to the associated act of spanking.[42] Rousseau himself was amazed at the power and persistence of a mental liaison that he viewed as quite contrary to the nature of punishment as well as "contrary to nature," that is, depraved and insane. He hints that these spanking fantasies inflamed his imagination during his solitary vice and in all his future erotic experiences.

In a most candid and dramatic fashion, Rousseau illustrated doctors' worst fears—"bizarre" and painful practices could become associated with genital pleasure and onanism. These unnatural passions could then become the sole focus of one's thoughts. Later, in the nineteenth century, pleasure in corporal punishment would be only one of an increasing number of erotic "monomanias," and the mastupratiomaniac could be baptized under the name of his or her particular type of "unnatural" stimulation.[43] As in Rousseau's case, this pleasure was usually viewed by physicians as the product of chance association and imaginary obsession. Early-nineteenth-century medical writers portrayed masturbation as dangerously hyperpleasurable even if for "bizarre" reasons. Largely echoing Rousseau, Dr. Léopolde Deslandes wrote in the *Dictionary of Practical Medicine and Surgery* that the masturbator had an imaginary object of pleasure with which he could endlessly play and thus delay the sexual dénouement: "His upheavals find here an imagination on fire, and senses prepared to feel them in all their energy. For this reason, masturbation produces on the organism *a more profound impression than coitus*" (1834, 369; emphasis added).

We can now begin to weave together the many conceptual strands of the "dangerous supplement" in Rousseau's erotic confessions and in the medical anti-onanism literature. Most evidently, masturbation represented a "dangerous supplement" to reproductive coitus. Although the morbid physical effects of onanism were worrisome, Rousseau and contemporary doctors especially feared that the "solitary vice" opened the Pandora's box of the imagination— the dangerous supplement to reality. Furthermore, these critics depicted sexual desire, particularly in puberty, as a supplement to "natural" living. But why were these supplements dangerous? Because they threatened to *supplant* that which they originally just *complemented*. Imaginary associations seemed frighteningly protean and tenacious. For example, the *Encyclopédie* warned that the only two healthy and "natural" ways of voiding superfluous seed were in "commerce and union with women" and "that [natural excretion] provoked during the sleep of celibates by voluptuous dreams which supplement equally, and *sometimes even surpass reality*" (20(2):990; emphasis added). Given the "fatal advantage" of its "convenience," the supplement—masturbation, imaginary representation, or sensual writing—threatened to surpass Nature and overwhelm Reason.

Critics who depicted Rousseau's *Confessions* and philosophy as dangerous also remarked on the ill effects of novel reading and imaginativeness on Rousseau's own life and philosophies. Elie Fréron in the *Année littéraire* highlighted Rousseau's confession of having spent whole nights reading novels; from this Fréron concluded: "One now understands the source of that chimerical mind, of that taste for falsity and lies which he conveyed to his philosophy; one is no longer astonished that, being nourished on novels in his childhood, he maintained in adulthood so many paradoxes and romanesque systems" (1782, 153). Fréron failed to see anything in Rousseau's project that had not been done in Saint Augustine's *Confessions*. The only distinction Fréron could identify was the utter shamefulness of Rousseau's avowals (147). But the shamefulness of these confessions was precisely the novelty of Rousseau's autobiography and its exploration of the erotic imagination.

## Speaking the Unmentionable

Writing about oneself is an ancient tradition; however, the word *autobiography* and critical interest in autobiography only date to the late eighteenth century with the rise of bourgeois culture and the modern conception of the subject and individuality. Literary scholars have specifically credited Rousseau with developing the modern autobiographical genre.[44] Although Rousseau labeled his autobiography a "confession," his literary product differs notably from its Roman Catholic predecessors. Traditional confessions, such as Saint Augustine's (I:1(1)), were constructed as pious and penitent monologues with God. The autobiographer, on the other hand, addressed his fellow men (the writer was usually a man addressing presumed male readers). So although autobiography furthered the cult of the self or the "myth of the ego" (Lejeune 1975, 340), it was not a solipsistic discourse: it fundamentally examined the relation between the modern subject and its civic setting.

Rousseau's first preamble to the *Confessions* makes explicit the social function of autobiography. Our understanding of other humans is generally just a reflection of our understanding of ourselves, he explained, but this self-understanding is usually quite limited since, as a social creature, an individual must compare himself with another being (*Confessions*, 1148). In order to further the "knowledge of mankind," Rousseau volunteered himself as the first-ever, brutally candid metric for all comparisons: "I will be truthful; I will be truthful without reserve; I will tell all; the good, the bad, in sum, everything" (1153). He dismissed all previous histories, confessions, and memoirs as merely accounts of *external* actions designed to glorify the author rather than reveal the truth. To know the *truth* of an individual, he emphatically claimed, is to understand the history and processes of the person's *inner* workings (1149).

Such a project, Rousseau declared, required that he invent a new language and a new style to untangle the chaos of his often vile but occasionally sublime sentiments:

> What trivialities, what miseries am I not obliged to expose, into what revolting, indecent, puerile, and often ridiculous details must I not enter to follow the thread of my secret dispositions, to show how every impression that left a trace on my soul entered it for the first time? While I blush at the mere thought of the things I must recount, I know that stern men will yet again treat the humiliation of these shameful avowals as impudence; but either I make these avowals or I disguise myself; because if I silence something I will not be understood on anything, it is all thus bound together, it is all one in my character, and that bizarre and singular assemblage requires all the circumstance of my life to be thoroughly unveiled. (1153)

Given this model of psychic development—in which every sensory impression shapes the soul—an understanding of the subject demands uninhibited revelation. We can therefore better understand Rousseau's need to confess his masturbatory habits, his erotic attachment to punishment, and his sexual entanglements. His confession of the "solitary vice" is special, however. Unlike the revelations of his coital intrigues, this is the sole erotic act that could have gone unmentioned without fear of ulterior revelation by anyone else. Its confession is thus the highest proof of his unreserved candor. The same can be said for Rousseau's confessions of his autoerotic punishment fantasies, to which no one would otherwise have had access. In Rousseau's construction of the "true knowledge" of humans, there is no better demonstration of naked truth than the revelation of one's erotic imagination.

Rousseau correctly predicted the reaction of his contemporaries to such disclosures. To those accustomed to hagiographic memoirs, Rousseau's erotic confessions seemed utterly gratuitous and revolting.[45] Elie Fréron sarcastically predicted that those who had thought Rousseau an ambitious slave of fame, "ready to sacrifice truth for glory," would now be convinced of his utter humility, for "how indeed could one not regard as the most modest and humble of men, someone who would unnecessarily make the most humiliating admissions, who reveals to his contemporaries and to their nephews the shameful frailties, the misery attached to humanity which we would prefer to hide from ourselves, in a word, who exposes himself, gleefully, to eternal ridicule in the eyes of his century and of posterity" (1782, 145–46). How paradoxical that one hostile reviewer in the *Journal des gens du monde* (1782, 112) complained that no one was a lesser seeker of the truth than Jean-Jacques! The critics were unable to accept Rousseau's premise that a truthful exploration of subjectivity demanded that propriety be sacrificed.

I reemphasize that, according to Rousseau, this candor is not simply for the sake of personal exhibitionism but for the purpose of social judgment. But behind Rousseau's philosophical and literary justifications lay a more pressing motivation for his confession. A libelous, anonymous pamphlet, "The Citizens' Sentiment," was distributed in Geneva on December 27, 1764. It accused Rousseau of a litany of sexual crimes: incest, abandonment of his bastard children, and bearing the traces of venereal diseases caught from his debauchery. The author was Voltaire, who lambasted Rousseau for "abjuring all the sentiments of nature just as he strips those of honor and of religion" (1764, 312). Rousseau's first reaction was to deny all accusations. Upon receiving the defamatory broadside, Rousseau had his editor in Paris print copies of Voltaire's text along with a point-by-point defense in the footnotes. Nevertheless, it was true that Rousseau had abandoned his three illegitimate children at orphanages. So, by early January 1765, he decisively resolved to write his *Confessions* to admit this and other "shameful frailties" so that he be known in "all the truth of nature." He must strip himself naked in order to expose himself to the judgment of his peers and of history. "Because my name must endure amongst men," Rousseau wrote in a prophetic voice, "I do not want it to carry a false reputation; I do not want to have attributed to myself virtues or vices that I did not possess" (*Confessions*, 1153).

So it was a sex scandal that fueled this "first ever" truthful autobiography. All the more reason, then, that Rousseau dedicated himself to displaying the secret vices of his erotic life—to the horror of his detractors.

Rousseau's gambit worked. Posthumously, the notion of virtue was tightly bound to his person and works; these were regularly invoked by Revolutionary orators justifying their political positions in the name of that exceptional Rousseauvian virtue.[46] However, the Rousseauvian confession of the secret depths was not always seen as salutary to the Republic—particularly when those depths lay in the erotic imagination.

## Imaginary Hygiene

While Rousseau hoped his erotic self-exploration and self-revelation would serve to clear his name and to contribute to social psychology, his contemporary critics argued otherwise. To them, Rousseau's personal and literary activities were matters of dangerous self-indulgence. Just as the "dangerous supplement" had helped the solitary Rousseau turn pain into his core erotic passion and "abjure the sentiments of nature," critics feared that "solitary pleasure" would turn other children into erotically self-absorbed, alienated, and antisocial beings.[47] Dr. Desruelles, for example, portrayed a typical life history of masturbation:

> A vague unease, an aimless desire, an uncertain discomfort, without real cause, at least for him, everything agitates, torments, pushes him involuntarily perhaps, towards a pleasure he has yet to know, for which he searches instinctually but which escapes him because of his innocence. Satisfied, that deceiving pleasure soon vanishes, inspiring a desire to see it reborn. An uneasy curiosity has begun, and the fleeting but attractive delirium of the senses terminates the shameful act that will devour his life, unless he renounce immediately. Somber, melancholic, hiding from himself, the masturbator seeks out isolation and obscurity; he has neither rest nor real enjoyment; without fondness for those around him, he is entirely possessed by his disgusting passion. (1822, 32–33)

This characterization of the habit of onanism as a "monomania" was commonplace in the early nineteenth century after Jean Esquirol developed the concept of the monomanias in 1810. The total obsession with a "bizarre taste" did not literally drive Rousseau to "the point of depravation and insanity," as he claimed in his *Confessions* (16), but physicians diagnosed many young people in which it supposedly did. Take, for example, a case reported by the preeminent hygienist A. J. B. Parent-Duchâtelet: an eight-year-old girl with "vicious and criminal penchants" whose addiction to masturbation from the age of four was so strong that she threatened to kill her parents when they tried to curtail her solitary vice. The Paris Commissioner of Police concluded that "only this mortal habit [of onanism] could have disturbed this child's intellectual organs, and caused the horrible monomania from which she suffers" (Parent-Duchâtelet 1832, 189).

In order to prevent the initial corruption of the innocent, doctors recommended a whole variety of physical restraints and forms of surveillance. But as the disease of masturbation was increasingly understood in the nineteenth century as a mental disorder involving a perverted imagination, they feared that conventional physical therapies were, at best, palliative. Dr. Claude François Lallemand in his widely reviewed volumes on "involuntary seminal losses" fretted: "The eyes may watch the book, the ears listen to the word of the schoolteacher, but who can stop the imagination from working? At night it will be more difficult yet; no surveillance could stop it, nor even observe it" (1836–42, 1:432).

If the imagination was the culprit, then it made sense to target it for treatment. The director of the lunatic ward of the Salpêtrière, Dr. Etienne-Jean Georget, therefore recommended that when signs of onanism are noted in children, the doctor "strike their imagination with lectures and prescribe rigorous surveillance in a severe tone" (1840, 79). Dr. Demeaux (an anatomist in the Paris Faculty of Medicine, the vice president of the Anatomical Society, and a fervent admirer of Lallemand) advocated exploiting the natural shame and timidity of the onanist by subjecting young people between the ages of ten and twenty to surprise inspections twice a year by a specially trained national corps of masturbation inspectors (1856, 1857, 1861). Those children who were not deterred from the "abominable maneuver" by the mere fear of detection, Demeaux reasoned, would at least be caught early in their addiction when intervention was still possible (1857).

Lallemand had proposed an even more radical intervention—fundamental ideological reform through a return to the "principles of the Revolution and the Convention": "It would be necessary to ground the base of a national education on the *duties of the country* towards its citizens, in order to extract from all the *physical, intellectual,* and *moral* dispositions the greatest possible benefit for the prosperity of society, for the happiness of each individual" (1:435). Lallemand makes it clear that, by the nineteenth century, the anti-onanism campaign was not simply aimed at preserving the health of individual children but, more important, the health of the state.

The Revolution first made "social medicine" an institutional reality, and during the Napoleonic period French "public hygiene" (or public health) rose to world prominence. The new public hygienists argued that the health of the individual body and that of the social body were closely linked.[48] As Dr. Julien Joseph Virey stated in his *Philosophical Hygiene, or Health in the Physical, Moral, and Political Regimen of Modern Civilization* (1828): "We inherit vigor or weakness from the social state; its constitution forms our own, inspires our customs, or deploys our passions."[49]

It was inevitable that hygienists would also view "solitary passion" not just as a matter of individual morbidity but, more ominously, as a symptom of social pathology. Alternating their critique between the individual and the social impacts of masturbation, Drs. Fournier and Béguin inveighed against juvenile onanism:

> Above all it is in young people of one and the other sex that masturbation causes the greatest ravages; it is all the more fatal since it strikes *society* in its element, so to speak, and tends to destroy it by enervating, from their first steps, the subjects who would efficaciously contribute to its preservation and splendor. How often we see these weakened, pallid beings, equally feeble of body and mind, owing only to masturbation, principal object of their thoughts, the state of languor and exhaustion to which they have sunk! Thenceforth, incapable of defending the *nation* or of serving it by honorable or useful work, they lead, in a society that despises them, a life that they have rendered void for others and often onerous to themselves. (1819, 101–2; emphasis added)

No longer was masturbation a devastating disease simply because children were malleable and vulnerable, but, more important, because children were the future wealth of the nation. Fournier and Béguin newly emphasized that self-pollution was not merely a matter of self-destruction but one of social despoliation.

In the nineteenth century, the economy between the individual and the social body was understood to run on the currency of "heredity"—a biological wealth that was increasingly perceived as a collective endowment.[50] France's vigor seemed particularly threatened given the nation's declining birth rate, which hygienists had noted since 1815.[51] Those who squandered and weakened their seed were therefore viewed as especially noxious to society. Public hygienist Joseph Henri Reveillé-Parise decried the catastrophic effects of "libertinage of the hand" on social strength:

> Masturbation . . . is one of those scourges that attack and soundly destroy humanity. . . . In my opinion, neither the plague, nor war, nor smallpox, nor innumerable other such evils produce as disastrous results for humanity as this fatal habit. It is the destroyer of civilized societies, and all the more active since it operates continually and saps the generations. (1828, 93)

He further warned that pale, nervous women exhausted by manustupration "could not exercise the functions of maternity," and likewise, weak, effeminate, corset-wearing men would transmit their masturbatory deterioration to future generations. "Thus the tree is mutilated right down to its roots," lamented Reveillé-Parise (93–94). Twenty-four years later, he would still be echoed by Dr.

Figure 3. Aba, an "idiot" at Bicêtre Hospital. In his treatise, *Des maladies mentales* (1838), J. E. D. Esquirol writes, "Aba is an onanist and robber" (93; Plate 22). "Idiots are extremely prone to masturbation, and they indulge in this deplorable practice to excess, without modesty, without shame and in the presence of everyone" (102). (Courtesy of the Department of Special Collections of the Van Pelt-Dietrich Library, University of Pennsylvania.)

Debourge, who condemned the "deplorable solitary maneuver" as a "potent cause of depopulation, whose effects are all the more fatally disastrous since, although it may not kill, it tends to bastardize, bestialize, degrade, and degenerate the species" (1852, 314). (See Figures 3 and 4.)

What emerges from the antimasturbatory literature of the nineteenth century is the perception of "deviant" individuals as viruses of the social corps—polluting its national strength and purity. Clearly, a profound change had occurred since Rousseau's and Tissot's warnings regarding the corrupting effects of civilization on the innocent, natural bodies of children. By the time of the Restoration (1814–1830), the vector of contagion had been reversed: Reveillé-Parise and other hygienists were denouncing "mastupratiomaniacs" as the "destroyers of civilized societies."

Figure 4. An insane masturbator (the iconography suggests he is Jewish). J. E. D. Esquirol notes that "Monsieur G. . . is an onanist. He abstains during the day because he is observed, but as soon as he is in his bed, if left alone, he abandons himself to his morbid practices, and ceases only when warned or if he notices he is under surveillance. . . . This plate represents this idiot in his habitual pose, the regularity of his traits is remarkable" (1838, 92 Plate 22). Note his fixed hand gestures. (Courtesy of the Department of Special Collections of the Van Pelt-Dietrich Library, University of Pennsylvania.)

While the condemnation of masturbation had not abated, during the intervening years the dramatic political, social, and ideological conflicts of the Revolution and First Empire had altered the French worldview. Neither the "state of nature" nor the "noble savage" were tenable Arcadian fictions any longer. Lallemand, for example, rejected Rousseauvian pastoralism and declared that peasants commonly engaged in onanism as well as sodomy and bestiality (1836, 1:440). The colonized "primitives" had also proven far from docile after the Revolution, particularly those of Haiti, where ex-slaves Toussaint-Louverture and Jean-Jacques Dessaline led a revolt that eventually ousted the French in

1803. The Rousseauvian ideal of the Noble Savage, free of civilized, societal constraints, paled further as early-nineteenth-century ethnographers returned from the "wild" with tales of barbaric "primitives" who were slaves to violent, natural drives.[52] Closer to home, the once idealized healthy, happy "productive classes" became the disgruntled industrial workers, and these urban poor, grouped into large crowds, were represented as volatile, rebellious, and primitive masses.[53] Even children, who Rousseau had represented as naturally innocent and good, were increasingly viewed with skepticism and distrust in the nineteenth century. Physicians compared the developing infantile nervous system and moral sense to those of "primitives." These, in turn, were represented as adults in a state of arrested cultural development. The author of a work on *Insanity in Children* observed:

> We well know how fears, hatred, jealousy, we could even say sentiments of vengeance, are frequent at an early age. . . . [The least incitement or praise unequally divided] suffices to ignite an explosion of truly morbid passions, of that egoistic jealousy, shall we say, that one finds among *uncivilized peoples, primitives, veritable infants*, having naught but sensual and nutritional needs, and going even further, that jealousy one likewise finds among *animals*. (P. Moreau 1888, 20–21; emphasis added)

Childhood onanism, he continued, produced an inevitable arrest in cerebral and mental development at a state of "moral imbecility," fixing the child's moral sense at a primitive, quasi-bestial level.[54] After the Revolution and with the political reaction that accompanied the First Empire under Bonaparte, even the fantasy of innocence was defunct.[55] Rather than waxing nostalgic over a childlike utopia, antimasturbationist writers worried about social decrepitude, or worse, atavism. And given the new public hygiene perspective, the onanist was less to be pitied than cursed as a canker on the vulnerable social body.

## Polluting Knowledges

Dorinda Outram (1989) has suggested that in the violent contests for political order that followed the French Revolution, the individual, private body was transformed into a necessary object for ensuring the order and productivity of the social corpus. I have argued that this reconfiguration of the body began before the Revolution, as *philosophes* and social theorists started condemning masturbation and the erotic imagination as dangerous supplements to Reason and Nature. Hygienists of the imagination reconceptualized seminal loss not merely as personally debilitating but also as socially enfeebling because "self pollution" infected society's phantasmic institutions: hereditary purity, moral fiber, and national strength. To heal the social body, this venom had to be squeezed to the surface. So even as it was being vilified, expression of the erotic was becoming essential to thorough expositions of the self.

Rousseau's words would, therefore, resonate with ironic truth throughout the nineteenth century:

> I recount very odious things about myself, which I would be loath to excuse; but it is also the most secret history of my soul, these are my confessions at all cost. It is just that my reputation expiate the ill resulting from my desire to preserve it. I fully expect public denunciations, the severity of judgments pronounced out loud, and I submit myself to them. But may each reader imitate me, may he enter within himself as I have done, and in the depths of his conscience dare he say to himself: *I am better than that man.* (*Confessions*, 1155)

Rousseau defies us to explore the most "revolting" and "indecent" chapters of the secret history of our souls. It is only these pages that offer society a true history of the self and thereby "further the knowledge of mankind" in general. His challenge was clear: "May mankind hear my confessions, may they moan at my indignities, may they blush at my miseries. May each in turn bare their heart with the same sincerity" (*Confessions*, 5). Throughout the nineteenth-century, growing numbers of people took up the Rousseauvian challenge. By their own volition or through medicolegal coercion, they would plumb the depths of their secret sexual beings at the behest of medical professionals devoted to healing onanism and other "bizarre" sexual tastes. As medical theories and social politics changed with time, so too did erotic confessions. Solitary, sensual reverie lingered, nevertheless, as a leitmotif in these emerging narratives stimulating, in turn, novel forms of sexuality and the public visibility of erotism.

# CHAPTER **2**

*Erotomaniacs:
Self-Representation
in Courts and
Asylums*

The patient spends her day lying on her back, her legs spread and bent at the knees. People have complained to her in vain about this posture; she says it is the only position she can tolerate because as soon as her thighs are touching, she feels a fiery heat in the genitals, followed immediately by extremely intense sensations and the venereal spasm. She adds that her imagination greatly contributes to augmenting these accidents, and she claims to have continuously present in her mind *seductive places* and *voluptuous images* which she struggles in vain to dispel. In a series of letters she has sent me, she describes at length the origin and gradual development of her illness. (Baillarger 1845, 147)

Mademoiselle G—— was twenty-four years old when she came to the attention of Dr. Baillarger, a member of the prestigious Medico-Psychological Society and co-founder of its journal, the *Medico-Psychological Annals* (where the case history was published). Born of an insane mother, Mlle. G—— suffered from the pallor, weakness, amenorrhea, gastric pains, and circulatory anomalies characteristic of the vague diagnosis of "chlorosis" (the "green" disease of young women).[1] The unusual and publishable aspect of her case was her "remarkable mental disorder": "The patient's imagination is constantly occupied with erotic thoughts. Mademoiselle G—— takes pleasure in reporting in the finest details the sensations she claims to experience quite often, despite herself, in her genital organs" (147). These descriptions were so explicit that her female neighbors had to discontinue their visits "because of the obscenity of her speech and the disgust it inspired" (147).

Only Dr. Baillarger (and his medical brethren) had the moral fortitude and scientific defenses to receive Mlle. G——'s written confession, which detailed the evolution of her voluptuous sensations. It all began around age four, she reported, with pains in her genitals. This was also when she began masturbating; however, her diagnosis was not simply "onanism" as in the many cases we encountered in the previous chapter. Her mental deviation seemed significantly different. With the onset of menstruation, her pains were accompanied by the vivid sensation that her "genitals opened wide." Her "imagination was assailed by voluptuous ideas and images, and at the same time intense desires." "All these things which happened with such a lively and continuous force in my imagination," she complained, "always procured me a great sensation of pleasure" (147–8). Her bedsheets even aggravated her genital heat. She slept less, worked continuously, recited religious poems, and even tried skipping rope to alleviate the genital fires and the images of seductive places and things that troubled her mind. But nothing succeeded in distracting her, she moaned: "Solitude, silence, the purity of the sky, bird songs, the beauty of the countryside were, or have been since then and still, pernicious" (148). Even when she tried entertaining herself with a doll, she wanted to dress it as a boy: "'That doll,' she says, 'would have become a pernicious object . . . the mere sight of it would have given me ideas'" (149). She had erotic dreams that woke her suddenly at night with acute sensations and violent spasms. She applied ice packs to the head and genitals and tried leeches and cupping "in her continual battle against her malady," but to no avail. "The mental desires totally mastered the imagination," reported Baillarger. "Then developed what Mlle. G—— calls the latest symptoms, those which she does not dare describe in her letters" (148). She confessed to Dr. Baillarger in person that "despite herself, she not only experienced spontaneous voluptuous sensations, but sometimes she had the distinct impression that those sensations were caused by a body introduced in her organs, in other words, there was a *complete reproduction of the venereal act*" (149; emphasis added). Baillarger diagnosed Mlle. G—— as an erotomaniac and had her placed in a hospice for the insane. After a few months of unspecified treatments, she was discharged as "perfectly cured of her chlorosis and erotic hallucinations" (149). Her long-term remission was assured by a prompt marriage.

Although Mlle. G—— represents the pornographic ideal of the freely available woman in perpetual heat, she also embodies the logical and terrifying product of masturbatory addiction: the imaginary pleasure of solitary vice ultimately produces a delusional addict, sensing venereal pleasure independent of actual coitus. Baillarger, however, quickly passed over the matter of onanism—by then considered a symptom rather than an independent diagnosis. More than a mechanical addiction, Mlle. G——'s disorder was understood as an illusion or hallucination produced in her body; she was driven insane by a "desire in the genital parts."[2]

The symptom that compromised her virginity and was most disturbing, particularly to G—— herself, was the imaginary "reproduction of the venereal act." Her insistence on describing in exquisite detail these voluptuous sensations—what we might call her "erotolalia"—was the most unbecoming and antisocial aspect of her disorder. It literally drove away all her female friends. Mlle. G——'s disorder totally set aside love or actual coitus. Instead, it centered on a pure sensual illusion and, most remarkably, the voicing of that erotic imaginary. Baillarger, therefore, turned to the diagnosis of erotomania, which as we will see had been used for centuries. In the early nineteenth century, however, alienists synthesized the prior associations of "love melancholia" and "monomania" with the emerging notion of *érotisme*—sexual obsessions and compulsions that were bizarre, antisocial, pornographic, or criminal. As medical interest shifted from love to sex, doctors were one of the few auditors who permitted, even compelled, Mlle. G—— to indulge in her erotolalia. To speak of her sensual experience and imagination was not just a matter of erotic self-expression, but also of her self-defense and medical therapy.[3] After a brief review of the erotomania diagnosis, I examine how the medicolegal framing of the erotic was a vehicle for sexual self-representation ("er*auto*graphy"). As we saw with the campaign against onanism, doctors portrayed the erotic imagination as a dangerous, morbid force requiring increasing analysis and regulation. Furthermore, forensic medicine and "social hygiene" in the early nineteenth century, for professional reasons, encouraged and even obliged erotic confessions. This self-representation took many forms: personal examinations of sexuality, medical confessions of the erotic imaginary, and legal self-defense. Through this rich outpouring of patient/defendant confessions, the protean diagnosis of "erotomania" broke down into increasingly fine varieties of *érotisme*. Finally, we will see how the erotic became embroiled in political strategies of perverse representation which insinuated the erotic into the social imagination of the time.

## From Heroic Love to Erotic Delirium

The diagnosis of erotomania was in desuetude in the twentieth century until it was officially recognized in 1987 by the American Psychiatric Association, which defined it as the delusion of being loved by another, usually of higher status.[4] Several psychiatrists have tried to legitimize the diagnosis by tracing its supposedly continuous history from Hippocratic cases to medieval *amor insanus* to Esquirol's nineteenth-century monomaniacs to Clérambault's Syndrome in the twentieth century.[5] In so doing, they often fail to note the dramatic changes in the characteristics of erotomania.[6] Most significantly, medieval love melancholy was a form of excessive, unrequited love for another, whereas contemporary erotomania is a delusion of being loved. Furthermore, nineteenth-century erotomania described manic patients, like Mlle. G——, with "perverse" *sexual* sensations, obsessions, and compulsions but who confessed no particular *amorous* interests at all. In other words, a connotation of deviant sexuality (*érotisme*) was introduced into the diagnosis of erotomania in the nineteenth century and later withdrawn from it in the twentieth. The nineteenth-century incarnation of erotomania is therefore central to the contemporary notion of the erotic: something "which is associated with physical love, which is of a sensual nature, sexual," or artistic works "which can incite the search for physical pleasure."[7]

As I mentioned in my earlier discussion of truffles, the association of *érotisme* with sensuality or the sexual drive only emerged in the nineteenth century. What would it have meant to speak of the *érotique* before then?[8] Since the Middle Ages, the noun *érotique* referred to an artistic form: chivalrous love poetry or songs. As a medical term, it referred to heroic, usually unrequited, chivalrous love leading to *melancholia*, that is, a humoral preponderance of "black bile." This variety of romantic melancholia entered the medical canon in the eleventh century with Constantine the African's *Viaticum*, which in its numerous recopyings used *amor heroicus* and *amor eroticus* interchangeably.[9] The diagnosis of *amor hereos* was predominantly applied to aristocratic men during the Middle Ages, but was increasingly employed during the Renaissance in reference to women.[10] Physicians of the time also began associating erotomania with disorders of the genitals.[11]

Jacques Ferrand, in his French treatise *On Love-Sickness, or Erotic Melancholy* (1610), followed in the medieval humoral tradition by identifying the "erotic" with melancholic love: "*Love, or this Eroticall Passion is a kind of Dotage, proceeding from an Irregular desire of enjoying a lovely object, and is attended on by Feare, and sadnesse*" (1640, 31). Unlike his medieval predecessors, he argued that "love-melancholia" affected women as well as men. The word *erotomania* appeared for the first time when his book was translated into English as *Erotomania, or a treatise discoursing of the essence, causes, symptoms, prognostics, and cure of Love, or erotique melancholy* (1640).[12] Among the symptoms of erotomania in women, Ferrand included the "green sickness" or chlorosis (as in Mlle. G———'s case) as well as *furor uterinus*. Ferrand claimed that *furor uterinus* (as well as satyriasis) were types of love melancholy (1640, 93). By the late eighteenth century the connections between "erotic melancholia" and frank sexual desire (nymphomania or satyriasis) were still uncertain. In *Nymphomania*, for example, Bienville clearly associated masturbation with "uterine fury," but he did not describe either of these phenomena as "erotic" or as forms of erotomania. Although the *Encyclopédie* linked the *érotique* to an "excess of corporeal appetite," it clearly distinguished "incensed love [erotomania] from uterine fury and satyriasis, which are also an excess of this passion, but in which all modesty has been lost, whereas those in love retain their modesty, often even accompanied by extremely respectful feelings, sometimes even to excess" (12(2):913). Love, not carnal desire, is the distinct feature of erotic melancholy. As far as the *Encyclopédie* was concerned, "erotomania"—whether totally chaste or tinged by sexual desire—was the result of inordinate love, whereas uncontrollable lust was characteristic of nymphomania and satyriasis.

This distinction was in force in two early-nineteenth-century cases of nymphomania and satyriasis.[13] A Lyonnaise noblewoman in her forties suffered from periodic fits of delirium characterized by obscene outbursts, sexual attacks on her chambermaids, and the insertion of various items in her vagina and between her breasts. Dr. Rodamel (1806) diagnosed her as suffering from nymphomania or hysteria (he used the terms interchangeably to denote a primary disease of the uterus).

Dr. Rony-Duprest (1801), of the Paris medical faculty, described a twenty-year-old man who had engaged in three years of excessive onanism in adolescence (up to fifteen times a day), weakening his strength and intelligence. The patient began having delusions that his employer's wife loved him, and he regularly had an erection and ejaculated each time she looked at him. Nocturnal pollutions became frequent. As in other onanism cases we have seen so far, the reading of fiction (in this case, Racine's *Phèdre*) was blamed for the patient's ultimate mental undoing. Imagining himself to be Hippolytus, he reenacted the climax of *Phèdre* by throwing himself at the feet of his employer (imagined to be Theseus) and declaring his illicit love. In spite of enforced separation from the fantasized Phædra, the patient continued to suffer from involuntary emissions until treated with antispasmodics and tonics. This poor shopkeeper-Hippolytus was firmly diagnosed with satyriasis, not erotomania or erotic melancholy. Like the aristocratic nymphomaniac, this was not a case of chaste, exalted love or melancholic disappointment. In the opinion of the examining physicians, both were cases of primary genital derangement with secondary lubricious, delusional thoughts.

Alienists had abandoned humoral theories of erotomania by the time Jean-Etienne Dominique Esquirol reclassified it in the 1810s as a form of "monomania." Esquirol applied the new diagnosis to those with a focal mental pathology or idée fixe in an otherwise sane mind: for example, an obsession with ambition, with murder (homicidal monomania), with fire (pyromania), with theft (kleptomania), and so on.[14] Although he eliminated the medieval image of heroic melancholy from his erotomania diagnosis, Esquirol retained its association with love. It was purely the mental fixation on love that was the defining feature of the disease (1815, 186). Unlike nymphomania and satyriasis—in which the genitals were the seat of morbidity—"in erotomania, love is in the head. The nymphomaniac and the satyriac are victims of a physical disorder; erotomaniacs are the toys of their *imagination*" (186; emphasis added). Esquirol's examples of classic erotomania are the love of Abelard and Heloïse, and Don Quixote's chivalrous love "which was practically epidemic in his time" (191). With Esquirol, erotomania shifted from being a somatic/humoral disease to a being a mental/nervous disorder predominantly due to "moral" causes (in the Enlightenment sense of psychological and environmental causation).[15] Esquirol's theory of the moral etiology of erotomania integrated earlier critiques of the imagination, novels, and onanism:

> Even though it may erupt at an advanced age, young people are nonetheless most vulnerable to this disease, especially young people [or young women, *jeunes personnes*] with a nervous temperament, a lively, ardent imagination, dominated by self-love, the allure of pleasures, idleness, the reading of novels, a vice-ridden education. Masturbation (in communicating to the nervous system a greater though factitious sensitivity) [and] continence (in impressing

upon it a very energetic activity) equally predispose to erotic delirium. (Esquirol 1815, 192)

Esquirol continued to distinguish nymphomania from erotomania even in his final treatise on mental diseases (1838).[16]

The dividing wall between the neuropsychological basis of erotomania versus the genital etiology of nymphomania, however, was starting to crumble at this time because physiologists perceived an intimate association between the body and the brain. Esquirol himself, in keeping with earlier critics of onanism, had warned that masturbation could make the nervous system hypersensitive and vulnerable to erotomania. Dr. Louyer-Villermay, in his entry on nymphomania in the *Dictionary of Medical Sciences,* initially distinguished this supposedly uterine disorder from erotomania ("insanity produced by the pains of love") (1819a, 576). Nymphomaniacs were sexually voracious madwomen driven by an unappeasable genital itch to obsessive masturbation or sex as well as lascivious gestures, obscene language, and lubricious conversation (563). The nymphomaniac's only salvation was a speedy marriage to a vigorous young man who could "cure her through the repeated delights of marriage" (588). Yet he also argued that nymphomania constituted "a particular species of alienation, a true monomania" (564). Therefore, Esquirol's "moral" (that is, psychological) therapy for erotomania could also be adapted to the treatment of nymphomania:

> The physician must take care to diminish this sympathy [between the uterus and the nervous system] by an active and busy life, by placid and varied distractions, in order to act in a favorable way on the imagination, to calm and rectify it. Additionally, he will strive to distance from the patient's sight and hearing all objects that usually excite their senses, such as statues, prints, *erotic* reading and conversations, and even music, especially that which is melodious. (Louyer-Villermay 1819a, 595; emphasis added)

In blurring the boundaries between nymphomania and erotomania, Villermay elided the *érotique* with the overtly sexual or obscene. The erotic arts were no longer those poems and songs evoking sublime love, but those charged with sensuality and thus likely to induce "disgusting obscenity" in the nervously susceptible. The behavior, language, and writings of the erotomaniac reflexively became characterized as "erotic," betraying the "sexual delirium" of his or her mental disorder. I have focused thus far on the transformations of *erotomania* as a medical term. But, as with onanism, erotomania also emerged as a matter of social disorder because manifestations of the erotic imagination sometimes came into conflict with the law and public morals.

## Committing Erotomaniographers

In 1816, a young scion of a distinguished family was confined to a Parisian hospital on grounds of insanity. The suspected patient, Mr. D——, immediately appealed to a lawyer complaining of false detention and calumny. His ultraroyalism, he claimed, had made him the victim of political persecution by the more constitutionally oriented Minister of Police. The lawyer asked Dr. Gandois-Hery to examine the supposed patient. After two interviews with Mr. D——, Dr. Gandois reported back to the lawyer that the "patient" seemed quite sane and that his plaint was reasonable. Deciding to represent the young man, the lawyer met the Police Commissioner only to discover a startling aspect of the case. Mr. D—— had been arrested for harassing a princess with loveletters "of the most disgusting obscenity and revolting drawings of the supposed pleasures he had enjoyed in her arms."[17]

Mr. D—— was eventually set free but again arrested in 1826. This time he had the distinction of being examined, defended, and then indicted by the leading alienists of the day: Esquirol, F. Leuret (Esquirol's leading disciple), C.-C.-H. Marc, and G. Ferrus.[18] Leuret published Mr. D——'s medicolegal dossier in 1830 in the *Annals of Public Hygiene and Forensic Medicine*. The case exemplifies the diverse professional concerns that made erotism the focus for social regulation of the imagination in the second third of the century.

Esquirol and C.-C.-H. Marc had founded the *Annals of Public Hygiene* just the previous year. It was an important forum for advancing the scientific status and broad social utility of medicine as advocated by Esquirol's circle of physicians.[19] The journal's prospectus was a manifesto for social medicine:

> Medicine does not have as its sole object the study and cure of disease, it also has intimate links with social organization; sometimes it assists the legislator in the creation of laws, often it enlightens the magistrate in their application, and it always keeps watch alongside the administration over the maintenance of public health. Thus applied to the needs of society, this part of our knowledge constitutes *public hygiene* and *legal medicine*. (Marc 1829, v)

Advances in the human sciences could only produce widespread good if legislators and judges allowed themselves to be enlightened by physicians. As we saw in the previous chapter, the advocates of public hygiene claimed the new sciences would aid in the "perfection of institutions" such as hospitals, schools, prisons, workplaces, cemeteries, and barracks, as well as society in general. Increasingly, physicians intervened in court matters under the justification that "faults and crimes are diseases of society which we must labor to cure" through the sciences of physiology and psychology which "lend their enlightenment to the science of government" (Marc 1829, vii). The monomania diagnosis was a particularly important vehicle for legitimizing the medical profession's incursion into legal affairs.

The title of Leuret's article on Mr. D—— betrays the professional interests behind this odd case: "EROTIC MONOMANIA Misjudged by People Ignorant in the Observation of the Insane." Leuret bluntly claimed that the differentiation of insane from rational people often was difficult and required special medical expertise. "The affair I am going to recount," Leuret continued, "is striking proof of what I advance; already known to the public in some of its details, it is interesting above all for the details ignored till now and which most strongly demonstrate the necessity of physicians' intervention to enlighten jurists and members of the jury when an accused person is suspected of insanity" (198). The case thus became an occasion to defend the monomania diagnosis and the exclusive ability of seasoned alienists in its determination. The moral of the case was that Dr. Gandois (who was ashamed to have been duped by Mr. D——) later became secretary-in-chief of the Royal Asylum of Charenton, and after daily contact with five to six hundred insane people "soon learned to recognize how numerous the varieties of mental derangement could be" (209). When, ten years later, Gandois heard that two lawyers, Messrs. Dupin and Tardif, had been duped into defending Mr. D——, Gandois immediately intervened to prevent another embarrassing professional snafu.

Mr. D—— in fact had a thirty year history as a writer and drawer of "erotic" materials. He had been repeatedly arrested for addressing pornographic epistles to Empress Josephine Bonaparte, Queen Hortense, Mlle. de Beauharnais, Mlle. Salysbury, and other noblewomen "of great power, merit, or beauty" (200, 218). He had also been arrested for surreptitiously entering the homes and carriages of noblewomen. Mr. D—— had been committed to Charenton five times and diagnosed as suffering from "erotic delirium." Each time he had been released because he disrupted the institutions: "he disturbed the imagination of the patients, or planned escape plots with them" (211).

Charenton, under the Old Regime, had been run by the Brothers of Charity not only as a hospital for lunatics but also as a prison for those detained under *lettres de cachet*. It was closed in 1795 but was reopened two years latter as the national asylum for the insane and a model institution for "moral therapy."[20] One of its most famous inmates, the Marquis de Sade, had also provoked the ire of Charenton's physician-in-chief because the "abominable man" and his asylum theater productions had a morbid influence on the imagination of the other patients. The doctor begged the Minister of Police to remove Sade to a prison because *"The man is not a lunatic.* His only delirium is that of vice."[21] Although Sade had been arrested in 1801 for his "immoral" novel *Justine* (which had sold without legal problems since 1791), it is more likely that Bonaparte objected to *Zoloë and Her Two Acolytes,* a recently published pornographic roman-à-clef. Although anonymous, it was widely attributed to Sade. The novel's heroine, Zoloë, was a thinly veiled representation of Josephine Bonaparte herself (Lever 1991, 588). The police commissioner noted that Sade would have remained in prison had he not "employed all the means his depraved imagination suggested in order to seduce and corrupt the young men" who unfortunately were detained on the same corridor as he. The commissioner concluded that "this incorrigible man was in a perpetual state of libertine dementia." He had Sade transferred in March 1803 to the Bicêtre hospice and the next month to Charenton as a "patient of the police."[22] "His family," wrote the director of Charenton, "in order to attenuate, if possible, the shame of his writings, sought to have the Marquis's perversity pass for insanity," and therefore made every effort to transfer him to an asylum.[23] So, indeed, Sade was not insane, but politically pornographic.

Similarly, the leading alienists of Paris could not detect a thread of mental instability in Mr. D—— despite numerous interviews. Nevertheless, Esquirol, Marc, and Ferrus declared that Mr. D—— suffered for twenty-eight years from intermittent "erotic delirium" and lacked the discernment for judging the gravity of his actions (Leuret 1830, 220).

The debates on the legitimacy of the monomania diagnosis/defense are especially fascinating in this case because of the patient's own intervention. After an evaluation by Esquirol, Marc, and Ferrus while detained in the hospital in 1826, Mr. D—— wrote to Dupin complaining that it was clear that

> the three doctors would like to establish the system according to which a man, although perfectly reasonable, can be accused of insanity based on a single fact that they would like to impute to him. They give that absurd system the name of monomania. Thus, in my case, they would have one assume: 1st. that the fact is real to prove my monomania; and 2nd. assume monomania to prove the alleged fact. What an absurd, extravagant, and vicious circle! (203–4)

Mr. D——'s critique is indeed impeccable. Not surprisingly, Dupin and Tardif originally accepted it and wrote in Mr. D——'s defense to the instructional judge. The two doctors got to the heart of the monomania controversy: "Monomania is a modern resource; it conveniently allows one either to wrench the guilty from the just severity of the laws, or to deprive a citizen of his rights arbitrarily. When one could not say, *he is guilty,* one would say, *he is crazy;* and one would then see Charenton replace the Bastille" (206). Dupin and Tardif were alluding to the fact that Charenton had compromised its status as a model mental asylum by taking in "police patients" (like Sade). However reasonable Mr. D——'s analysis of the monomania diagnosis as a vehicle for the arbitrary institutionalization of undesirables, his arguments only served, in Leuret's eyes, to further justify the diagnosis, since the most dangerous monomaniac is precisely the one who most convincingly seems sane. This truly was a vicious circle!

What was to be done with Mr. D——, who had been volleyed back and forth between prison and hospitals, Dr. Gandois asked. Imprisonment or deprivation of civil rights was unjust and could be a "terrible means of oppression and eternal captivity" (213). He used the case to argue for the establishment of special institutions for treating such monomaniacal patients who were believed curable. Unless such people were speedily expedited to Charenton, they would probably become incurable waiting for provincial justice to be served (213). Gandois pleaded for special insanity laws, echoing Esquirol's plea in 1819 for a national asylum system. (This system would eventually be instituted through the law of June 30, 1838.) Gandois recognized that it was necessary to balance "the interests of public safety and prompt treatment against the safeguarding of individual liberty" (214).

It was precisely in "the interest of public safety" that medicolegal professionals increasingly examined, classified, and institutionalized the behaviorally and sexually deviant.[24] Erotomaniacs were thus pawns in a number of professional debates over the monomania diagnosis, the forensic authority of the medical profession, and the demands for a public asylum system. But at the same time, the label itself was undergoing a major transformation. Although Leuret unproblematically labeled Mr. D—— as an erotic monomaniac, the case is clearly different from eighteenth-century descriptions of erotomania, or even Esquirol's 1815 definition. Mr. D—— was never described as melancholic (nor even manic); he denied any love for the women in question, and his form of expression was far from gallant. These "more or less erotic letters" displayed "disgusting obscenity" (207, 200). In Mr. D——'s case, "erotism" lost any connotation of love and was transmogrified instead into pure lascivious vulgarity. Mr. D—— was an "erotomaniographer" of a new erotic world, a pornographer in the present sense: a producer and circulator of sexual texts. While the distribution of these texts and images brought him into conflict with the law, it was the mere production of them that physicians took as a symptom of insanity. Like the chronic onanists discussed earlier, Mr. D—— was described as being driven by the irresistible impulse of his "erotic and *solitary* delirium" (211). The "deviation of his vagabond and solitary imagination" was to picture himself in voluptuous scenes with noblewomen (210). He had "fits of delirium which made Mr. D—— take pen in hand to inflame his erotic verve" (208). For the examining doctors, it was quite simply his erotic self-representation—the writing and drawing of his sexual fantasies—that constituted Mr. D——'s filthy folly ( *folie ordurière*) (200).

Although the medicolegal experts claimed to represent Mr. D—— in court, they primarily used the case as grounds for professional authority battles. Ultimately, Mr. D—— had to engage in judicial self-representation. However, even his two letters of self-defense were employed by Leuret as counterevidence of Mr. D——'s sly monomania and of the need for expert alienist examiners. This is, of course, a recurrent danger of erotic self-expression in the medical setting: doctors could turn a "patient's" confessions into evidence of pathology and simultaneously recast those "obscene" stories into therapeutic "meta-pornography," or medical tales about curing the erotic. Thus, through the proliferation of scientific discourses on sex, the medical profession was an accomplice to the "outrages to public decency" it denounced.[25]

## Distinguishing Morbidity from Morality

Erotomania and the monomanias were essential for the medical profession's campaign to gain a foothold in the courtroom and the legislature, but they were slippery platforms since they obliged doctors to uphold conflicting positions. As in Mr. D——'s case, doctors used the erotomania diagnosis to "defend" him from what they portrayed as an unsympathetic society and a harsh legal system which was ignorant of the pathological basis of his misdemeanor. Yet physicians simultaneously portrayed themselves as defenders of "public morals." The resolution of these opposing interests lay in the subtle discrimination between willful vice and true "morbid" eroticism deserving of legal and social clemency and condescension. The diagnostic criteria of erotomania made it possible to integrate moral and social values into the developing conception of the "erotic."

How was erotic monomania different from old-fashioned libertinage (epitomized by Sade)? This was a critical question that concerned Henri-Louis Bayard, a future expert and author on medicolegal matters (1843). Bayard had written his medical thesis on "utero-mania" and presented its medicolegal considerations in an article in the *Annals of Public Hygiene* (1837).

He thoroughly agreed with Villermay's position (discussed above) that nymphomania was a variety of monomania. Furthermore, he made it clear that the confinement of nymphomaniacs was important not only for the protection of the public, but also for the protection of individual families and the institution of the family. Quoting E.-J. Georget, Bayard pointed out that libertinage in itself was not a mental disorder, but in cases of well-born, well-bred people "above need, who forget their dignity, their affections, the interest and honor of the family, to the point of descending without remorse, or even with pleasure to the rank of the most vile creatures, in those cases could not one, as a last resort, justify their interdiction and sequestration because of *a profound moral perversion*, as much as for the depravation of the inclination toward sexual union?" (Bayard 1837, 418). Given the importance he lent to class status in distinguishing immorality from insanity, Bayard most likely would have declared Sade mentally ill. So, although French law was rather permissive in matters of private adult sexuality, doctors could argue that "erotism" demanded regulation because it promoted social disorder and class embarrassment.

The socially disruptive effects of *sensualité sexuelle* were also an important focus of C.-C.-H. Marc's *Of Madness Considered in Its Relation to Medico-Judicial Questions* (1840). Marc was one of the founders of the *Annals of Public Hygiene* and a long-standing member of the Health Council.[26] By 1840, Marc had risen to professional prominence as First Physician to King Louis-Philippe. In Marc's medicolegal treatise he tried to distinguish between the passions and the "lesions of will" as causes of crime. Those suffering from lesions of will (for example, imbeciles, children, lunatics) had traditionally been judged as not responsible for their actions. The forensic doctor's task was to "determine as far as possible those circumstances in which passions, taken to their highest degree, could be assimilated before tribunals to lesions of reason which exclude or at least attenuate guilt" (1:130). Only the "innate or natural" passions could be excused in court, not the "factitious or acquired" passions— those that "result from appetites, penchants or repugnances, and ills resulting from the state of society in which we live" (1:130). "Among the innate passions," Marc noted, "those born of love deserve the first place, because, taken to extreme, this emotion often brings before the tribunal defendants whose extravagance or atrocity of actions afflicts society. Above all, we can agree that sexual union is the main motive" (1:131). He warned that this dangerous sexual appetite often lay hidden under a vague, moral attraction, especially in women.

Marc had diagnosed Mr. D—— as an erotic monomaniac in 1823 but later refined his position on the case by distinguishing Esquirolian erotomania from nymphomania and satyriasis. He designated nymphomania and satyriasis jointly under the neologism *aidoiomania*, from the Greek *aidoia*, meaning pudenda or shameful parts. (This unisex term does not seem to have been adopted by anyone else.) Marc understood both male and female aidoiomania to be "instinctive monomanias" and therefore lesions of the will. He warned that authentic, organic aidoiomania and erotomania had to be carefully distinguished from the simulated variety or commonplace vice and libertinism, which deserved no leniency (2:218–21). However, this distinction between the "natural" and the "acquired" passions proved rather difficult given his list of causes of organic aidoiomania: a soft, sedentary life; puberty or menstruation; continence as well as onanism and libertinism; warm climates (one reason sexual insanity was supposedly less common in France than in the Orient or Italy); professions executed in positions that encourage blood circulation to the genitals (2:194–95). In other words, acquired vice (such as libertinism) could eventually result in organic disease.

In addition to echoing the etiological theories of Tissot on the ill effects of masturbation and idleness, Marc incorporated into his construction of erotomania a heavy dose of anticlericalism. He emphasized the morbid influence of ecclesiastical celibacy or religious devotion, and went so far as to suggest that the temptation of Saint Anthony was really a symptom of satyriasis (2:191–215). Since the Middle Ages, the continence of priests, seminarians, and nuns had been blamed for causing spermatic blockage, hysteria, nymphomania and satyriasis. With the development of the erotomania diagnosis, anticlerical analysts would also diagnose fervent love for Christ or the Virgin Mary as forms of "religious erotomania." This anticlerical conflation of religiosity, hysteria, and eroticism would be most thoroughly and graphically achieved in the 1880s with Charcot's comparative study of saintly and hysterical postures (Charcot & Richer 1887).[27] Charcot's erotic pathologization of religiosity relies on the earlier construction of female erotomania, when alienists stripped the *érotique* of its associations with love and painted it instead as sexual, particularly in a fashion perceived to be dangerous to public manners and values. The sensational case of the "Vampire of Montparnasse" drew public attention to this novel medical sense of the *érotique* and to its broad social threat.

## Necrophilic Appetites and Corrupt Politics

In the winter of 1848, a pair of grave desecrations in Montparnasse Cemetery alerted Parisian authorities to a cluster of similar violations throughout the city.

The Parisian press soon began reporting on the gruesome exploits of the "Vampire of Montparnasse." Vigilance having failed, cemetery guards set explosive traps. These severely wounded an intruder in the early hours of March 15, 1849. Later that day, an injured man limped to the gates of the Val-de-Grâce Hospital and was kept under surveillance as the suspected Vampire. The patient, twenty-five-year-old sergeant major François Bertrand, slowly recovered. During his convalescence, his physician, surgeon-in-chief Marchal de Calvi, encouraged Bertrand to chronicle his life and thoroughly confess his crimes. Finally on July 10 Bertrand appeared before the military court of the Seine. Journalists described him as a slim, handsome man with "lively yet melancholic eyes." During his interrogation, he freely admitted to having exhumed and mutilated corpses from common graves for over two years.[28]

During the trial, Bertrand shocked the packed courtroom not only by his descriptions of unearthing, disarticulating, and eviscerating putrid corpses, but also by his utter equanimity throughout these grisly revelations.[29] Called to the witness stand on Bertrand's behalf, Marchal de Calvi read selections of Bertrand's hospital confessions. These painted a picture of a melancholy, solitary youth, who had always been fascinated by lugubrious places like cemeteries. He had been brought up in a staunchly Catholic family in Voisey, Haute–Marne. After attending a theological seminary, he entered the army in 1844 and had been an exemplary soldier. Although Bertrand denied preferentially exhuming female corpses, these were the only ones he mutilated. His doctor/confessor, Marchal de Calvi, discreetly suggested that Bertrand's destructive monomania was complicated by an even more horrible excess: erotic monomania.

Bertrand's descriptions of his mutilatory sexual practices and sensations were so gruesomely explicit that Marchal de Calvi chose not to make them public during the trial. Instead, they appeared later in various medical publications, and are an excellent example of er*auto*graphy: erotic self-representation.[30] From an early age, Bertrand delighted in mutilation—working his way up from objects to dead animals to live dogs and finally corpses. As had become standard in medical reports of sexual perversity, Bertrand related his masturbation history, paying special attention to his imaginary pleasures. Early in puberty, his onanistic fantasies had begun to incorporate the torture and mutilation of women:

> At thirteen or fourteen I knew no limits; I masturbated up to seven or eight times a day, the mere sight of women's clothing excited me. While masturbating, I transported myself in my imagination to a room where women were

at my disposition; there, after having quelled my passion on them and having amused myself at torturing them in every manner, I imagined them dead and exerted upon their cadavers all sorts of profanations. (Epaulard 1901, 43)

His fantasies of "annihilating" female bodies were always accompanied by masturbation. In his memoirs, Bertrand declares that he was madly in love with women, and objected to any vulgarity in their presence. This declared respectfulness is oddly linked to his violent erotism, as in his description of one encounter:

I embraced every part of that woman's body, I held her to me with enough strength to break her in two; in a word, I proffered upon her all the caresses that a passionate lover would make to the object of his love. After having played with that inanimate body for fifteen minutes, I applied myself to mutilating it, to pulling out its entrails like all the other victims of my furor. (47)

This merging of "love" and the mutilation of women seemed imperative and "natural" to Bertrand, and would even appear in subsequent fiction.[31] Medical analysts did not remark on his distressing association between sex and violence toward women since aggressiveness was the hallmark of the "normal" masculine sex drive. Instead, medicolegal experts debated the relative diagnostic significance of Bertrand's mutilatory versus erotic drives in their evaluation of his criminal responsibility.

In the courtroom and in the medical press, the Bertrand case was the occasion for two battles: a heated professional dispute between physicians and lawyers, and a debate within the medical profession about the classification of mental diseases. Like other cases at the time, the Bertrand trial was used by the medical profession to assert the authority of science and the legitimacy of the "monomania" diagnosis and defense. As Dr. François Leuret wrote, concerning Mr. D——'s case of *monomanie érotique,* the profession had to "demonstrate the necessity of medical intervention in order to enlighten jurists and members of the jury whenever a defendant is suspected insane" (1830, 199). Ever since Esquirol introduced the monomania diagnosis, the legal profession resisted its increasing use as a mitigating circumstance in cases of homicide, arson, theft, and other crimes.[32] Lawyers accurately perceived that physicians were using the monomania diagnosis as a means of claiming judicial authority based on the presumption that medical knowledge had higher scientific and humanitarian worth than arbitrary legal doctrines.

While the medicolegal witnesses at Bertand's trial were confident of the superiority of scientific knowledge, their expertise did not lead to a consistent diagnosis in the case. They all agreed that Bertrand was monomaniacal, but they disputed the exact variety of his monomania. Some argued that he was a "destructive monomaniac" driven to sudden and uncontrollable acts of mutilation. Another camp believed the violence was secondary to, perhaps just a cover for, his erotomania and his perverse appetite for "unnatural" coitus. There was even debate whether Bertrand had cannibalistic tendencies, since it appeared that one female cadaver's genitals had been chewed on. In spite of the sexual explicitness of the confession, Bertrand himself, in a daring rebuttal to Dr. Claude François Michéa (Secretary of the Medico-Psychological Society), asserted that destructive monomania preceded his erotic monomania. At this time the label *necrophilia* did not exist; however, after the term was coined by the Belgian alienist Guislain, doctors regularly mentioned Bertrand as the "classic" necrophile.[33] In 1849, however, only the term *erotomaniac* could have been applied. As we have seen, the diagnosis had long since dropped its meaning of "melancholic, heroical love." Furthermore, as Dr. Félix Jacquot noted in a letter to the *Medical Gazette of Paris,* there could have been no love present when Bertrand "disinterred the cadavers of women, hideous debris, already green with putrefaction, which he kissed erotically with even greater excitement than living flesh palpitating with life" (1849, 575). Therein lay the real basis of "perversion of genesic instinct," argued Jacquot, for do not grieving mothers throw themselves on the bodies of their daughters? Do not passionate lovers lend beauty, wit, and virtue to an ugly, brutish, and sullied woman? "Isn't love all an illusion?" Jacquot exclaimed (576). In claiming that all *eros* is error, Jacquot began to trace a dangerous line of continuity between the "normal" and the "pathological."[34] He continued listing a variety of "perverse genesic appetites" for corpses, animals, pain; and anal stimulation that had been reported in sane military men and priests (targets which are historically meaningful).[35] He also noted that pederasty was common among the Muslims and the ancient Greeks, and suggested that venereal aberrations are common in all settings in which men are sequestered together and expected to be celibate.

Dr. Jules Guérin, the editor of the *Medical Gazette of Paris,* recognized the danger in blurring the line between immoral acts and deranged minds. Guérin warned in a concluding footnote to Jacquot's comments:

> In this letter, interesting on many counts, our learned colleague has not perhaps established a sharp enough difference between depravation of manners and depravation of instincts. This confusion is problematic for many reasons: physicians especially, who hold the key to progress, must not open the door to abuses. (Jacquot 1849, 578n.)

The "key to progress" was biomedical science. More to the point, in the Bertrand case the key to social progress and "true" knowledges of man was the key of sexuality. It could open the door of progress by joining the dark space of the present with the knowledge-lit space of the future. Yet it was perceived as a dangerous key because it could open opposed doors: that of progress and that of abuses, of discrimination and of permissiveness. In the darkness of non-scientific knowledge, it was unclear to nineteenth-century physicians whether these doors could be distinguished. Herein lay one of the great dilemmas of the period: the uneasy confidence that the single key of sex-knowledge would establish a sharp distinction between progress and regression.

The medicolegal experts' failure to arrive at a definitive diagnosis for Bertrand may have led the judge to reject the monomania defense. This worked in Bertrand's favor since the court instead found him guilty of criminal violation of the sanctity of mortal remains. He was condemned to the maximum sentence of one year in prison, after which time he was set free. For Bertrand, as in other cases of sexual misdeeds, a criminal conviction led to a shorter internment than a judgment of insanity. As Dr. Michéa noted (1849, 339), had Bertrand been judged monomaniacal he probably would have spent the rest of his life in an insane asylum. So at that time, claiming insanity mitigated one's guilt but most likely lengthened one's sentence.

Guérin made it clear that the stakes in the medical involvement in Bertrand's trial were far more important than just one "perverse" sergeant's future. His and other cases of erotomania at the time posed major medicolegal challenges to the discrimination between the criminal versus the pathological, and normal versus perverse appetites. The politics of perverse appetites had a much broader social impact and quickly spread beyond the trial of the Vampire of Montparnasse. In an article that began with a discussion of Bertrand, Dr. Jean Raimond (1849) turned to "an aberration or perversion yet more unusual, and which alienists have yet to attend to": the *Club des Grands Estomacs* (the great stomachs club). The young aristocratic members of this club gathered every Saturday for eighteen-hour, Pantagruelesque banquets in Paris, "that vast receptacle of all disorders, all debaucheries, and all vices." Raimond represented Paris itself as an infectious place—a corrupt body seething with disease. He reproduced one of the club's sumptuous menus, which included twenty-three courses, twelve bottles of wine, and a bottle of eau-de-vie per person! Naturally, such gross appetites and consumption would eventually lead to generalized paralysis and delirium, Raimond concluded. However, he claimed that their primary problem was not merely overeating but a fundamentally perverse instinct due to their aristocratic breeding and Parisian milieu. Thus the body of the aristocracy itself was as corrupt as the city of Paris. As in Bertrand's case, doctors were carving a new niche into the medicomoral regulation of society by broadly reconceptualizing "aberrations of appetite" as "perversions of instinct." Matters of unorthodox choice were biologized as pathologies of body and mind.

At the same time in the Assemblée Nationale, a battle was raging over philosophical and political ideologies in medical education and, ultimately, in science itself.[36] At issue was the reintroduction of parochial schools in France and the admission of clerical and spiritualist teaching in the Faculty of Medicine of Paris, which was otherwise dominated by philosophical materialists. The combatants enlisted metaphors of perverse eroticism, particularly necrophilia, to attack each other. Referring to the resurgence of reactionary politics in science, a left-leaning doctor complained,

> We are witnessing a sad spectacle. The human mind seems to be regressing. . . . [Religious reasoning is invading philosophy, politics and science, turning back the progress of millennia and especially that of 1789.] There is a general travesty of thinking. That which yesterday was the object of violent opposition, of derision and sarcasm, is respected today and the object of homage and veneration. Some declare a return to ideas, to principles, to beliefs we thought were *dead forever;* and history, when she will wish to characterize the current situation, will call the present period the *age of exhumations.*
>
> What is the reason for these strange transformations?
>
> One sole cause, fear. . . .
>
> Search only there for the motive for these strange conversions, these incredible regressions, these *monstrous alliances.* (Latour 1849c, 389; emphasis added)

Latour slanders his ideological enemies with metaphors of necrophilic perversion (which was in the news thanks to Bertrand's trial). Not surprisingly, a great deal had been made of Bertrand's upbringing in a seminary. Dr. Lunier had observed, "That type of education perhaps also developed in him a bizarre excitability of the genital organs, as is quite common [in religious institutions]" (1849, 369). Lunier added that priests or ex-seminarians were responsible for the majority of known cases of "cohabitation with the dead" (369).

On the opposing proclerical side, critics of the materialist Parisian medical monopoly did not fail to employ the same strategy of "perversification." Noting the danger of opening the door to abuses along with the door to progress, Dr. Edouard Carrière debated Amédée Latour in an ongoing series of articles entitled "On Authority in Medicine." Carrière warned,

> These philosophers are like certain novelists, working in the name of moral-
> ity, stripping vice naked, while they believe they are following the road of
> morality, they arrive at absolutely the opposite result. Realize also that every-
> thing in science is linked, that the tree of the scientific encyclopedia has such
> close connections, that a disturbance at one point can produce *great perver-
> sions* in the whole. (Carrière 1849, 443; emphasis added)

It was not just the perversion of science that doctors on the right complained
of, but the perversion of medical students' minds in Paris: "The young people
who arrive in Paris imbued with the religious education of the domestic hearth,
necessarily must lose it at the [Paris Medical] School. It is impossible for them
to defend themselves against those doctrines of egoism and revolt which are the
moral consequence of those scientific principles that they are taught [i.e., ma-
terialism]."[37] As in the case of Bertrand and the aristrocrats with *grands estomacs,* Paris was depicted as a site of contagion. In much the same way in which
the seminary was blamed by the Left for Bertrand's erotomania, Paris was represented as the locus not just of perversions of moral appetite but also of a virulent philosophical and political perversion. Supporters of parochial education
warned that these young doctors posed an even greater threat to the nation after
completion of their medical indoctrination in Paris:

> Those vices of organization are all the more grave because medical education
> is important to the state not only for the physical well-being of individuals,
> but it is also important politically. Physicians disperse, in the cities and coun-
> tryside, the science and ideas that they acquired during their student life. . . .
> It is only too true that, among men of knowledge and intelligence who have
> mixed with the country people, there are too many that became apostles of
> that socialism which we have seen begin its effects in Paris. We should not at-
> tack this as a vice of the heart but as a profound mental deviance determined
> by a vice-ridden education. (Latour 1849a, 409)

Just like the cholera epidemic then raging in Europe, an epidemic of socialism
was spreading from Paris to the provinces. Especially after the Revolution of
1848, provincials depicted Paris as a canker of radicalism (Pick 1989, 58). The
Right proclaimed that "to end such evils one must go to the source, and attack
them in the nest where they originate; this is the reason for the reform which is
being prepared through the means of free education" (Latour 1849a, 410). In
the eyes of the proclerical Right, free medical education would be the way of
clearing out the materialists—those philosophical prostitutes who were per-
verting pure, religious minds and initiating a syphilis-like epidemic of social-

ism. This fear of socialism and Parisian radicalism contributed to Louis-Napoleon's successful rise to power and his conservative social policies during the early years of the Second Empire.

In these three very different cases—Bertrand, the Club des Grands Estomacs, and the education debate—the medical profession utilized the perverse appetite of necrophilia as a rhetorical weapon in professional power plays and internecine political battles. Doctors argued that "perversity" was not a random individual event but represented a profound nervous and constitutional deviance that was a threat to professional and social order. The opposing ideological camps sought to represent diverse forms of deviance (sexual, gastronomic, political) as embodied qualities. Bodily needs (for sex, food, association) had certain socially acceptable manifestations, but they were driven by some supplement to their rational manifestation, some force that overwhelmed reason and will—a delirious supplement of nature that challenged socially conventional order and threatened to undermine it.

## Diversifying the Politics of Erotism

Bertrand's case was regularly resurrected in the nineteenth century, each time taking on different diagnostic and social tones. In 1864 Henri Legrand du Saulle, a leading medicolegal expert, discussed the case in the context of *érotisme,* not *érotomanie* or destructive monomania (the diagnosis was no longer used by then). His category of *érotisme* included love sickness, satyriasis, nymphomania, senile demented licentiousness, and "erotic depravations," under which rubric he grouped Bertrand, Gilles de Rais, and Sade. Ambroise Tardieu, in his discussion of sexual assault, diagnosed Bertrand with "sexual psychopathia" or "perversion of the sexual instinct" (1857, 113), emphasizing that Bertrand's *érotisme* was a socially dangerous, criminal sexuality. For Dr. Auzouy, physician-in-chief of the Fains mental asylum, *érotisme* was a social threat because it was one of the "perversions" of the "natural" affections: the love of God, self, family, and nation (1858, 56). The Vampire of Montparnasse case exemplifies the emergence of *érotisme* as a term of accusation, transgression, criminality, and pathology.

*Érotisme* became a versatile embodiment of certain social anxieties in a period of governmental, economic, populational, military, political, and religious instabilities. The "delirious supplement" of the erotic was a useful model for turning socially troubling phenomena into proper pathological objects of a science of man. This science promised to restore the rational, natural law and order that many people longed for, particularly after the Revolution of 1848. One doctor expressed a commonplace worry: "In our time, time of transition, of transformation, the principle of liberty has dissolved the principle of authority; the disaggregated molecules flee and search for each other, attract or repel" (Maugras 1849). Ironically, the medical rhetoric of erotism uncovered yet more chaos and "abuses." Physicians found that under the aegis of their intense interrogation, erotolalia—the speaking of the erotic—took new liberties. As they broadened their scope on sexual behaviors and as they projected the model of dangerous erotism onto society, physicians paradoxically discovered that the distinctions between the "natural" and the "acquired" or the "normal" and the "perverse" were not clear—as Dr. Jacquot had controversially suggested in the Bertrand case (1849, 578). As the knowledge of sex was increasingly construed to be central to a knowledge of society, the "sharp difference" between perverse manners and perverse instinct became blunt. The study of the pathological, which was meant to cast light upon the normal, proved to cast an embarrassing light upon an expanding variety of erotisms lurking in the recesses of normality: inversion, fetishism, masochism, sadism. Aspects of perversity were increasingly revealed in culture and politics as erotism proved to be an effective rhetorical weapon for portraying opponents as constitutionally depraved.

"Perversification" remains a common political rhetorical strategy today. Even the rather obscure diagnosis of erotomania made a memorable comeback in October 1991 when Alabama Senator Howell Hefflin dryly asked, in his Southern drawl, "Are you a spurned woman, Professor Hill?" His query provoked thunderous laughter from the audience during the tense interrogation of law professor Anita Hill at the Senate Judiciary Committee's U.S. Supreme Court confirmation hearings for Judge Clarence Thomas. Whether meant as a serious hypothesis or a sly tactic to ridicule the very scenario of the delusional enamorata, the accusation of erotomania had been flung by Hefflin—playing lawyer and diagnostician—onto the floor of the hearing room and the living rooms of millions of television spectators.[38] It would be up to the supporters of Judge Thomas to make the label stick to Professor Hill as a means of discrediting an otherwise credible and sane woman and her claims of sexual harassment. Thomas, in turn, was accused of indulging in pornographic films. His opponents specifically raised the specter of Long Dong Silver, a famously well-endowed black porn star. As in the Bertrand case, sexual violence and aggression against women was hidden under a diagnostic label. The hearings became a political battleground with opposing camps using erotism to slander each other.

Currently in the United States, the most politically inflammatory form of erotism is perhaps homosexuality. Struggles over gay civil rights, same-sex marriage and adoption, homoerotic art, and gays in the military are being fought at every level of the legislature and judiciary. As we will see in the following chapter, same-sex erotism inherited the politicization of erotomania. "Inversion," from the time of its medical discovery in the mid-nineteenth century, was embroiled in complex matters of gender and nationalist politics.

# CHAPTER 3

*Inverts:*
*Pointy Penises,*
*Hysterical*
*Mollies, and*
*Literary*
*Homosexuals*

To start, here is the patient's own narrative of the bizarre phenomena that he experiences and that he associates with his so-called sensuality: "My sensuality," he says, "manifested itself from the age of six by a violent desire to see boys of my age or men, naked. . . . At about the age of fifteen, puberty arrived; masturbation gave me even greater satisfaction; furthermore, I provoked erection and its consequences as much by imagination as by manipulation; more than once I had an erection, an amorous convulsion, and seminal loss at the mere sight of a man's virile member. . . . I love female attire; I love to see a woman well dressed, because I tell myself I would like to be a woman to dress similarly. From the age of seventeen, I dressed as a woman during carnival and experienced an indescribable pleasure in dragging my skirts through rooms, wearing wigs, and going shoulderless. . . ."

The patient thus describes the characteristics of this irrepressible obsession of which he is fully aware.

This sick person, what is he? (Charcot & Magnan 1882, 54–56)

Indeed, what is this thirty-one-year-old man with "voluptuous sensations" provoked by the sight of naked men and male statues, or even by "obsessive memories of these images"? Furthermore, how is his "bizarre" sensuality related to other elements of his clinical history: "neuropathic tendencies in the ancestors; disproportion between the age of the father and mother. . . . From ages 5 to 8, a propensity for theft.—Habits of onanism until age 22.—Hysteriform attacks from the age of 15"? Jean-Martin Charcot and Valentin Magnan, two of the most prominent neurologists of the Third Republic, presented this patient as the first case of *inversion du sens génital*.

This man was not, however, Patient Zero of "inversion of the genital sense," just the first reported *French* case. Charcot and Magnan included him as fresh clinical evidence in their review of the foreign medical literature on the subject. They acknowledged that their German colleague, Karl Westphal, had first labeled such patients in 1869 with the diagnosis of *conträre Sexualempfindung* (contrary sexual sensation). In 1878 an Italian forensic doctor, Arrigo Tamassia, had described the first Italian men suffering from *inversione dell'istinto sessuale*—the term that Charcot and Magnan simply rendered into French. And, most recently, a Viennese physician, Julius Krueg, had published similar cases of a male and a female whom he diagnosed with "perverted sexual instinct." After reviewing the existing European medical literature, Krueg concluded that there were only "thirteen well-established cases of this affection [*sic*]" (1882, 369). Although contrary sexual sensation or inversion of the genital sense was a rare and new diagnosis in the late nineteenth century, its incidence was apparently on the rise. Or, at least, it had become a hot research topic for elite European physicians.

Today it is commonplace to identify "inversion" as a radically new sexual identity and the "invert" as the immediate ancestor to the modern "homosexual."[1] The birth of the invert is more historically complex, however, for he did not spring fully formed from the mind of German physicians in 1869. This chapter will show how Charcot and Magnan molded inverts out of prior neurological and medicolegal theories concerning pederasts, hysterics, and neurodegenerates—figures who were culturally and socially well recognized in the late nineteenth century. The emerging medical investigation of "perverted sexual instincts" was not simply an isolated, objective research program but also a manifestation of larger cultural concerns beyond the hospital. Therefore, my genealogy from the "pederast" to the "homosexual" interweaves biomedical theories and "extrascientific" strands of influence: professional concerns, class and gender anxieties, natalist preoccupations, national rivalries, and literary controversies.

Here, as in the previous settings, *belle-lettristes*—whether medical professionals or scientific dilettantes—played a crucial role in shaping the medical discourse. Some (such as Marc-André Raffalovich) wrote from personal experience to defend homosexuality. Others (such as Emile Zola and J.-K. Huysmans) took it upon themselves to condemn the epidemic of "perversity." But apologists and censors alike argued for fiction's power to shape disciplinary knowledges, social stereotypes, and even intimate experiences of inversion. Throughout these intertwined narratives, I will highlight the trope of inversion: a radical contradiction between the interior being and the superficial appearance. This device recurs in the description and condemnation of these supposed physical and moral "degenerates": sodomites, male hysterics, and inverts. Due to this contradiction, effective diagnosis hinged on the detection of subtle external signs that betrayed and defined these degenerates.

## The Pathognomy of Pederasty

"Fiers mignons, malgré l'art du poudre et du rouge,
Vous sentez tous la mort! O squelettes musqués,
Antinoüs flétris, dandies à face glabre,
Cadavres vernissés, lovelaces chenus,
Le branle universel de la danse macabre
Vous entraîne en des lieux qui ne sont pas connus!"
        Charles Baudelaire, "Danse macabre" (1857)*

Eighteen fifty-seven was an especially active year for sexual and somatic surveillance. Baudelaire's poems *Les Fleurs du mal* and Gustave Flaubert's novel *Madame Bovary* were both published that year and their authors put on trial for contravening the *loi de Serre*. This 1819 law criminalized books or pamphlets

---

*"Proud mollies, despite the artifice of powder and rouge, you all stink of death! Oh, musky skeletons, withered Antinoüses, smooth-faced dandies, enameled cadavers, doddling gigolos, may the universal sway of the Dance of Death drag you off to unknown places!" From Baudelaire's "Danse macabre," *Les Fleurs du mal*. *Mignons* are cute boys, or the very effeminate favorites of Henri III. Antinoüs, a beautiful Bithynian boy, was the beloved of the Emperor Hadrian. Both were commonly used nineteenth-century terms for designating sodomites.

deemed by the courts to be an "outrage to public and religious morality, or to good morals."[2] It was also the year, as we saw in chapter 1, that Dr. J. B. D. Demeaux published his recommendations for eradicating onanism from schools by means of surprise inspections by a national board of specialized doctors. Also in 1857, Dr. Bénédict A. Morel published his *Treatise on Degenerations*, a work that shaped French cultural anxieties for half a century. And in the same year, Ambroise-Auguste Tardieu published his influential classic of forensic medicine, the *Medicolegal Study of Assaults on Decency*.

During the first half of the Second Empire, when the government was pursuing an extremely conservative domestic policy, it seemed imperative to detect moral corruption and prevent its imitation, transmission, or inheritance. As we saw in chapter 1, pathognomy, the study of the signs of passions and diseases, was a central feature of the "scientific" approach to masturbation. Demeaux assured the Minister of Public Education that specially trained physicians could almost infallibly detect stigmata of masturbation on the bodies of young onanists and thus curtail erotic morbidity. Even literary traces of the erotic, however subtle, had to be nipped at the bud to prevent a social epidemic of indecency. A good example is the scene of Emma Bovary's adultery, which was marked merely by a shower of shredded paper from a cab window during her recklessly long ride with her lover Léon. The passage had been suppressed in its original 1856 serial publication by the *Revue de Paris* out of fear that it would provoke legal condemnation, as it later did.[3]

Tardieu was the first to bring this subtle quality of scientific scrutiny and interpretation to bear on the positive detection of sodomy. Tardieu was a medicolegal expert and collaborator on the *Annals of Public Hygiene and Legal Medicine*. His *Medicolegal Study of Assaults on Decency* gained him the professorship in forensic medicine at the Faculty of Medicine of Paris and the tome was hugely successful: it was reedited six times over twenty years and almost doubled in length. It covered three imbricated issues: public offenses against decency, rape and sexual assault, and pederasty and sodomy.[4] While recognizing that pederasty was hardly a new subject, Tardieu rightly claimed that it had never been the object of serious, scientific analysis in the way that even prostitution had been scrutinized in Alexandre Parent-Duchâtelet's *Prostitution in the City of Paris* (1836).

Unlike prostitution, there was no legal regulation of sodomy per se because the Constituent Assembly in 1791 had abrogated Old Regime laws concerning "crimes against nature." Nevertheless, police continued to arrest men suspected of sodomitic solicitation under the Penal Code of 1810: Article 330 (which condemned "public offenses against decency") and Article 334 (which made it a crime to corrupt young people).[5] Public concern about and private titillation over sodomy had grown since the Enlightenment with the emergence of sodomitic subcultures and the proliferation of pornography.[6] In eighteenth-century Paris, undercover agents (known as *mouches* and "pederasty patrols") had entrapped suspected sodomites. These had been sentenced to Bicêtre Hospital if they were poor or Saint-Lazare Hospital if they could pay. During the several days to months they were confined in the hospital, they were encouraged to implicate others. Aristocrats usually went free. No wonder one eighteenth-century police official had declared that "pederasty can only be a vice of gentlemen."[7]

Although the legal environment had changed by the time of the Second Empire, the police and the public were increasingly concerned about sodomy and pederasty (two terms that were, by then, used interchangeably).[8] Tardieu attributed this heightened interest to more active police surveillance, an extraordinary public taste for scandal, large blackmail rings, and the perceived connection between sodomy and murder.[9] Tardieu echoed the opinion of an eminent judge that "pederasty is the school in which the most able and audacious criminals are educated" (195). Although pederasts were accused of debauching minors, Tardieu nevertheless noted that pederasts were usually the *victims* of murderers, blackmailers, or rings of crooks posing as agents of the vice squad.

If entrapped "legitimately" or caught in flagrante delicto by the police, pederasts were increasingly subjected to medical examinations to determine whether they were indeed sodomites. For this reason, sodomy had taken on considerable importance in the practice of legal medicine. It was Tardieu's extensive personal experience with this sort of examination that permitted him to "discuss with more certitude and more authority the history of the signs of pederasty" (197). He dismissed prior writers for merely circulating errors based on few observations or copied from an outdated treatise by Paolo Zacchia (1651). Tardieu boasted that he, in contrast, had personally performed over three hundred meticulous physical examinations of suspected pederasts. His data led him to conclude that pederasty was a far more common phenomenon than previously thought. It was widely distributed throughout the age groups (with the highest prevalence among fifteen- to twenty-five-year-olds) and throughout professional or class categories (especially domestics, merchants, military men, and tailors) (208).[10] This data confirmed that sodomy could not be considered a privilege of the aristocracy as it had been popularly represented in the eighteenth century.

Evidently, demographic factors could not aid the forensic doctor in detecting "true" pederasts. Tardieu relied instead on his extensive familiarity with sodomites' bodies "to establish . . . that the vice of pederasty leaves, in the conformation of the organs, material traces far more numerous and significant than hitherto believed, the knowledge of which will permit the forensic doctor, in the majority of cases, to direct and confirm the lawsuits that are of such great interest to public morals" (213). He believed that pederasts were exclusively "active" or "passive" (that is, either penetrative or anally receptive). Based on this assumption, he claimed that chronic, passive pederasts exhibited flaccid buttocks, a funnel-shaped deformation of the anus, relaxation of the anal sphincter, and other anal characteristics (see Figure 5). As if to confirm that these physical findings were definitively associated with anal sex, he insisted that women and prostitutes who indulged in sodomy exhibited the same anal traits.[11] Habitual active pederasts, on the other hand, demonstrated penile peculiarities: either thin, pointy penises like dogs, long, tapered penises with a large muzzlelike glans, or, in the case of those also addicted to masturbation, club shaped penises.

Tardieu repeatedly insisted that the determination of pederasty was to be based on positive physical findings, however subtle they might be. Nevertheless, for him and his predecessors, sodomy was not an organic disease but a *vice*, that is, an immoral choice. The same was true of what he regarded as the most common form of sex "against nature," conjugal sodomy (198). In Tardieu's opinion, pederasty and sodomy were not matters of mental illness. There were, however, two important exceptions: those who crossed either class or gender boundaries were probably insane. He observed that certain pederasts, "apparently distinguished by education and fortune," consorted with individuals of "profound degradation and revolting filthiness." He knew of one pederast of high social rank who descended to the lowest level of depravity by seeking voluptuousness in passionate submission to sordid street urchins. It was undoubtedly the horror of class debasement, as much as the spectacle of abjection, that moved Tardieu to describe such cases as examples of "the saddest and most shameful insanity" (213). Despite these exceptional cases, Tardieu warned against broadening the aegis of the insanity diagnosis to protect pederasts:

> I have said that the weakening of the intellectual and affective functions could be the final term of the shameful habit of pederasts. But one must not confuse that state, in some ways secondary, with the excesses of debauchery and the extremes of depravation. However incomprehensible, however contrary to nature and reason the acts of pederasty may appear, they should not escape the responsibility of conscience or the just severity of the laws, nor, above all, the loathing of upright people. (255)

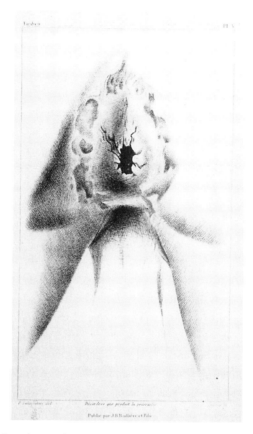

Figure 5. Funnel-shaped anus of a passive sodomite. From Ambroise Tardieu's *Medicolegal Study of Assaults on Decency* (1857). (Courtesy of The Boston Medical Library in the Francis A. Countway Library of Medicine, Boston.)

According to Tardieu, the revolting irrationality of pederasts' actions could not in itself justify a diagnosis of primary mental imbalance. Nevertheless, he did go so far as to suggest that male pederasts had characteristic mental peculiarities.[12] Under the rubric of "the exterior of pederasts," Tardieu discussed their reputed effeminacy—an association already firmly established in the eighteenth century and probably linked to the even more ancient notion of the *molles:* "soft" or unmasculine men.[13]

To illustrate the connection between pederasty and effeminacy, Tardieu provided a colorful portrait of the typical *tante* (auntie):

Curled hair, made-up skin, open collar, waist tucked in to accentuate the figure; fingers, ears, chest loaded with jewelry, the whole body exuding an odor of the most penetrating perfumes, and, in one hand, a handkerchief, flowers, or some needlework: such is the strange, revolting, and rightfully suspect physiognomy that betrays the pederast. . . . Hairstyles and dress constitute one of the most continual preoccupations of pederasts. (216–17)

Although he did not report any anatomical femininity, Tardieu suggested that pederasts' sartorial and behavioral effeminacy constituted a clear, fixed psychological and ontological marker. Pederasts' "depraved tastes" were exclusive despite attempts to dissimulate them behind sham marriages and mistresses, or efforts to exploit the general belief that sodomitic habits were incompatible with (normal) sexual relations (254).[14] Pederasts' deceitfulness demanded that, despite the distinctive characterological markers, forensic doctors had to rely on physical, exterior traits to unmask sodomites who denied their shameful behaviors.

The sodomitic masquerade—the discordance between the public surface and the secret depths—distressed Tardieu most viscerally: "A trait no less characteristic, and which I have observed a hundred times, is the contrast between this false elegance, the exterior bodily cult, and the sordid filthiness that alone would suffice to distance one from these wretches" (216). Effeminate refinement was merely a thin container for sodomitic sewage. Ever since the eighteenth century, dressing above one's station—in the effeminate refinement of the aristocracy—was a sure way of attracting public and police suspicions of pederasty.[15] Tardieu, likewise, reported that pederasts had a predilection for grandiose sobriquets (such as "the Queen of England") and for sartorial finery (217). He worried generally about pederasts' deceptions, their factitiousness expressed as inversions of class, gender, and hygiene. What might appear to be an elegant lady, in fact was a squalid, lowbred auntie. For example, at the prostitution trial of the "Queen of England," one reporter exclaimed: "Can it really be a man?" (218).

Although Tardieu insisted on a clear pathognomy of pederasty, it was commonly feared that, thanks to secret signs, pederasts of all classes could recognize *each other* even more easily than they could be recognized by doctors. Pederasts thus formed a "shameful free-masonry" (218). Dr. Fournier-Pescay referred to the "confraternity" that recognized its vile members through "something distinctive in their dress" (1821, 446). Sodomites were thus simultaneously condemned both for their democratic and subversive commingling of classes and for organizing into an elitist, secret order of the cloth.

Tardieu's masterwork betrays a variety of anxieties provoked by pederasts. These deceitful debauchees could only be detected by knowledgeable doctors, yet they possessed a mysterious means of identifying one another that eluded the analytic gaze of medicolegal experts. They disrupted public morals by their gender and class deception, not because they were physically, anatomically effeminate but because they performed travesties of class and gender.[16] The social concern for preserving clear gender distinctions was so great that transvestitism was made a punishable offense in 1853 during the early, conservative years of the Second Empire.[17]

Tardieu's concern over the classification and detection of stigmata of hidden disease were shared by other colleagues. For example, the alienist Bénédict A. Morel had described the supposedly pathognomonic features of insane men's penises (1851, 567).[18] Morel is perhaps better remembered for his *Treatise on Degenerations* (1857), which associated physical stigmata with mental disorders within his general theory of hereditary decay. Relying on Lamarckian principles of inheritance, Morel proposed that an array of somatic and nervous disorders could be the product of an accretion of hereditary damage due to climatic conditions, diet, and the consumption of alcohol and toxins.[19] Unchecked, this gradual process of hereditary degeneration from the original Adamic type eventually led to cretinism and infertility (see Figure 6). This generalized and protean degenerative process, Morel believed, could be detected through a variety of physical and psychological stigmata. The theory's vagueness made it a powerful explanatory tool in accounting for a bewildering variety of social "diseases": criminality, anarchy, depopulation, immorality, foreign national characteristics, urban poverty, and so on.[20] Degeneration theory therefore played an important role in bolstering the professional and scientific credibility of French alienists and their demands to shape social policy.[21]

Morel's theory placed a premium on the family medical history in the diagnosis of degeneracy. In order to justify the diagnosis, physicians had to carefully inquire after every nervous or degenerative disorder in a patient's relatives. Degeneration theory served as a conceptual bridge between the anatomico-pathological mode of thinking of the Paris School in the first half of the century and the psychiatric approach to an expanding list of mental illnesses at the turn of the century.[22] Similarly, the quest for the pathognomy of pederasty gradually shifted from Tardieu's hunt for the *physical stigmata* of sodomy on the patient's body to a search for *hereditary taints*—particularly of a mental nature—in the patient's family medical history.

In a presentation to the prestigious Medico-Psychological Society on March 27, 1876, Dr. Henri Legrand du Saulle addressed the hotly debated question: "Are there physical signs in reasoning insanity?" (1876, 433).[23] He made it clear that a firm "Yes!" was essential to maintaining the respectability of medicine before the courts, the public, and the other sciences. His professional

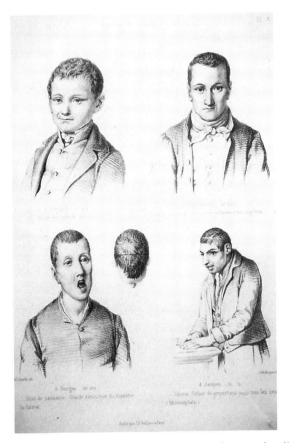

Figure 6. Vicious conformations of the head. In his *Treatise on Degenerations* (1857), Dr. Bénédict Morel described his twenty-three-year-old patient Jean Baptiste (upper right) as having: "Obtuse intelligence. Bad tendencies. Angled forehead" (Plate 10). (Courtesy of The Boston Medical Library in the Francis A. Countway Library of Medicine, Boston.)

concerns were not unlike Tardieu's. For physicians to be credible, especially in the courtroom, they had to rely on positive, physical traits and not obscure psychological theories.[24] Legrand du Saulle argued that *héréditaires* (hereditary degenerates) exhibited a variety of cerebral disorders and bodily stigmata—for example, cranial deformities; eye, ear, and buccal cavity peculiarities; and facial anomalies and tics. His original contribution was to suggest that during puberty *héréditaires* suffered a variety of mental disorders: hysterical suffocation, mysticism, anorexia, eccentricities, mania, melancholia, masturbation, and criminal tendencies. He further proposed that many *héréditaires* presented genital abnormalities (such as hypospadias, phimosis, small or absent testicles) and, most relevant for us, "genesic perversions."

Legrand du Saulle presented several such cases; for example, a twenty-year-old youth who had been apprehended, along with an old man, for mutually exhibiting their genitals at a public urinal.[25] Unlike other degenerate patients who displayed some "intellectual deficits," this young man had a degree in literature and possessed a "very ornate mind." He was, however, morose, solitary, contemplative, and "expressed a striking repulsion for women in general. . . . He felt himself, on the contrary, invincibly attracted to men, to images, paintings, and statues representing male nudes" (446). Thanks to Legrand du Saulle's care, this young man (whom police undoubtedly considered a pederast) escaped any legal and moral condemnation. Contrary to Tardieu's admonition regarding the medical exculpation of sodomites, the "patient" was never labeled a "pederast" but was instead diagnosed as suffering from *perversion génésique* (reproductive perversion) due to reasoning insanity. The telltale stigmata were his penile deformities (which Legrand du Saulle promptly treated surgically). The fact that this patient's mother was a hysteric provided even stronger evidence of his degeneration. This intelligent young gynophobe with the hysterical mother—rescued from the ignominy of arrest for a crime against decency and caught instead in the diagnostic net of degenerationist neuropsychiatry—is a perfect figure for demonstrating the confluence of the legal pursuit of the "vicious" sodomite and the neuropsychiatric treatment of the hysterical male.

## (En)gendering Hysterics: The Lunacy of Effeminacy

A hysterical man—the juxtaposition seems unremarkable given the current usage of the word *hysterical:* suffering from the psychoneurosis called *hysteria* or expressing excessive emotionality. Yet the term *hysteria* remains gendered because of its etymology and history. As a disease ascribed by Hippocrates to suffocation of or by the womb (*hystera* in Greek), hysteria had long been considered a disease almost exclusively of women.[26] The gendering of the disease changed decisively in the nineteenth century as physicians increasingly insisted that it was a neurological disorder and, therefore, could also afflict men (Louyer-Villermay 1819b, 6–10; Georget 1820, 541). In the public arena and much of the medical literature, hysteria nevertheless remained (and probably still remains) a female-gendered disorder because its symptomatology represents a caricature of "femininity."[27]

Hysterical males in the nineteenth century were regularly accused of effeminacy and of possessing an excessively impressionable imagination like that of those creatures most vulnerable to erotic disturbances: children and women. Some early case descriptions used coded language to convey the patient's effeminacy. Dr. Mouchet (1848), for example, opened his description of a nineteen-year-old hysterical male by noting his "blond hair, fine, white skin." But most physicians were quite forthright in their descriptions of *féminisme*. Mourette (1869) reported on a boy with a "delicate complexion and feminine appearance." Yver presented a twenty-nine-year-old man with a feminine appearance: thin, beardless, fine, white skin, cute face, and hyperexcitability. This patient's mother was, most significantly, hysterical.[28] After Morel's *Treatise on Degenerations* (1857), doctors not only sought stigmata of effeminacy but also traces of nervous debility in patients' mothers to establish a diagnosis of male hysteria.[29] Jacques-Joseph Moreau (de Tours), one of the early, vocal supporters of hereditarian theories of mental illness, argued in *Morbid Psychology* (1859) that fathers contributed most to the somatic constitution of their children while maternal heredity had a greater impact on the offspring's mental state.[30] Maternal mental illness was therefore quite ominous, leading August Klein, in his work on *Hysteria in Men* (1880), to conclude that "in cases in which direct hereditary transmission is noted, it almost always comes from the mother and the mother is almost always hysterical" (10).

In an earlier treatise on hysteria, Pierre Briquet (1859) argued forcefully that the disease was neurological but with an environmental etiology: the social demands placed on women (marriage, motherhood, family, work, home economics) constituted too great a challenge to their impressionable nervous systems. Applying the same environmental mechanism to males, he proposed that men with hypersensitive nervous constitutions were also likely to succumb to hysteria. Although Briquet (1881) denied that the genitals were to blame for hysteria, he nevertheless supported the theory that seminal loss was a predisposing cause.[31] Similarly, Dr. Michéa had described the case of a man whose childhood epileptiform crises became more frequent and violent when, at age eighteen, "he contracted the morbid habit of masturbation and abandoned himself to it with an incredible furor" (1865a, 42). Dr. Hirtz also had blamed "frenetic masturbation" for provoking hysteria in a male.[32] As we have seen, "excessive" seminal loss through onanism had long been held responsible for impotence, so it was physiologically reasonable at the time to claim that a man, "losing his virile attributes to bear those of a woman, and thereby becoming vulnerable to the diseases of the weaker sex, could end up with hysteria" (Bonnemaison 1875, 675). Even those who rejected the gonadal etiology of hysteria, nevertheless, found that deviation from the "normal" sexual organs and psychology was a common trait of the male hysteric.

The best informed reconciliation of these contradictory elements was proposed by Paul Fabre, physician at the Vaucluse Asylum and corresponding member of the Medico-Psychological Society.[33] His article on "Hysteria in Men" in 1875 (a year of numerous publications on male hysteria) drew on the work of Morel, Magnan, and especially on Briquet's theory of nervous impressionability. Fabre reported cases of male hysterics with feminine traits, poorly developed genitals, frequent masturbation, and diminished interest in coitus with women. He noted that the character of one Mr. X——, a man-of-letters, "resembles in many ways that of a woman: despite his exterior appearance, which is totally virile, Mr. X—— loves to be dominated, he cries and laughs easily according to the circumstances; emotions have the greatest influence upon him . . . his venereal appetite is almost null" (363–64). By the same token, Fabre rejected the old association between female hysteria and nymphomania or "uterine fury." Instead he claimed that hysterical women generally had a diminished interest in sex and were often sterile or less fertile than healthy women. The reason for this infertility lay not in their genitals but in the indeterminate gender of their nervous systems: "The individuals stricken with this neurosis offer certain psychological and physical analogies that seem to distance them from the sex to which they belong, to direct them to a new sex, so to speak, whose neutrality and exaggerated impressionability are the principal attributes" (365). For Fabre, hysteria in both sexes presented a neurological gender inversion—literally a female brain in a male body, and vice versa—that could account for the "genesic perversions" of hysterical males like Mr. X——.

Certainly, in the popular imagination, hysteria was not just for women anymore. Mr. X——, the hysterical writer, was in good company since novelist Gustave Flaubert also bore the diagnosis of hysteria.[34] On January 12–13, 1867, Flaubert wrote George Sand complaining about his isolation at his country home:

> The sensibility is unduly exalted in such a milieu. I suffer palpitations for no reason, rather understandable, all told, in an old hysteric like myself. For I maintain that men are hysterical like women and that I am one. When I wrote *Salammbô*, I read "the best authors" on the matter and I recognized all my symptoms. I have the ball [*globus hystericus*] and the nail in the occiput. (1980–91, 3:592)

On May 1, 1874, he wrote to Mme. Roger des Genettes, "Dr. Hardy . . . calls me a hysterical old woman. 'Doctor,' I told him, 'you are quite right'" (1926–54, 7:137). To his long-time friend Marie-Sophie Leroyer de Chantepie, he similarly had written on March 18, 1857 that he had the nervous irritability of a kept girl (1980–91, 2:692).

The diagnosis of hysteria stuck to Flaubert even into the twentieth century when René Dumesnil (editor of the Pléiade edition of Flaubert's works) retrospectively examined Flaubert with the intention of dispelling persistent rumors that the novelist had been epileptic, sexually frigid, and afraid of women (that is, homosexual) (1905, 88). Dumesnil determined, supposedly in Flaubert's defense, that the novelist's nervous crises were the product of "epileptoid hysteria with a strong neuropathic tendency" (94). Flaubert's superior literary abilities could thus be attributed to his neurodegeneracy since "his mania for analysis is pushed to exaggeration, and this is a trait common to all intellectual neuroses and superior mentality" (95). The excessive imaginativeness and hypersensibility of the hysteroepileptic placed Flaubert on the dangerous edge between insanity and literary genius. Fortunately, as the son of the physician-in-chief of the Rouen Hôtel-Dieu, Flaubert was endowed with a medical mentality and steely surgical literary style that prevented him from falling into the abyss. Relying on persistent hereditary degenerationist theories, Dumesnil concluded that Flaubert united the ardent imagination and romantic character inherited from his mother with the superior intelligence and scientific spirit of his father (317).

The image of Flaubert as hysteric was most evident in his first published novel, *Madame Bovary* (1856). Flaubert identified so closely with his heroine that he reportedly exclaimed, "Mme. Bovary, c'est moi!" In a review of the work, Baudelaire also declared that Emma was the female incarnation of Flaubert, and inversely that,

> despite all his zeal as an actor, [Flaubert] was unable not to infuse virile blood into the veins of his creature, and that Madame Bovary—for all the energy and ambition she may have in her, and also her dreaminess—Madame Bovary remains a man. Like armed Pallas [Athena], springing from the brain of Zeus, that bizarre androgyne has kept all the seductions of a virile soul in a charming feminine body. (Baudelaire 1857, 652)

Baudelaire found this double act of gender inversion—Emma as Flaubert in drag, and vice versa—the product of literary genius. Contemporary physicians were far more wary of hysterical gender inverts and their novels.

Dr. Ernest Lasègue in an article on "Hysterics, Their Perversity, Their Lies" (1881) warned colleagues against the willful malevolence and irresistible deceitfulness of the hysteric's imagination. Hysterics and lunatics both told untrue stories, Lasègue noted, but the great danger was that "the latter are unbelievable, whereas *the novels of hysterics* impose themselves by their verisimilitude" (1881, 114; emphasis added). The same principle could be applied more broadly, Lasègue suggested: "Do we not have something analogous in the wide field of human inventions? This is the novelist who, commencing with a premise furnished by the imagination, allows himself to be led by this to the point of believing that everything he creates actually happened" (112). The novels of hysterics and hysterical novelists seem to collapse into the same category through their shared traits: hypersensibility, overimaginativeness, deceitfulness, and self-delusion. Doctors also uncovered these characteristics in the novels and lives of "inverts"—the literate, fin-de-siècle perverts who emerged in the 1880s. Heeding Lasègue's warnings concerning hysterics, physicians were on guard against inverts' seductive narratives.

## Perversion and Nationalism

The diagnostic and nosological characteristics of sexual inversion had been gradually accumulating in the nineteenth-century medical literature: sodomy, pederasty, effeminacy, effeminate hysteria, somatic and psychic gender crossing, same-sex erotic attraction, and lack of "venereal appetite" for the opposite sex. Yet none of these elements constituted "inversion of the genital sense" as it would emerge in the 1880s and be transformed soon thereafter into an array of "sexual perversions." As noted earlier, the history of inversion per se began with the description of "contrary sexual sensation" by German forensic physicians at mid-century.

The fact that the diagnosis arose first in Germany and not France is probably due to the greater legal repression of sodomy in Prussia and, after 1871, all of Germany. As noted earlier, sodomy in private between adults had been decriminalized in France, but this was not the case in central Europe. Paragraph 143 of the Prussian penal code established "unnatural lewdness" as a criminal offense. The newly unified German Empire in 1871 extended this law as Paragraph 175 of the penal code.[35] Given the climate of legal persecution, accused sodomites claimed mental irregularity and sought the assistance of liberal German doctors. Although Hermann Kaan (1844), like Tardieu, insisted that pederasty was a perverse choice, he also suggested it might be a constitutional aspect of personality. In 1852 Ludwig Casper argued that the disposition to pederasty could be innate, and Wilhelm Griesinger (1868–1869) proposed that it might be a psychopathic condition mitigating legal responsibility. A psychological theory of congenital, same-sex love was advanced by a Hanoverian legal official, Karl Heinrich Ulrichs (under the pseudonym Numa Numantius), in his autobiographical and legal brochures pleading for the decriminalization of "unnatural acts" (1864–1879). Ulrichs coined the word *Urning* to identify the "third sex" to which he and his fellows belonged.[36] He proposed the classic model of gender inversion: *Urnings* were female souls caught in male bodies.[37]

Ulrichs argued that their nature was a physiological condition without intellectual deficits and should not be the object of legal persecution.[38]

It was through the writings of Ulrichs that Karl Westphal, editor of the German *Archives of Psychiatry and Nervous Diseases,* became interested in what he called *conträre Sexualempfindung.* Westphal described it as a symptom of a neuropsychopathic condition in either sex, associated with hereditary taints and occasionally mania, melancholia, and inclinations to theft. Additionally, these patients often betrayed traits of hysteroepilepsy and moral insanity (1869, 106–7; 1876). Westphal's article was followed by a flurry of German publications on contrary sexual sensation.[39] Even so, in 1877 Richard von Krafft-Ebing (who became the leading fin-de-siècle German sexologist) could only identify eighteen cases in all the preceding medical literature.[40]

The Germans had invented and monopolized the study of contrary sexual sensation until the 1880s, so it is hardly surprising that French writers—still burning with animosity in the wake of the Franco-Prussian War—referred to inversion as the "German vice" (Dubarry 1896b). Nationalist rivalry was as fierce and vituperative over the study of inversion as over other scientific and political issues. The initial French foray into research on inversion was launched in 1882 with Charcot and Magnan's article mentioned at the beginning of this chapter. They not only reviewed foreign publications on the new disorder, but also presented new clinical material and laid out a theory of inversion pathology strongly at odds with the Germans' hypotheses. The first part of the article presented the patient introduced earlier, who ejaculated at the sight or mere thought of naked males. Charcot and Magnan were clearly perplexed by his constellation of perversities when they exclaimed, "This patient, what is he?" They proceeded to create him out of the clinical materials at hand.

Jean Martin Charcot was the charismatic chief physician at the Salpêtrière Asylum during the Third Republic who restored the popularity of the hysteria diagnosis. Valentin Magnan interned at Bicêtre and the Salpêtrière before his appointment to the new Saint-Anne Asylum in 1867. He spent the rest of his career there and promoted the degenerationist theory of neuropathology.

The two neurologists found that in spite of the patient's exceptional intelligence, education, and achievements (he was a university professor), he had a degenerate family history, especially on the mother's side. The grandfather was "agitated" and consorted with artists; the grandmother was "eccentric"; the mother engaged in "exaggerated religiosity" and wore gaudy clothing. Since the age of fifteen, the patient had suffered convulsive fits, which the two neurologists believed were hysterical rather than frankly epileptic. Under the label *inversion of the genital sense* Charcot and Magnan fused the two diagnoses examined in the previous two sections: the elite pederast and the effeminate, degenerate male hysteric.

In itself, this innovation in nosology was quite an accomplishment, but the two doctors seemed unaware of their diagnostic hybridization. They intended to make a different taxonomic contribution. This became clear in the second installment of the article, the title of which was lengthened to include their new diagnostic term: "sexual perversions." They reported four additional cases that broadened the scope of the sexual perversions: a melancholic onanist (with a hysterical mother), erotically obsessed with buttocks; a hysterical man obsessed with boot nails; a son of eccentrics who was obsessed with night bonnets; and a man who stole aprons to masturbate on them. Today we would identify these as examples of "fetishism," and this is precisely how Alfred Binet reclassified them when he coined the notion of "erotic fetishism" in 1887.[41] Charcot and Magnan, however, presented these cases as fundamentally the same class of disorder as sexual inversion. Like dipsomania (alcoholism), these "impulsive states" were all congenital variants of degenerate heredity characterized by a compulsive obsession:

> Should in the place of boot nails, night-bonnets, or white aprons the obsession have man for its object, the phenomena unfold in the same manner; and we must recognize that the histories of all these patients are closely related. They are, so to speak, fashioned in the same mold, they do not differ except in the more or less acute degree of intellectual degeneration. (321–32)

The doctor's underlying objective was to collect all the sexual perversions under the same diagnostic rubric rather than develop increasingly fine, phenomenological categories as had the Germans. Krafft-Ebing, for example, had hypothesized that inverts suffered from a degenerate heredity, but he had distinguished same-sex inclination from what he grouped as opposite-sex perversions: lust-murder, anthropophagy, and necrophilia.[42] He thereby justified lobbying for the repeal of antisodomy laws.[43] Westphal had also argued for the abrogation of antisodomy laws in hopes that this would allow more contrary sexuals to seek medical attention and thus further the scientific study of the condition (1869, 108).

By lumping rather than splitting the sexual perversions, Charcot and Magnan resisted any greater legal or social acceptance of same-sex eroticism than already afforded by the liberal French penal code. Instead, they forcefully argued for the psychopathologization and paternal medical treatment of inversion alongside all varieties of compulsive, degenerate desires. They warned that "these obsessions, these impulsions which, by the sole fact that the patient is aware of them, affect certain allures of benignity, are, on the contrary, always the manifestations of a very grave state" (322).

Dr. Jules Falret echoed these sentiments in his comments on Magnan's lecture on sexual perversions presented at the Medico-Psychological Society. Betraying concerns about national priority and purity, Falret warned that hereditary reasoning insanity (*folie raisonnante*), of which inversion was just a variant, represented the lowest state of degeneration short of imbecility or idiocy; it was not just the first step below sanity. He sharply criticized the Germans for focusing on inversion as a special case rather than examining it as just one aspect of the genital perversions of the hereditarily insane (Magnan 1885a, 473).

So, in a storm of Franco-German rivalry, *sexual inversion* had firmly entered the French lexicon.[44] The term was nevertheless "too vague," as Tamassia himself noted when he coined *inversione dell'istinto sessuale*. It collapsed two distinct issues into one label: psychological gender inversion, or the sensation that one's psychological gender is the opposite of one's physical sex; and the preference "to satisfy [one's] sexual instinct with individuals of the same sex."[45] Physicians well into the twentieth century would overlook this confusion between what today we distinguish under the terms *transsexualism* and *homosexuality*. Charcot and Magnan were not concerned with this ambiguity. Charcot wrote no more on inversion. He instead turned to male hysteria and made every effort to characterize it as a disorder of all classes of men, not necessarily of the effeminate.[46]

Magnan, in contrast, became increasingly interested in the sexual perversions (Sérieux 1921). He developed a system for classifying the perversions, including inversion, according to the presumed neuroanatomical location of their pathology, whether spinal, posterior spinocerebral, anterior spinocerebral, or anterior cerebral. These hypothesized lesions from the "lower" to the "higher" neurological centers were matched with behaviors ranging from the most automatic, reflex genital acts of the "spinal" idiots who masturbated mechanically, to the sexual insatiability of nymphomaniacs, the sexual perversions of inverts and pedophiles, and, finally, the obsessive platonic love of "anterior cerebrals" (see table). As had been the case with pederasty, the interest in sexual perversions arose mainly because of forensic considerations. Magnan concluded his article by stating that "despite their reasonable appearance, these patients are at the mercy of their impulsive desires, [and] could not be considered responsible" (1885a, 472).

Forensic interest in the sexual perversions was such that medicolegal journals quickly dominated the scientific discourse of inversion and sexual perversion. Particularly prominent among these was the *Archives of Criminal Anthro-*

### Classification Systems for "Perversions of the Sexual Instinct"

MICHÉA (1849)
1. Greek love or love for one's sex
2. Bestiality
3. Attraction to inanimate objects
4. Attraction to human cadavers

LACASSAGNE (1884)*
I. Pathological quantity
    1. States of augmentation: erotic temperament, onanism, satyriasis, nymphomania
    2. States of diminution: frigidity, impotence
II. Pathological quality
    1. Inversion of the genital sense
    2. Necrophilia
    3. Bestiality
    4. Love for inanimate objects (or "nihilists of the flesh")

MAGNAN (1885B)
1. Spinals: mechanical, automatic sexual stimulation (e.g., idiot onanists)
2. Posterior spinocerebrals: reflex orgasms (e.g., nymphomaniacs)
3. Anterior spinocerebrals: perverse love objects (e.g., pedophiles, fetishists, inverts)
4. Anterior cerebral or psychics: purely platonic love (e.g., erotomaniacs)

*From Lacassagne's lecture delivered November 1884 (qtd. in Chevalier 1885, 9–11).

---

pology, *Criminology, and Normal and Pathological Psychology*, which Drs. Alexandre Lacassagne and Gabriel Tarde founded in 1885. Lacassagne, the professor of forensic medicine at the Faculty of Medicine of Lyon and a leader in the discipline, had lectured on the topic in November 1884. Unlike Magnan's speculative neuroanatomical system of sexual perversions, Lacassagene had proposed a simple phenomenological classification system that elaborated on an earlier one by Michéa.

By 1885 the French medical journals were pullulating with these queer new creatures, and Dr. Julien Chevalier, one of Lacassagne's students, had ample material to write a thesis on *Inversion from the Medico-Legal Point of View*. Chevalier mainly summarized previous publications, adding Lacassagne's new report on an effeminate invert with a hysterical mother. This case study of *la femmelette* adhered to the dominant theory of the degenerate etiology of congenital inversion (Chevalier 1885, 130). Chevalier's original contribution was a theory of the relationship between history and sexuality. He noted that, although the word *inversion* was of recent origin, it described an ancient phenomenon. It was therefore necessary to know its "historical filiation" in relation to the evolution of humanity in order to understand why the phenomenon existed. Freely adapting Auguste Comte's classification of the evolution of human intellect, Chevalier identified four historical stages: fetishism, polytheism, monotheism, and the present. This historical progress was marked by the cultivation of the mind in place of "primitive" sentiments and instinctive drives. He nevertheless agreed with Lacassagne's appraisal that even Christianity and (Western) civilization had not succeeded in extirpating these animal passions. The taming of primitive drives had happened to the greatest degree among the elite, but the masses merely exhibited a veneer of civilization. Chevalier continued, quoting Lacassagne:

> If one goes to the bottom of things and looks at what is below the apparent, one finds that even the believer in the most refined religions has remained, as far as ideas are concerned, the primitive man who lives in the grotto of the quaternarian era. . . . Taken as a mass, humanity has remained what it was in the beginning: purely fetishistic. (25)

Magnan's neuroanatomical system of sexual perversions represented inversion as a pathological descent to inferior, "primitive" cerebrospinal levels. Chevalier's and Lacassagne's model of sexuality, in turn, portrayed inversion as historical atavism: a regression to pre-Christian moralities. In their different ways, the emerging nosologies of perversion explained sexual inversion as a multilayered inversion of historical orders. Not only was inversion a neuropsychological counter-evolution but also a historical and cultural regression. Inversion was theorized as a retreat from the intellect to the passions, from the real to the imaginary, from the civilized to the primitive—typically feminine regressions consonant with the effeminacy associated with male hysteria and sexual inversion.

The conflation of diverse sexual and gender anxieties in the diagnosis of inversion is evident in the dizzying panoply of designations for the illness: "contrary, inverse, perverted, [or] inverted genital sense; —contrary, inverse, [or] perverted sexual attractions, impulsions, [or] sensations; —attraction of same sexes; —crossed sensation of sexual individuality; . . . —perversion, [or] inter-version of the sexual instinct, [etc.]" (Chevalier 1885, 14). Some order needed to be brought to this field of confusions; therefore, in 1894 another of Lacassagne's students in the laboratory of legal medicine, "Dr. Laupts," undertook a national survey on inversion through the *Archives of Criminal Anthropology*. His extensive questionnaire included items on the heredity, physical and psychological status, and medical and legal history of inverts. The survey was addressed not only to doctors but also to professors, lawyers, and *novelists* (1894, 105). Laupts argued that the study of inversion was not simply a matter of scientific curiosity but of vital interest to French society, and indeed the entire human race:

> These days, no one doubts that the number of degenerations, of cerebral derailings—expressed by the tendencies towards suicide, by phobias, etc.—results in large part from the fact that in our nation the genital functions are often not accomplished as they should be. Therefore, it is necessary, from the point of view of the vitality, of the future of the race, to study the morbid causes, to discern the dangerous and evil elements, among which must be ranked for an appreciable part the creature stricken with sexual perversion: the pervert, the feminiform, congenital invert. (1896, 104–5)

This vitriolic indictment makes it clear that the diagnosis of inversion consolidated numerous disorders and dreads: immorality, effeminacy, degeneration, mental illness, genital "abuse," national decay, and genocide. The sexual perversions, particularly sexual inversion, conveniently knotted together fin-de-siècle medical, social, and moral preoccupations that stemmed from declining French fertility, growing class tensions, and the demoralization of the nation after its humiliating defeat in the Franco-Prussian War.[47] It was therefore appropriate that the first published reply to Laupts's survey came from a major cultural figure who shared these concerns—not a physician, but the novelist Emile Zola. Zola's contribution and the ensuing nationalist medical debates on inversion show how the fin-de-siècle construction of homosexuality was a broad literary and cultural affair with repercussions beyond the confines of medical texts and knowledge.

## Novelizing Inversion

*Monsieur Emile Zola, Paris*

It is to you, Monsieur, who are the greatest novelist of our time and who, with the eye of the savant and the artist, capture and paint so powerfully *all* the failings, all the shame, all the ills that afflict humanity that I send these *human documents* so cherished by the cultivated people of our age.

This confession, which no spiritual advisor has ever learned from my lips, will reveal to you a frightful illness of the soul, a rare case—if not, unfortunately, unique—that has been studied by learned psychologists, but which till now no novelist has dared to stage in a literary work. (Invert 1894, 212)[48]

So opens a truly unique "human document" of the late 1880s: a bundle of letters and postcards mailed anonymously to Emile Zola by a twenty-three-year-old Italian aristocrat. In florid, raunchy detail alternatingly exuding hubris and shame, Zola's correspondent narrates the feverish evolution of his "frightful illness," *an erotic passion for men.* He recounts his early cross-dressing experiences and masturbatory addiction, his youthful infatuation with stable boys, his secret love affair with a fellow military officer, and his seduction by an older man. In a final postcard, he gleefully reports being sodomized by an elegant Milanese gentleman met the previous night! Although he experienced profound moral ambivalence about his erotic inclinations, the young man ultimately hoped that he would be reborn as a hero in a great Zola novel: "I do not know if you can do anything with the terrible passion I have confessed to you, but in any case I am glad to have confessed it to you. If the misery which afflicts me can find a place in the sublime descriptions of human misery, I beg you, Monsieur, do not render me too odious" (135). By providing an abundance of authentic documentation, Zola's mysterious correspondent hoped his unusual "deviation" might be represented more extensively and candidly by the inventor of the "experimental novel": the author who declared that "the dream of the physiologist and the experimental doctor is also that of the novelist who applies [Claude Bernard's] experimental method to the natural and social study of man" (Zola 1880, 1188). Zola's self-made image as paternal doctor clearly seduced the young Italian, for he wrote, "Please forgive my horrible scribble, but I [write] with my heart on my sleeve, as if I were confessing to a doctor or a friend, and I have not paid attention to the form or the spelling" (Invert 1895, 231).

Despite this false modesty, the Italian's autobiography actually adopted the form of the medical case history. His appropriation of the medical genre reflects the cultural currency of hereditarian theories. The Italian himself boasted of his familiarity with the works of "learned psychologists" and with Zola's novelistic representations of hereditary degeneration. As in the case studies of male hysterics, the Italian began with family antecedents: "My father is of a very impressionable and nervous temperament, an artist to the tips of his fingers. He had a rather adventurous life with considerable highs and lows" (213). The Italian invert's grandfather was also a handsome and well-respected gentleman, but died at an early age of heart disease. The maternal line was more severely tainted neurologically and psychologically, primarily because it was Jewish.

My mother was very pretty in her youth, although emerging from a very *ugly* and *vulgar* family. She always had few wits and I still reproach my father for having allied himself to a family that is so ugly and with such little distinction. . . . She cannot read a little sentimental anecdote without crying; she has little memory and her only excuse is her great goodness. . . . I still think it is one of the qualities or defects inherent to the race from which she descends and for which I have no sympathy, rather, a certain repulsion. (214–15)

The racial "taint" of the Jews would soon preoccupy France with the eruption of the Dreyfus Affair. The Italian, however, primarily blamed his Jewish heredity for ugly physical traits, particularly in his brothers. His own superlative looks came from the paternal side, but his nervous, impressionable temperament was clearly the product of both his mother and father. His beauty was, however, distinctly feminine. Like Ulrichs before him, the Italian invert argued that his nature and physique were congenitally female:

> Whenever I see my nanny, she always tells me that all the women she knows had named me *the little Madonna,* I was so cute and delicate. . . . I still recall the shiver of joy and pleasure that coursed through my little person when I went out in my little puffed-up blue piqué dress with blue bows and my big Italian straw hat [as was common among boys of his social class].
>
> When I was four, they took away my little dresses to put me in trousers and a little jacket. Once they had dressed me as a boy, I experienced profound shame—I remember it as if it were today—and I quickly ran to my nanny's room to hide and cry; to console me, she had to dress me again as a girl. They still laugh whenever recalling my cries of despair in seeing them take away those little white dresses which were my greatest joy.
>
> It seemed as if they were taking away something that I was always destined to wear.
>
> That was my first great sorrow. (215)

Even his first erotic inclinations towards males were of a distinctly feminine quality: "I always imagined myself to be a woman, and all my desires since then have been those of a woman" (371). He recollects that, even before puberty, he had a vague idea of his sexual difference and a premonition of his erotic destiny. At age thirteen he developed a crush on one of the servants and regularly invited him up to his bedroom to recount sexual adventures. These libertine tales filled him with desires: "I wished he had slept beside me, to feel his blond, polished body; I wanted to embrace him and have him by me to take his pleasure and to return it." On one of these occasions,

> I was suddenly driven to know him thoroughly and without shame, and as if in jest, I begged him to show me his member in order to persuade me that it

really was as large and handsome as he claimed. At first he refused, but finally after making me promise never to tell anyone, he opened his trousers and completely revealed himself in the state of erection that our talk had provoked. He approached my little bed where I was panting with desire and shame. I had never seen the member of a big person and I was so stunned that I couldn't say a word. Propelled by I know not what force or what innate desire, I seized it with my right hand and vigorously rubbed it mumbling, "My it's beautiful, my it's beautiful!"

I had a furious desire to do something with that member which filled my whole hand and I desired ardently to have a hole in my body in which to insert the object of all my desires. (372)

Reflecting a century of medical writings on the dangerous power of the imagination, he reveals how, from the youngest age, he "took refuge in an imaginary world" populated with princesses and queens whom he imitated and Greek heroes whom he loved (368–70). He even fantasized of being Andromache in order to embrace the muscular Hector. The Italian invert recalled that after being rebuffed by a handsome stable boy,

I sought to persuade myself through my imagination that I was his wife, and at night I placed my bolster alongside me and kissed and bit it as if it were a living person. I thought of the handsome young man so robust and so fresh, and I sought in my movements to procure the illusion of sleeping with him. In doing this, and almost unwillingly, I corrupted myself and I felt my own semen flow for the first time. (730)

Much like the young Rousseau, the pubescent Italian was terrified by this seminal loss. Despite occasional attempts to abstain from the solitary vice, he abandoned himself wholeheartedly since: "My lively imagination lent me the most convenient images and I delighted in that terrible pleasure whilst evoking images of men who pleased me and with whom I wanted to be." Further echoing Rousseau, the Italian reports that, fortunately, he was of a hardy constitution, otherwise such indulgence "would no doubt have killed anyone else" (730).

This Rousseauvian confession of the most intimate, shameful, morbid, yet poignant aspects of inner experience impressed Zola, who felt the subject was extremely important:

I was struck by the great physiological and social interest [the letter] offered. It touched me by its absolute sincerity, because one senses the flame, I would even say the eloquence of truth. . . . [T]ell if he does not achieve, in certain passages, the moving style of sentiments profoundly experienced and expressed.

It is a total, naïve, spontaneous confession that very few men would dare make, qualities that render it quite precious from many points of view.

Zola even hoped that its publication might "inspire some pity and a modicum of equity for these wretches" (1896, 1, 3). Given all these scientific, literary, and social virtues of the invert's manuscript, Dr. Laupts naturally asked: "Why did [Zola] not discuss inversion, why did [he] not dedicate one of his novels to inversion? The subject is worth the effort" (1907, 833).

The Italian invert wondered the same thing. He later wrote: "With each of Zola's new novels, I hoped to finally discover a character who was the reproduction of myself, but I was always disappointed and I was finally convinced that the writer had lacked the courage to stage so terrible a passion."[49] Zola was hardly one to shy away from controversy. Even before the Dreyfus Affair and his famous essay "J'accuse!" (1898), Zola's naturalist novels had been condemned for their vulgarity, sensuality, and morbidity. Some of his harshest critics were those people he claimed as his colleagues: physicians, who nevertheless considered him a "scientific dilettante." Like Flaubert before him, Zola had also been deemed a pathological writer, and he had been "diagnosed" as an epileptoid degenerate, a "superior degenerate," an olfactory fetishist, and a sexual psychopath.[50] Yet he continued to portray the great spectrum of physical and moral degenerations: alcoholism, prostitution, monomania, adultery, and homicide. Therefore, Zola's literary impotence on the topic of inversion is quite revealing. He could never have edited the Italian's manuscript, he confessed, because,

> I was then in the roughest hours of my literary battle; critics treated me daily as a criminal capable of all vices and all debaucheries. . . . First of all they would have accused me of entirely *inventing* the story from personal corruption. Then I would have been duly condemned for merely having seen in the affair an occasion for base speculation on the most repugnant instincts. And what a clamor if I had permitted myself to say that no other subject is more serious or more tragic; that it is a far more common and deep wound than pretended and that still the best thing for healing wounds is to study them, to expose them, and to treat them! (Zola 1896, 2)

Despite Legrand du Saulle's dictum (regularly cited in sexological works)— "science like fire, purifies everything it touches"—the social taint of "inversion" was clearly too much even for Zola, the *scientific* novelist. Privately, Zola admitted: "I have encountered [inverts] . . . and in shaking their hand, I experience an instinctive repulsion I can barely overcome" (Laupts 1907, 833). And to another correspondent, Zola wrote, "If I am full of pity for those whom you call Uranists, I have no sympathy for them, no doubt because I am different."[51]

Zola had become increasingly fervent about the birthrate in France—a concern most clearly voiced in *Fécondité* (1899). He was extremely anxious about all forms of nonprocreative sex, and once moaned: "How much seed wasted in one night in Paris—what a shame that all of it does not produce human beings" (Laupts 1907, 832n.). On the threat of inversion, Zola was even more vehement: "An invert is a disorganizer of the family, of the nation, of humanity. Man and woman were certainly not placed on earth to do other than bear children, and they kill life the day they no longer do what is necessary for this" (1896, 4). As we have seen, Zola's concern with seminal waste and non-procreative sexuality was shared by contemporary French doctors and anthropologists. Therefore, Zola submitted the Italian's confessions to Dr. Laupts to be published as the first response to Laupts's survey on sexual inversion.

Dr. Laupts introduced the "document" in a style more suited to the back cover blurb of a racy "true crime" novella: "It is the true story of a man who bore a great name, a very great name in Italy. As exact as a scientific observation, as interesting as a novel, as sincere as a confession, it is perhaps the most complete and most endearing document of this genre" (1894, 212). It is not clear what genre Laupts is referring to, but the text borrows from numerous forms: eighteenth-century confessional letters in *Onania*, epistolary novels, Rousseauvian autobiography, licentious literature, and the hereditarian case study of sexual perverts. Laupts clearly agreed with the Italian that the confession was a "precious document" for it was reprinted in Laupts's anthology of articles and documents on homosexuality, *Taints and Poisons: Sexual Perversions and Perversities* (1896).

Strolling down a street one day, the Italian was startled to discover Laupts's volume in a bookstore window. He immediately wrote to Laupts that he was elated to find himself "printed in *living color*, although I would have much preferred to be reborn in the pages of a novel and not in a medical science treatise" (Saint-Paul 1930, 116). Indeed, the Italian dandy repeatedly suggested that he fashioned himself a *belle-lettriste* and that he envisioned his life itself as a work of art:

> I unburdened my soul somewhat [in my confessions to Zola] and I wrote with a retrospective voluptuousness of the abominable and ardent scenes in which I was the actor. . . . I therefore want to complete the study of my person, whom I often consider favored by nature because she made me a creature that even the most audacious poets have been unable to create (Invert 1895, 231–32).

Ironically enough, his "true" confession was printed verbatim but under the title "The *Novel* of an Invert."

Just like most of Zola's novels, the confession was published serially, and Laupts had a knack for breaking the action at moments of sexual climax. For example, in the third installment, "Youth—First Acts," we learn of the Italian's first sexual experience, an encounter during his military service with a handsome young officer:

> He was half undressed and seated on my legs right up against me. I spoke to him as if enchanted. . . . [S]uddenly he leaned over, embraced me in his arms and applied a long kiss to my cheek; at the same time he plunged his hand under the sheets and firmly grasped my flesh. I thought I would die and an immense joy suddenly seized me. We remained a few seconds like that, resting one head against the other, our fiery cheeks touching, my mouth in his in the warmth of the pillow. I was never so happy!!
>
> The lamp on the floor cast faint rays upon the immense dormitory where, in the distant beds, my companions were sleeping, and left the corner where we were thus ecstatic in the deepest darkness.
>
> (*To be continued.*) (Invert 1894, 737)

Readers had to cool off for two months before the hard-core action resumed. *But is it science or is it fiction?* As Zola feared, some foreign writers were convinced it was entirely his own fabrication,[52] and it did not help matters that Laupts labeled it a novel. Perhaps Laupts felt the text deserved the designation because of its intrinsic literary qualities: the richness of its figurative language, the well-developed characterization of its hero, or its exceptional length for a medical "article" (almost forty eight pages). Perhaps it was safer to label it "The Novel of an Invert" than "The Pornography of an Invert," for the work is indeed pornographic. As had already become standard practice in the work of Krafft-Ebing, the sexually explicit passages were "cloaked in the decency of a dead language"—Latin. For the literate medical and lay audience who purchased these books, the Latin passages in italics were that much easier to find and enjoy. For example, the Italian recalls the scene of seduction by an older friend of his father's, a cavalry captain (the italicized paragraph is in Latin in the original):

> [The captain] rose suddenly, locked the door and closed the shutters, then returned to me who was panting with desire, shame, and fear. He undressed me in the wink of an eye, all the while running his hands over my body; he even took off my stockings and shoes, cast away my shirt, and carried me like a little

child into his bed. In an instant he too was completely naked and lying beside me; I felt I was in a dream and was no longer conscious of my acts and thoughts.

*He lay on top of me, panting and groaning loudly, and he clasped me so tightly in his arms that I almost suffocated; he began stroking himself on top of my body. He had a huge member which, when rubbed over me, gave me an extraordinarily pleasurable sensation. Meanwhile, he sucked my ears, inserted his tongue in my mouth, and caressed my entire body with his hands. He kept saying the sweetest nothings to me in a broken voice. When he emitted his semen, he inundated me and didn't cease thrusting, but roared like a bull. Meanwhile I had ejaculated copiously, and for a long time we clung to one another as if unconscious and indeed glued together; in fact, we struggled to unstick ourselves.*

I was not in the least bit ashamed at that moment, and he too seemed totally happy. (Saint-Paul 1930, 94–95)[53]

This sort of Latinized pornography was finding its way ever more frequently into the pages of medical texts under the cover of science. Tissot and his Enlightenment colleagues had worried that even vague descriptions of masturbation might enflame young imaginations. A century later, the medical literature on sexual perversions equaled eighteenth-century licentious literature in sexual explicitness, but unlike its illicit counterpart, sexological works were sold openly in bookstore windows.

Recall that the Italian invert had read some of this medical literature and had even discovered his own story in a bookseller's vitrine. Rather than being dismayed by Zola's breach of confidence, the Italian was delighted to see his words in print. He wrote to Laupts, praising the doctor as a "savant . . . and a kind and indulgent man." The Italian even contributed dozens more pages of self-description directly to Laupts because "like every sick person who sees in a doctor a friend, . . . I am filled with friendship and gratitude for those who occupy themselves with the odious illness that haunts me, and . . . I seek to render them service by exhibiting that which they painfully seek, and which I, on the contrary, know so well: *by innate science*." He, nevertheless, left it up to Laupts to draw theoretical conclusions from this data: "I have told you the causes and the effects; now it is up to you to study them and profit from them for the sake of science and humanity" (Saint-Paul 1930, 116, 128). He recognized that the business of creating scientific knowledge was not entirely in the hands of physicians: researchers depended on him for data, and by being an informant, he could engage in the "voluptuous," exhibitionistic self-representation and self-exploration he adored.

Perhaps it was precisely because the invert had played such a strong, autonomous role in shaping his own narrative that Dr. Laupts decided to place the "true confession" under a cloud of suspicion with the title "The Novel of an Invert." The label *novel* distinguished the first-person patient confession from the "objective" medical writings surrounding it. The "novels of hysterics" had been roundly denounced as deceitful. Laupts may have wanted to cast the same doubt on the Italian's confession, despite its author's claim that "it is pointless to reassure you that everything in my story is true" (Invert 1895, 231). However, in dealing with inverts and their masquerades, one could never be too wary. "This autobiography resembles those of all effeminate Uranists who have gone public," warned the second respondent to Laupts's investigation.

> This novel of an invert will teach nothing to those with experience in psychiatry. . . . Unbridled vanity and lust are especially demonstrated in the relations between the invert of the novel and the Captain. . . . Repugnant or dangerous acts will generally occur between people united by debauchery, vanity, or interest. (Raffalovich 1895b, 333)

The author, Marc-André Raffalovich, was a newcomer to the field of sexology. Generalizing further, Raffalovich cautioned that "one should not dwell on such autobiographies or attach much importance to them" (1895a, 116). We must be careful in evaluating Raffalovich's comments, however, for he too was an invert. But then so was Dr. Laupts, if only literally: *Laupts* was a fictional name, the inversion of his real name, St.-Paul. Even better, he was a writer of literary and fictional works: North African travelogues, war stories, farces, short stories, poems, and a melodrama about syphilis (1907). All of this was published under his second pseudonym G. Espé de Metz—a name adopted when bibliographers, to Georges Saint-Paul's horror, started cataloguing Laupts's texts with *German* authors (Saint-Paul 1930, 5).

Deceptions and counterdeceptions, charges and countercharges were especially rife in the medical literature on inversion, particularly because of the active participation of inverts themselves in the scientific fashioning of "homosexuality." Raffalovich especially inflamed the Franco-German national and scientific rivalries. The writers who addressed him as "Dr. Raffalovich" ignored the fact that he had no medical degree.[54] In his day, however, Raffalovich was the most provocative and prolific "medical" writer in French on homosexuality. He enunciated positions so divergent from dominant French medical opinion that they appeared radically prohomosexual. Yet like the Italian, Raffalovich betrayed a deep moral ambivalence about sexual inversion, and his campaign to normalize homosexuality was fought by sacrificing a stigmatized group of "perverse" inverts. In many ways his scientific opinion was the forerunner of the political strategy employed by current homosexual apologists who campaign for the rights of "good" homosexuals by perpetuating the marginalization of "bad" ones: cross-dressers, sadomasochism enthusiasts, flamboyant effeminates, and so on.[55] Pitting virile homosexuals against effeminate, degenerate ones had far broader fin-de-siècle repercussions: it resonated with internal tensions in scientific rhetoric as well as nationalist conflicts in social analysis.

## Homoaesthetic Politics: Raffalovich, Wilde, and Huysmans

> Amat avidus amores
> Miros, miros carpit flores
>     Saevus pulchritudine:
> Quanto anima nigrescit,
> Tanto facies splendiescit,
> Mendax, sed quam splendide!
> Hic sunt poma Sodomorum;
> Hic sunt corda vitiorum;
>     Et peccata dulcia.
> In excelcis et infernis,
> Tibi sit, qui tanta cernis,
>     Gloriarum gloria.

Lionel Johnson, "In Honorem Doriani Creatorisque Eius"*

Just two years after his brief response to Laupts's inversion survey, Marc-André Raffalovich published an extensive monograph, *Uranism and Unisexuality: A Study of Different Manifestations of the Sexual Instinct* (1896), in Lacassagne's "Library of Criminology" series. In 1897 Raffalovich was entrusted with writing the "Annals of Unisexuality," a journal-within-a-journal in the *Archives of*

---

*Excerpt of "In Honorem Doriani Creatorisque Eius," a poem written in gratitude to Wilde for a copy of *The Portrait of Dorian Gray*. "He avidly loves strange loves and, fierce with beauty, he plucks strange flowers. The more sinister his spirit, the more radiant his face, lying—but how splendidly! Here are apples of Sodom, here are the very hearts of vices, and tender sins. In heaven and hell be glory of glories to you who perceive so much" (trans. Ellman, 1988, 323–24).

*Criminal Anthropology,* and his work met with professional approval among German and British reviewers. Dr. Paul Näcke, for example, praised Raffalovich as one of only six non-German experts on inversion (1908, 111n.). Despite his remarkable publication history, Raffalovich was treated with hostility by French doctors. He remained a mysterious character, in part because he did not live in France or belong to the small circle of Parisian academic physicians.

Raffalovich came from a Russian Jewish family that had made its banking fortune in France. His mother, Marie, was a beautiful, intelligent socialite and an intimate friend of Claude Bernard, a leader in experimental physiology. It was Bernard who recommended that Raffalovich become a doctor. After completing his early education in Paris, he was sent to Oxford to study medicine but never completed his studies because of his weak health. Instead, he established himself in grand style in London, publishing poetry and novels and hosting the literary stars of the time: Henry James, Aubrey Beardsley, Pierre Louÿs, Stephan Mallarmé, and, the most notorious of aesthetes, Oscar Wilde.

Raffalovich and Wilde were intimate friends until their vicious falling out in the early 1890s, apparently over some indiscretion of Wilde's. Later, Wilde openly mocked Raffalovich's unattractiveness and portrayed him as a pretentious, nouveau riche foreigner. "Poor André!" Wilde once quipped, "He came to London with the intention of founding a *salon,* and he has succeeded only in opening a saloon."[56] Their mutual friend, Arthur Symons, introduced Raffalovich to Wilde's companion, a pretty-boy and budding poet named John Henry Gray. *A Portrait of Dorian Gray,* with its secret dedication to John, was published in 1891, but the next year Wilde met the younger and more angelic Lord Alfred Douglas. Raffalovich, who had become enamored of Gray, caught the suicidal poet on the rebound and they became lifetime companions.[57] They coauthored a play called *The Blackmailers* (1894) which the dramatic critic of the *Times* described as "a sordid and repulsive picture of blackmailing practices carried on in society." In this play, an older scoundrel induces a young man into blackmailing scams "whose game appears to be perfectly well understood by the society in which they move."[58] Blackmail and scandal concerning allegations of sodomy were all too common in England (as they were in Paris), and such scandal moved from the stage to the courtroom with the *Wilde v. Queensbury* trial in 1895.

The Wilde Affair perturbed London's dandies, including Raffalovich and Gray who took off for Berlin before the trial ended. Within a few years both of them turned to Catholicism. Raffalovich converted in 1896 and two years later became a lay Dominican under the name Brother Sebastian. Gray decided to enter the priesthood and began seminary training in Rome at Raffalovich's expense. Raffalovich later subsidized the construction of Saint Peter's Church in Edinburgh where Father Gray was installed as parish priest in 1907. A great benefactor of the Dominican Order, Raffalovich also donated funds for the construction of Saint Sebastian's Priory in Pendleton, Manchester.[59] In 1905 Raffalovich moved into a house next to Saint Peter's. While he and Gray did not live together, Raffalovich's wealth was held in a joint account with Gray. The reportedly met every day for tea until Raffalovich died on Saint Valentine's Day 1934. Gray was much distressed by the loss and followed Raffalovich to the grave just four months later.[60]

Perhaps it was through Arthur Symons, a close friend of John Addington Symonds and Havelock Ellis, that Raffalovich was introduced to the burgeoning scientific study of inversion and to Ellis and Symonds's groundbreaking *Sexual Inversion* (1896).[61] Raffalovich's unpublicized "unisexuality" and his familiarity with the dandy literary set in London would be important factors in the positions he took on inversion in the French medical press. As we have seen, until 1894 French medical writers on inversion had stressed several points: inversion was a variety of degenerate insanity characterized by hysterical gender-crossing; it was a form of primitive nervous activity; and it was frequently criminal.[62] Given this history, Raffalovich's reply to Laupts's questionnaire in 1894 must have seemed extraordinary. Raffalovich brazenly claimed to know several inverts, not as patients or as criminal suspects, but socially. He assured readers that it was perfectly safe to be friends with a congenital invert. Inverts, he claimed, were no longer satisfied with Ulrichs's model of the female soul in a male body. On the contrary, some inverts were *more* virile than regular men and were attracted to men because of the invert's fondness for masculinity. This attraction-of-similars was the true key to their condition, he claimed: "their passion is comparable to that elicited by sexual dissimilarity" (1894a, 216). Raffalovich was pointing out that the inversion model paradoxically maintained—at the psychic level—the paradigm of heterosexual attraction of opposites.[63] Physicians could only imagine that a feminine man (the invert or "psychosexual hermaphrodite") could fall in love with a masculine (normal) man. Love between two inverts was inconceivable.

Raffalovich, therefore, claimed that *inversion* was a misnomer and proposed instead *unisexuality:* "As men, they love men; but they affirm that were they women they would love women" (216). In other words, he first introduced into France the contemporary conception of *homosexuality:* a "form of sexuality in which sexual attraction is directed towards a person of the same sex."[64]

Raffalovich (1896b) was also the first French writer to report Havelock Ellis's early claims that male "homosexuality" could be present in apparently normal men and was just a variant of human sexuality. He firmly rejected Tardieu's model of pederasty as well as the degeneracy model that had monopolized French medical literature. "There are already enough thinkers and observers in accord in recognizing that inverts are not necessarily either degenerates, or sick people, or criminals," Raffalovich wrote; "they even discover that inverts cannot be divided into passives and actives" (1897a, 87–88). He mocked those doctors who "search, almost with desperation, for stigmata of degeneracy" in virile inverts (1896b, 429). Inverts could not be degenerates, he added, "except in the sense that would make *all men* degenerates: absolute physical and psychological harmony is not to be found" (1897a, 87n.2).

Even though he tried to strike a dispassionate, scientific tone, Raffalovich's position on the social status of homosexuality was even more radical than his psychiatric claims. "It is difficult to do justice to inverts," he opined, "just as difficult as it would be to do justice to heterosexuals if one occupied oneself solely with their sexual life. . . . Because heterosexuality is not repressed, homosexuality should be equally favored" (1895a, 107). These suggestions were received with profound skepticism by French physicians. Slyly hinting at Raffalovich's homosexuality, one reviewer of *Uranism and Unisexuality* accused Raffalovich of having "a very personal opinion on degeneration—and I fear a very isolated one—to believe that there might exist sexual inverts who are neither degenerates nor mentally unbalanced" (Raffalovich 1897a, 87n.2). Another physician insisted that uranism was a sickness and "a deviation contrary to social utility"; therefore, "the invert does not have the right to inversion" (Tournier 1897, 714).

Raffalovich's claim for the "normality" of unisexuals came with an important caveat: he argued that there were major distinctions between virile, congenital unisexuality and effeminate, acquired inversion.[65] Congenital unisexuality was purely sexual and in no way tainted the moral sphere. On the other hand, effeminate inverts were the product of vice; they tended to be dishonest perverts and seducers of the young, just like heterosexual perverts (1894a, 217). He assured his readers that unisexuals could not recognize each other by special traits. While everyone could recognize the flamboyant, effeminate invert, the self-respecting unisexual would never exhibit himself thus: "they detest women too much to be effeminate" (216). Raffalovich thus attempted to dispel the fears surrounding the trope of inversion by insisting that the masculine unisexual's exterior truly matched his interior. They were the superior, interesting, honest, and moral ones, and "one could say that (and this could be a general rule), the greater the moral worth of a unisexual, the less he is effeminate" (216).

In addition to his controversial assertion that there were normal, masculine, congenital homosexuals, Raffalovich also proposed that childhood sexuality was normal. As we have seen, French medical writers tended to view any trace of autoeroticism and *érotisme* in childhood as pathologic. Laupts even argued that masturbation and inversion were fundamentally equivalent. "The solitary vice is autophilia [autoeroticism], and *autophilia* is *inversion*. To love oneself sexually, is to invert oneself; to love one's own organs is to prepare to love those of ones neighbor. In any case, all inverts, or nearly all, in one way or another are autophiles" (1896, 337).

Adopting theories by France's scientific rivals—the German sexologists Albert Moll and Max Dessoir—Raffalovich instead proposed the universality of childhood sexuality and the basic psychological equivalence of homosexuality and heterosexuality.[66] Most unisexuals were born that way, Raffalovich claimed, and they manifested their sexuality at an early age. There was no reason to believe that they were sexually precocious, as so many physicians had suggested. "We still know too little about children's sexuality," he concluded, "to know if heterosexual tendencies really develop much slower, or rather if we do not notice them when we encounter them" (1895a, 105). He recognized that a heterosexual bias influenced and even blinded scientists' supposedly objective observations.

Raffalovich sketched out the *normal* psychosexual development of the homosexual child. Much like Rousseau's Emile, this child could arrive at puberty physically innocent so long as he was protected from all bad counsel. He might be timid and ignore his body, but homosexuality would be florid in his imaginary life. Raffalovich's evocation of this infantile, homosexual fantasy life has an uncanny resemblance to that of the Italian invert. By age five or six, Raffalovich explained, the homosexual child would imagine being kidnapped by brigands and would "dream of the warmth of their chests and their nude arms" (1895a, 106). He would love paintings, statues, and pictures of beautiful men. Laborers, servants, and soldiers would attract his attention: "he already experiences the invert's passion for anything that resembles a uniform" (106). The homosexual boy would retreat into a special fantasy world where he was a hero loving other heroes, or he would project himself into a sentimental novel as a heroine. In parallel with this romanesque, "blue story" world, the invert child would begin to experience a carnal attraction to men, which he did not quite connect with this fantasy world (107). His imagination would be enflamed when he studied the classics and read of "Greek love." Raffalovich suggested that the apparent sexual precocity of homosexuals was just an artifact of their delayed sexual enlightenment in a predominantly heterosexual society. He sketched what today we would call the typical Euro-American "coming out" narrative:[67]

> The time arrives in the existence of every invert when he deciphers the enigma of his homosexual tastes. It is then that he reclassifies all his memories, and, to justify himself in his own eyes, recalls always having been what he is now since his earliest childhood. Homosexuality has colored his entire young life. (105–6)

While some youngsters were congenitally predestined to be homosexual or heterosexual, Raffalovich explained, others were born sexually indifferent and malleable: "they exhibit all the nuances between absolute homosexuality and absolute heterosexuality" (122). Life experiences, friendships, literature, and other incitements of the erotic imagination "determine little by little the form of the growing child's sexuality" (122). Education and experience not only mold the sexuality of the undifferentiated child but also influence the moral tone of both congenital homosexuals and heterosexuals. The greatest danger to society, he warned, is the production of true moral perverts—whether homosexual or heterosexual, male or female. These "hypocrites and cynical debauchees who try to deprave or do deprave children, young boys, or very young men, are treated by the public opinion with the justice and disdain they merit" (118). In what seems a thinly veiled allusion to Oscar Wilde, Raffalovich warned that "the sweet talker, the clever wit whose life is squalid does more evil to young men that the brazen debauchee. . . . The man of the world who addresses himself to one of these [boy prostitutes] knows the hazards and scarcely merits the pity he receives were one to imagine the consequences of his folly" (108; 118).

Pity is certainly not what Wilde received at the hands of the judge, jury, or public opinion in his trial against the Marquess of Queensbury just a few months after Raffalovich published his article on childhood sexuality. Raffalovich was equally merciless in his subsequent article on "The Oscar Wilde Affair" (1895c). Wilde was not guilty for his inversion per se, Raffalovich wrote, but he certainly deserved punishment for his corruption of youth. He shared this guilt with British society, which had tolerated and even lionized him for so long while knowing of his internal corruption (445). Raffalovich's denigration of Wilde's literary style is particularly revealing, for it fuses the earlier analysis of inversion with a personal vendetta against Wilde: "People balked when [Wilde] wrote *Dorian Gray*, a novel that is rather unoriginal (Oscar Wilde never was very original), artificial, superficial, effeminate. The unisexual reigned there, but without vigor, in the penumbra, in affectation and fear (Raffalovich 1895c, 450). He condemned Wilde, not for writing about unisexuality but for doing so flaccidly and languidly, for restricting himself to "artificial, superficial, effeminate" inverts. Raffalovich had earlier condemned these "inferior" homosexuals whose lives, autobiographies, and art were just reflections of their egoism, vice, and perversity. It was only the inferior inverts who wrote autobiographies, Raffalovich warned. Superior, virile homosexuals accomplished great military and artistic deeds and, therefore, had biographies written about them. Echoing Lasègue on the novels of hysterics, Raffalovich exhorted doctors and the general public alike to beware of the stories of corrupt inverts—such as Wilde or the Italian aristocrat—not only because their confessions might be deceitful fictions but, more seriously, because these novels were socially noxious. Raffalovich warned that literature reflected the true inner moral state of its creator just as the portrait of Dorian Gray (and Wilde's novel itself) reflected the true corrupt and corrupting soul. Conversely—appropriating Wilde's dictum that "life imitates art"—Raffalovich claimed that literature shaped the moral character of its readers.

As we have seen, artistic representations had long been criticized as dangerous to the malleable brains of women and children. Raffalovich, however, argued for their *salubrious* use in the treatment of the imagination. With poetic grandiloquence, he lectured novelists from the bully pulpit of medicine about the connection between fiction and social hygiene:

> I call upon our French novelists. . . . I would tell them: Because your readers, your admirers permit you to say anything, why not deliver them real observations? You have them. Describe then that passion of the strong for the strong, of Hercules for Colossus, of robust flesh, as they say, for robust flesh; show that it is not only the female but also the effeminate who is of no interest to these virile [homosexuals]; draw back the veils of ignorance and of falsehood . . . the clichés must be shattered. . . . We must contemplate the education of our children, of our grandchildren. (1896b, 431n.1)

Raffalovich inaugurated a battle not just over the fictional representation of homosexuality but over the fictionality of its scientific representation. His response to Laupts's monograph on perversion and inversion cuts to the quick of French medical analysis. "It seems to me," Raffalovich complained, that the fundamental error of [Dr. Laupts's] work is that he is driven to study inversion through books rather than an impartial and penetrating observation of life, and at more than one moment personal scruples trouble the experimenter. Dr. Laupts's imagined ideal of man interrupts his science and science contradicts his ideal. Also, he really is far too sensitive to study sexuality; he writhes, he pushes himself, he retreats, he defies himself, he knots himself up. All of a sudden that mysterious modesty that unisexuality imposes upon so many men strips him of his courage. (1897a, 198–99)

Raffalovich wryly pointed out that the French crusaders against sexual perversity often cringed like sissies before the horrors of inversion. Their observations did not "penetrate" the truth, and their analysis was "interrupted" by prejudice. He criticized another physician who, like his French compatriots, "discusses inverts as if they were newly imported savages that had been unknown in Europe, and who cite the very interesting, sober, and dignified work of Moll as one would cite an explorer" (1895a, 126). Raffalovich excused himself for highlighting such "fatuity" but continued: "If men of science collect such erroneous details, if they ignore what every psychologist can know, what classical antiquity already knew well, I will be forgiven my reproaches and my arrogance" (126). French scientists' cowardice was further demonstrated by the way their "pseudoscience" caved in to prejudiced public opinion (1896a, 23, 26). Even the Italian invert had noted that Zola, the supposed scientific novelist, "lacked the *courage* to stage so terrible a passion." Like the effeminate novels of inverts, the hypersensitive, timid writings of French scientists were not to be trusted. Instead, Raffalovich ambitiously proposed that his own "Annals of Unisexuality" would discard all these "theoretical delusions," "these dated and retrograde assertions," these clichés: "We will no longer invoke nature only to pretend that she constantly contradicts herself; we will guard against defamatory epithets . . . we will remember that the scientific and moral point of view is neither heterosexual nor homosexual" (1897a, 88). His "Annals of Unisexuality" would be "stamped with that healthy, male psychology that alone can help us know and understand unisexuality" (87).

Here was the invert outdoing the French doctors in their games of masculinist science. Doubts about the vigor and veracity of French science and scientists became even more acute when German sexologists became embroiled in the debate. Ironically, this was instigated by Raffalovich's publication of the observations of another nonscientist. In a 1904 article, Raffalovich contrasted the "Sodom of Paris" with homosexual gatherings in Berlin. The first part of the article consisted of anonymous excerpts from a private letter (by novelist

J. K. Huysmans) describing a descent into the seedy and criminal Parisian sodomitic underworld where the classes mixed promiscuously and profitably. "It made me think of Hell," Huysmans wrote on April 19, 1986.

> Imagine this: the man who has this vice willfully *withdraws* from association with the rest of mankind. He eats in restaurants, has his hair done at a coiffeur, lives in a *hôtel* where the patrons are all old sodomites. It is a life apart, in a narrow corner, a brotherhood recognizing itself by their voice, by a fixed gaze, and that sing-song tone they all affect.
>
> Furthermore, that vice is the *only* one which suppresses the castes, the decent man and the rogue are equal—and speak to each other naturally, animatedly without distinction of education. . . . It is rather strange and disquieting. (Allen 1966, 216)

Huysmans was echoing fears and accusations voiced earlier by Tardieu. The description of the homosexual underworld is probably accurate in part; however, there were also elite bars for homosexual men and women, and many fin-de-siècle artists and socialites were coveted precisely because of their homosexual notoriety.[68]

In the second part of Raffalovich's exposé, he contrasted this "Sodom of Paris" with Dr. Paul Näcke's description of the relatively open, middle-to-upper-class, well-mannered world of homosexuals in Berlin and of the meetings of the Scientific and Philanthropic Committee established by Magnus Hirschfeld for the defense of homosexuals.[69] Näcke was so moved by the narratives of these homosexuals' sufferings and their struggles with their parents that he wondered, "Why doesn't someone write unisexual novels?" (Raffalovich 1904, 931). Raffalovich again hoped to indict French society for its general immorality, irreligion, and ignorance of the psychology of healthy, sympathy-provoking bourgeois unisexuals. "Heterosexuals, by their example and behavior," Raffalovich complained, "have created many inverts" (935).

Näcke replied to Raffalovich in the next volume of the *Archives,* chiding him for uncritically presenting the most horrific vision of Parisian homosexuals. Näcke estimated that Paris had fifty thousand homosexuals (maybe twice that many), most of whom were upstanding and uneffeminate, and had numerous respectable venues for socializing. He rejected the implication that most homosexuals were "pederasts" (that is, practitioners of anal sex). Yet he slyly cast aspersion upon the French by suggesting that this "specialty" was more common in Latin cultures than Teutonic ones (1905, 184). In a subsequent article in a German journal, Näcke suggested that the French generally suffered from more degeneration than the Germans (1908).

Dr. Laupts immediately took umbrage at these affronts to French masculinity (1908a, 1908b). He shot back at both Raffalovich and Näcke that the French were no more degenerate that the Germans. Furthermore, Laupts insisted, "*I know* that homosexuality does not exist save as a *rare* exception in the entirety of continental . . . France. . . . *I know* that the vast majority of my (noncolonial) compatriots experience an undissimulated and *extreme* disgust for homosexuality" (1909, 693, 696). (Laupts was evidently less certain of the sexual normality of France's colonized subjects.) This was in dramatic contrast to the situation in Germany, where notable doctors, such as Westphal, Krafft-Ebing, and Näcke, had taken up the defense of homosexuals and had favored the deletion of antisodomy laws from the penal code. Laupts feared that homosexuality was contagious and was spreading in both France and Germany precisely "because it is studied, and spoken, and written about" (1909, 694). The very fact that German doctors had done so much work on the subject was proof of (and presumably cause of) the higher incidence of homosexuality in Germany than in France (Laupts 1908b, 741). In retort to Raffalovich's insult that Laupts's work on homosexuality was in "a literary tradition," Laupts accused Raffalovich of being "a bit too literary, too inclined, in any case to introduce into a scientific debate considerations of a moral nature that have no place there and are. . . somewhat absurd" (1909, 695).

These accusations and counter-accusations that scientific research was merely fictional "literature" continued to be flung across national boundaries thanks to essays by Eugène Wilhelm, a homosexual Alsatian lawyer, who had already published several articles on German sexology in the *Mercure de France.* Under the pseudonym "Dr. Numa Prætorius," Wilhelm accused Laupts of being utterly misguided: there might even be more homosexuals in France, including the countryside, than in Germany. Wilhelm indicted Laupts and his French colleagues for being practically ignorant of the existence of homosexuality in France because their old prejudices prevented them from broaching the subject with their patients and, thereby, discovering how many of these, in fact, were homosexual (1909, 201). He chastised French men of science for generally neglecting sexual questions and hurled Laupts's slur of "literariness" back in the face of French physicians: "They seem to want to leave this terrain to literature and superficial popularizers; one could say that a certain false shame, an ill-placed prudishness prevents them from studying these problems in detail and methodically" (Wilhelm 1912, 301). Wilhelm was right: men of letters, heterosexual and homosexual alike, did have an especially significant role in shaping the French discourse of homosexuality. But one can hardly accuse the *belle-lettristes* of having perverted science; rather, they informed the very fictions science was dedicated to spinning. Raffalovich and Wilhelm thus turned the trope of inversion on French physicians themselves, showing how the construction of the invert was a travesty of science: What was advertised as objective information was really prejudiced and willful disregard for knowledge.

## Un-Knowing Female Inversion

On issues of homosexuality, "un-knowing" emerged as a virtue for scientists both in their dealings with their patients and in their scientific research.[70] While Raffalovich and his fellow unisexuals complained about the malicious medical ignorance of their confreres, there were more serious victims of French doctors' un-knowing of inversion: female inverts, aka "tribades," or "lesbians." Women were occasionally mentioned in the literature on pederasty, hysteria, degeneration, inversion, and homosexuality. Tardieu, for example, discussed "assaults on modesty" committed by women (mainly nannies and servants) against little children and girls; however, he mentioned these actions under the rubric of "rape and sexual assault" rather than pederasty (1857, 65–71). Although sodomy between women (with dildos or enlarged clitorises) had been a concern of legists and moralists since the Middle Ages, Tardieu considered sodomy an action perpetrated exclusively by men on women or other men.[71]

The German medical literature, on the other hand, always identified "contrary sexual instinct" as a "disorder" of both sexes. German sexologists, such as Krafft-Ebing, Moll, Näcke, and Hirschfeld, continued to study lesbianism into the twentieth century. Charcot and Magnan cited the German cases of female inversion, but they explained that such observations were rare since women could better disguise their "instinctual disorder" (1882, 303). As with boys, the condition was deemed a degenerate psychopathic state that was innate, imperative, accompanied by cross-gendered behavior (virility and male dress) and onanism (304–5). Despite the declared severity of their condition, lesbians were rarely mentioned in the French sexological texts.

The French had become inured to the pornographic spectacle of tribadic couples in the eighteenth century and to the fantasmatic titillation of sapphic lovers in nineteenth-century literature. Balzac, Gauthier, Baudelaire, Louÿs, Monnier, Feydeau, and Zola had all depicted lesbians.[72] Havelock Ellis (1895) specifically remarked on French novelists' and poets' fascination with lesbianism. Precisely for this reason, doctors such as Chevalier criticized French artists for making "tribadism" unduly acceptable through its frequent and arousing representation in novels. He attributed the novelistic prevalence of tribadism to the fact that male authors could easily tolerate the vice in women, whereas ped-erasty evoked disgust in "normally constituted" men. These male authors, Chevalier concluded, represented *lesbius amor* as a neurosis of idle, decadent, upper-class and bourgeois women (1885, 69–74). Even Raffalovich men-tioned female unisexuality only to dismiss it as uninteresting. For him, misog-yny was one of the characteristic qualities of normal, virile homosexuals (1894a, 216). He even blamed women, particularly fashionable older women, for creating an insalubrious vogue for effeminate male inverts (218). As we have already seen, Raffalovich also made masculinity the essential attribute of good, objective science. Despite their awareness of "sapphic love," French physicians were truly satisfied with leaving it "to literature and superficial popularizers," in other words, viewing lesbianism as an unthreatening or even titillating fictional existence.[73]

Male inverts, on the other hand, were quite threatening, even if their lives were turned into fictions. The almost exclusive focus of French medicine on male inversion is a product of the material from which it was constructed: sodomy, hysteria, and degeneration. As we have seen, it was the confluence of anxieties over the class and gender-crossing of the sodomite and anxieties over the neurohereditary gender-crossing of the male hysteric that gave rise to the in-vert of the 1880s. The inversion model, in turn, left its impression on the un-derstanding of "homosexuality." As historian Robert Nye (1989) also argues, the French medical obsession with the effeminate male (particularly after the Franco-Prussian War) was a manifestation of a broader anxiety over waning masculinity and, by extension, cultural inversion and national impotence.

## Science Fictions and Inversions

In his scathing critique of degenerate, fin-de-siècle culture, Dr. Max Nordau fumed: "Does [Zola] think that his novels are serious documents from which science can borrow facts? What childish folly! Science can have nothing to do with fiction" (1893, 2:437). As we have seen, however, the scientific literature on inversion was especially dedicated to fiction, both the fictions it studied and the fictions it sponsored. To label the scientific literature on inversion a "fic-tion" is not to dismiss it as untruthful. "There is the possibility for fiction to function in truth," Foucault has argued,

> for a fictional discourse to induce effects of truth, and for bringing it about
> that a true discourse engenders or "manufactures" something that does not as

yet exist, that is, "fictions" it. One "fictions" history on the basis of a political
reality that makes it true, one "fictions" a politics not yet in existence on the
basis of a historical truth. (1980, 193)

The novelizing and fictioning of "homosexuality" served to advance the
underlying goals of defenders and derogators of homosexuality alike: on the
one hand, to reify the notion of a normal, virile homosexual; on the other hand,
to fashion a monster of perversity embodying all the degenerations and insecu-
rities that plagued the cultural imagination of fin-de-siècle France: intellectual,
artistic, therapeutic, military, and racial impotence.

While perfectly consonant with the latest scientific, biomedical "truths" of
the day, the medical debates on the nature of inversion were, nevertheless, also
molded by the cultural and political preoccupations of the time. The nationalist fires of Franco-German rivalry continued to burn on the terrain of science
well after France's defeat in the Franco-Prussian War. The construction and
counting of inverts was just one amongst many ideological weapons (just as it
is, albeit under different scientific and political conditions, in the United States
today).[74] The fictioning of what would later be called "homosexuality"—embellished as it was by associations with effeminacy, hysteria, and deceitfulness—was especially critical in bolstering fantasies of national potency and scientific virility.

In the case of inversion, fiction and nonfiction were blurred on a stage
bustling with novelists in medical drag and physicians passing incognito as novelists or inverts. Inverts and homosexuals found their "true" confessions turned
into scientific fictions under the fear that their narrative productions partook of
the deceitfulness and self-delusion of their sexual natures. Homosexuals also
played an active part in the "fictioning" of their experience. Not only did they
write anonymously or under pseudonyms to disguise themselves, but, like the
medical researchers of "sexual perversions," they found it necessary to invent a
new history for themselves. Manufactured in the political cause of homosexual
emancipation and decriminalization, this *histoire homosexuelle* or historical
coming-out narrative advanced seemingly contradictory claims of a long tradition, beginning with the "Greek vice," and of historical novelty. Likewise, the
scientific *histoires* simultaneously asserted the congenital nature of homosexuality and its acquired, even contagious, nature (Laupts 1909, 695, 694).

In the promiscuous intercourse between doctors and novelists over the societal poison of "sexual perversion," science itself served as a potent but ambiguous elixir. As Jacques Derrida (1972) points out in his exegesis of Plato's

*pharmakon* (meaning both *elixir* and *poison*), symbolic language is unmasked as a dangerous supplement to "true learning": superficially, writing appears to be a technique for remembering, but ultimately it produces forgetfulness since people will write down what they otherwise would be obliged to memorize.[75] Like the female soul disguised in the male body, the mechanism of poisoning is that of inversion: what superficially appears to be one thing is, at its core, the poisonous reverse. Physicians and *littérateurs* played a similarly dangerous game with the *pharmakon* of science which—like the novels conceived by Zola, Raffalovich, and the Italian invert—had the seductiveness of a social panacea. We have seen that Raffalovich, although critical of French sexologists, put his trust in science. The Italian invert was also delighted to find his confessions finally represented by science. Even while attempting to condemn and contain perversity, the scientific fictions of inversion were embraced by the inverts themselves, who used science to defend their "naturalness," consolidate an identity, and disseminate their stories of passion and "robust flesh." Where better than in scientific journals could the Italian invert "cry [my joy] from the rooftops" for finally having been sodomized (Saint-Paul 1930, 115)?

In addition to science, the *pharmakon* of history itself cannot be overlooked. Of all the human technologies, none is more inherently dependent on fabricating and forgetting than history. History figured prominently in the fin-de-siècle medical analysis of homosexuality. A patient's individual case history or anamnesis (reminiscence), often printed as a confession, was connected to other family histories and anamneses of supposedly related disorders. Doctors and inverts regularly alluded to the "Greek vice" of antiquity. Yet, as Raffalovich astutely noted, these historical connections were un-remembered in the convenient science fiction that "inversion" was a new syndrome of organic degeneration and social disintegration. Inverts were thus concocted as a terrible social and cultural poison through the conventions of amnesia and anamnesis: the inversions of forgetting and reminiscence, the masquerade of intolerance as sympathy, the travesty of ignorance as knowledge.

# CHAPTER **4**

## *Fetishists: Cults, Consumption, and Erotic Dramas*

Marie D——, widow of A——, housewife, forty-nine years old. . . . Father alcoholic, reportedly committed suicide at age sixty. Mother reportedly committed suicide. Brother very manic, was institutionalized.

Born and raised in the provinces. From the age of seven to eight, she indulged in masturbation, either solitary or reciprocal. "I played mommy and daddy with another little girl, on chairs." . . . Her passion for silk manifested itself early. "I married so I could have *a beautiful black silk dress that would be stiff.* . . . Silk has a *froufrou,* a *cricri* that gives me pleasure." To hear the word silk pronounced or even to represent silk in her thoughts provokes in her an erection of the genital parts. Total orgasm is produced with contact and *a fortiori* by the rubbing of silk against that region. . . .

She indulged in masturbation daily. Normal sexual relations procured, she insisted, *no pleasure.* . . . She recalls having lived in Paris, around 1888, with a sailor and then another man of whom she says: "He beat me, I love him still, but he doesn't want to speak to me any more. *At times when he beat me, I experienced an enormous pleasure.*" . . .

> She has stolen innumerable times from the department stores. . . . Often, when appearing before the court, she has refused to respond. . . . At the end of 1904, she entered a department store driven, she says, by a veritable impulsion. . . . "In the silk department, a light blue dress fascinated me, *it was very stiff.* Silk that isn't stiff does nothing for me. I took that *girls' dress,* I slipped it under my skirt, in a big pocket, and holding the dress by one end, *I masturbated myself in the middle of the store,* near the elevator, then in the elevator, where I have the maximum pleasure. In those moments my head swells, my face becomes flushed, my temples pound, I can no longer have pleasure except by that means. . . ." She adds: "Masturbation alone doesn't give me much pleasure, but I complete it by thinking of the tickling and sound of silk. Sometimes, at the moment I am masturbating with silk, I nevertheless think of men, although they leave me cold." (584–85)

The case of Marie D——, reported by Dr. G. G. de Clérambault in 1910 as an example of silk fetishism in females, crystallizes the many associations that had been accreting around the problem of the erotic imagination: precocious masturbation, degenerate heredity, criminality, immorality, obsessive fantasies, irrational compulsions, and loss of heterosexual attraction (to list just the most salient ones). The diagnosis of *fetishism,* however, added new layers to the medical theorizing and popular understanding of the erotic imagination. Furthermore, the diagnosis allowed analysts to explain the erotic motivations of strange behaviors even when their actors refused to confess.

Psychologist Alfred Binet coined the term *sexual fetishism* in 1887, five years after Charcot and Magnan first discussed *sexual inversion.* Describing fetishism as the "cult of trinkets," Binet drew his term from the anthropological literature on the idolatrous practices of "primitives."[1] The word *fetish* was traced back to the Latin *factitius:* man-made, artificial, fake. Just as Marie D—— supplemented the waning pleasures of manufriction with the associated sensations of silk, department-store eroticism, and beating, the notion of fetishism supplemented medical understanding of the psychology of eroticism with associations of "primitive" religious cults, modern consumption practices, and the myriad sensory triggers of sexual pleasure: touch, color, sound, taste, odor. Certain of these, such as tactile, olfactory, and gustatory sensations, had long been viewed as "primitive" senses (recall Brillat-Savarin's analysis of the erotic power of truffles). In drawing together the new "sexual perversities" under the heading of fetishism, Binet and subsequent sexologists further stigmatized the perversions as abnormal, primitive practices. However, by theorizing fetishism so broadly, by connecting it to the sensory perils of department stores and crowded cities, as well as the primitive senses and drives of even the most "civilized" people, fin-de-siècle sexologists captured everyone who experienced an erotic sensation or fantasy into the diagnostic dragnet of sexual perversity.

Although fin-de-siècle sexologists represented the supposedly artificial, fake pleasure of fetishism as a supplement to "normal" reproductive sex, they increasingly discovered that fetishism was the catalyst of *all* erotism. Furthermore, they suspected that secret or unconscious eroticism was the culprit of all varieties of unconventional or irrational crimes and improprieties. Conversely, fetishism in all its varieties—religious, economic, and sexual—acutely called into question the reality or nonfictiveness of religious faith, economic value, and erotic experience. In order to show how fetishism is a nexus of these three major domains of human experience and culture I begin by examining the origins of fetishism in literature on religious cults and Portuguese explorations. I connect these ethnographic observations with nineteenth-century French discussions of pathological religiosity or "theomania." Turning to Marx's analysis of "commodity fetishism," I trace the links between the "kleptomania" diagnosis and anxieties over the new bourgeois culture of consumption. Kleptomania would be associated with "fetishism" proper after Binet's article on "amorous fetishism" (1887a), which opened the floodgates of "sexual perversity" research. Olfactory fetishism, in particular, drew attention as a form of "primitive," atavistic sensuality. We will see how this pathology was brought to life in Huysmans's neurodegenerate hero des Esseintes, who embodied not only sexual perversities but also the closely associated culture of decadence. Finally, I turn to the other major subcategory of fetishism that arose toward the end of the century: sadism and masochism. As we have repeatedly seen, literary figures played an important role in shaping medical knowledge on *érotisme,* and in this section, the reemergence of Rousseau—not as onanist but as masochist—is indicative of a new hermeneutics of erotic suspicion in the reading of patient histories. Sexuality, which had been presumed to be firmly grounded in the dictates of "Nature," was proving to be a highly variable and artificial figment of the erotic imagination.

## The Cult of the Holy Parrot

And the censers on their fine chains were in full swing. An azure vapor rose to Felicity's room. She advanced her nose, inhaling with a mystical sensuality, then closed her eyelids. Her lips were smiling. The movements of her heart slowed beat by beat, each time more distant, softer, as a fountain dries out, as an echo fades; and when she exhaled her last breath, she thought she saw, in the opening heavens, a giant parrot, hovering over her head. (Flaubert, "Un Cœur simple," 622)

In "Un Coeur simple," one of his most subtle, poignant, and unpretentious works, Flaubert relates the life story of a simple servant, Felicity, in the service of a *haute-bourgeoise* widow and her two children living in a small Norman town. Orphaned young, jilted by her one and only suitor, silently mourning the death of a beloved nephew in America, she leads a quiet life of devotion to her mistress, "who, it must be said, was not an especially agreeable person" (591).[2] In her dotage, Felicity's devotion increasingly turns to her parrot, Loulou, the gift of departing neighbors and an animal whose American origins remind her of the mysterious land where her nephew died of yellow fever. She teaches it to say "Hail Mary" and, as she grows old and deaf to every voice but the parrot's, it becomes "practically a son or a lover" (615). She cries bitterly when it dies and she walks all the way to Honfleur to deliver it safely to a taxidermist. In her tiny room—part chapel, part bazaar—the stuffed Loulou takes the place of honor amongst an incongruous shrine of religious trinkets and peculiar memorabilia: rosaries, crosses, several statues of the Blessed Virgin, a coconut holy water font, saints' medals, and relics of lost loved ones (617). Beside the stuffed Loulou she places a reproduction of a painting representing the Holy Spirit as a brilliantly plumed bird "such that, in the same glance, she saw them together. They became associated in her mind, the parrot thus sanctified by this relation with the Holy Spirit, which in turn became more alive and intelligible in her eyes" (618). Thereafter and unto her dying moment, Loulou will be the repository of all Felicity's hopes for salvation.

Flaubert's portrait of the idolatrous Felicity is drawn with such tenderness that one might miss his criticism of the bourgeoisie—which had been far from subtle in *Madame Bovary*. While Felicity ecstatically dies amid the apotheosis of the Blessed Loulou, the townsfolk are celebrating the feast of Corpus Christi. Just outside Felicity's window, they have laid the golden monstrance on an altar cluttered with flowers, an enameled sugar bowl, crystal pendants, two Chinese screens, and Loulou herself, which Felicity had bequeathed to the parish priest. Like Felicity's chapel-bazaar bedroom, this altar—where sacred and profane, material and spiritual commingle amidst the mystical sensuality of incense—is a precious figure for the multifaceted character of the "fetish."

Fifteenth-century Portuguese explorers of the west coast of Africa used their native word *feitiço* to describe the talismans or objects of veneration that the "savages" wore on themselves or installed in special places for worship. As I alluded to earlier, *feitiço* is believed to be derived from the Latin *factitius* (man-made, fake, unnatural, magical). *Feitiçeros* were magicians or sorcerers, and *meu feitiçinho* could even be used as a term of affection meaning "my little fetish or darling" (Müller 1878b, 64). Anthropologist William Pietz (1985, 1987, 1988), in an excellent analysis of the etymology and history of the fetish in early ethnological accounts, points out that the word *feitiço* had previously been used rather broadly by the Portuguese in reference to idolatry and witch-craft. It was also applied to merely vain religious practices and objects that were deemed by the medieval Church to be worthless in comparison with legitimate sacramental objects (such as the host, chalices, sacred relics, crucifixes, mon-strances, and altars). As the nineteenth-century orientalist Max Müller (1878a, 56) pointed out in his thinly veiled anti-Catholic study of the ethnographical literature on fetishism, the reason the Portuguese could choose the word *feitiço* to describe the savages' trinkets and talismans was because the Portuguese sailors themselves were fetishists and undoubtedly possessed rosaries, crosses, images of saints and Madonnas, and all sorts of other good-luck charms. Even seventeenth-century Dutch Calvinist explorers compared African fetishes to Roman Catholic sacramental objects (Pietz 1987, 39). As Flaubert pointed out in "Un Cœur simple," the cult of trinkets is still practiced in "civilized" Euro-pean cultures.

The notion of "fetishism" as a religious system (as distinct from the sim-ple object called a "fetish") was first described by a Frenchman, Charles de Brosses, who named Australia and Polynesia (although he never actually ex-plored them).[3] Frustrated by the confusion of ideas concerning the mytholog-ical and religious systems of different cultures and of different times, he wrote *On the Cult of Fetish Gods, or Parallels Between the Ancient Religion of Egypt and the Present Religion of Nigeria* (1760). De Brosses coined the notion of fe-tishism as a religious principle, not just of Africans but of "all nations whatso-ever, in which objects of reverence are animals, or inanimate beings which they deify . . . things endowed with divine virtues, oracles, amulets, and life-saving talismans" (10). De Brosses thus universalized fetishism as the transhistoric and transcultural religious system of all those with a "savage mind," which he believed was like that of children. The savage mind is permanently stalled at a mental age of four, de Brosses claimed; therefore, savages lack a proper sense of causality, and they attribute life to their fetishes just as children believe their dolls are animated (185–86). In shifting from "the fetish" to "fetishism," de Brosses impressed on the notion of fetishism many of the characteristics that would adhere to the term until Binet applied it to "sexual perverts." Fetishism was theorized as a universal, originary, primitive or infantile form of thought characterized by the arbitrary or even random devotion to "worthless" items. As distinct from idolatry, fetishism was the worship of objects in their *materiality* rather than in their *symbolic* capacity as transcendent icons or representations of divinity.[4] Although primitive, the fetishistic tendency to overvalue and animate objects was a "natural metaphor of man" whether savage or civilized, de Brosses concluded. "Although [the civilized], do not always really imagine, any more than [the savage], that these physical things, good or evil to man, are in fact endowed with affection and feelings, this usage of metaphors nonetheless proves that there is in the human imagination a natural tendency to figure things thus" (216). The primitive's belief in the power of fetishes is fundamentally the same as ignorant and superstitious, civilized people's belief in nymphs, fairies, and ghosts (216). So however misinformed de Brosses may have been on the practices he christened *fetishism,* he notably broadened the term's applicability across space and time.[5]

While de Brosses claimed the "chosen race," Judeo-Christianity, had skipped fetishism or polytheism and gone directly to monotheism, Auguste Comte in his *Course on Positive Philosophy* (1830–1842) proposed that fetishism represented a common, primordial attitude of man towards the world: "Man everywhere began with the most coarse fetishism, as with a well-characterized anthropophagy" (5:26).[6] At this earliest stage of thought—common to the savage, children, and higher beasts—one's fears of the world were overcome thanks to the theological mode of thinking. According to Comte's natural history of human progress, this theological stage was eventually abandoned for metaphysical and then rational modes of thought and practice. The new sciences, especially his postive philosophy, augured the future positive stage of humanity. Philosophical treatises on history and religion were not the only rationalist critiques of theological modes of thought. As we have seen in previous chapters, many members of the medical profession (also steeped in Enlightenment materialism and rationalism) presented religiosity as not only irrational and primitive, but positively insane or, at least, monomaniacal.[7]

C.-C.-H. Marc, physician to King Louis-Philippe, dedicated a whole chapter of his medicolegal text on insanity to "religious monomania and demonomania" (1840, 2:222–46).[8] The former usually appeared as a variety of melancholia with religious idées fixes and excessive religious observance. Demonomania was similar but usually accompanied by visual and auditory hallucinations leading patients to believe themselves persecuted or possessed by the devil. In the materialist spirit of the Paris School, alienists "diagnosed" historical cases of witches, demonic possession, and divine visions as cases of insanity promoted by superstition and collective hysteria. "Was the Temptation of Saint Anthony," Marc asked, "anything other than a case of satyriasis?" (2:200). Marc especially warned of the nefarious effect of credulity, superstition, and love of the marvelous on the development of religious monomania. He also blamed the belief in magic and witchcraft for prompting crimes. Just as de Brosses saw an infantile, superstitious imagination at the root of fetishistic religiosity, the followers of Esquirol's doctrine of monomania viewed the credulous, simple-minded laborer as the typical victim of religious monomania. We hear the echo of this attitude in Flaubert's judgment of Felicity: "For such souls the supernatural is a simple matter" ("Cœur simple," 609).

This infantile, peasant, or primitive hyperreligiosity was closely tied to the "cult of the erotomaniac." Recall that Esquirol, in his original definition of erotomania, stated that it was "a mental affliction in which amorous ideas are fixed and dominant just like religious ideas are fixed and dominant in theomania" (1815, 186). To illustrate the overlap of theomania and erotomania, Marc (one of Esquirol's disciples) offered the case of a nineteen-year-old girl who, like Felicity, was a servant in an older woman's home. The young domestic fell madly in love with one of her mistress's sons. "To conquer her penchant, she resorted to practices of devotion. Almost constantly in church, she sought to calm her illness through sermons and religious offices," Marc reported. These went unnoticed until, one day, they failed to control her passions, and she rapidly declined into a state of delirium. She shouted biblical and mystical texts, made "the most obscene propositions," and threw herself naked on the floor, "abandoning herself to the most revolting actions."

> Her forces declined, and the patient, whose religious ideas were confused with erotic ideas, preserved an automatic movement of the whole body which could not be suppressed. By rubbing the thighs, or through mere oscillation of the hips, she procured the most acute pleasures, which were reflected in her facial expressions. (Marc 1840, 2:216–17)

The patient died two days later; the autopsy was uninformative. Marc nevertheless concluded that "erotomania was the determining cause of the religious delirium," and her break from sanity was "the result of the abuse of solitary pleasures" (2:217).

The line of demarcation between fervent devotion and insanity, particularly erotomania, was a fine one.[9] The line would be further blurred by anticlerical physicians during the Third Republic.[10] One writer proposed what might have seemed a scandalous question: "Is not [pathological religion] simply the exaggeration, perhaps even . . . the perfection of [normal religion], and is there not between the two an undetectable gradation, rather than a drastic leap, as is generally believed?" (Santenoise 1900, 144).[11] Even priests recognized the existence of religious erotomaniacs and "priest lovers" whom they called "confessional bugs" (*punaises de confessional*) or "font frogs" (*grenouilles du bénitier*).[12] "They demonstrate," doctors remarked, "the frequent association of mystical and erotic delirium" (Leroy & Juquelier 1910, 248). Writing on the topic of "erotic insanity," Dr. Benjamin Ball extended the pathologization of religion to include the clergy as well:

> For those who know the filiation of ideas in the minds of the sick, there is no doubt that the sublime cult that many priests have vowed to the Holy Virgin, that the admiration that shines in so many of the works of the most serious theologians, is the effect of an erotomania unknown to them; it is the love of women that speaks beneath all the appearances of piety in those good celibate men's ardent cult. Their chastity would necessarily predispose them to this aberration. (1887, 194)

Ball also described cases of epidemic erotic insanity in convents (1887, 262). Comparing paintings of saints to photographs of hysterical patients, Charcot drew parallels between states of religious ecstasy and stages of "grand hysteria" (Charcot 1885; Charcot & Richer 1887). Although especially pronounced during the Third Republic, an undercurrent of anticlericalism was present in earlier writings on "theomania" from members of the Faculty of Medicine of Paris. We encountered a similar skepticism about the sanctity of members of religious orders in the Bertrand case, where seminaries and monasteries were presented as cauldrons of sexual deviance. Going further back, eighteenth-century pornographic literature abounded in lascivious and scabrous tales of licentiousness in monasteries and nunneries. Even if formal clergy or religious institutions were not involved, the erotomaniac's unshakable devotion to the object of his or her "pathological love" was described as a cult or religious devotion (Legrand du Saulle 1864, 254). Whether talismans, rosaries, or stuffed parrots, another central element of the "pathology" of fetishism—the "cult of trinkets"—was the worthlessness of the venerated objects (at least in the eyes of anthropologists and physicians). Starting with the cultural clash between Renaissance European explorers and African natives, and continuing until the fin-de-siècle confrontation between doctors and "sexual perverts," diverse analysts have represented the fetish as an economic folly: a defect or delusion in the valuation of material objects.

## Commodity Obsessions

The mystery of the commodity lies simply in the fact that the social character of men's own labor is reflected as an objective character of the product of labor itself. . . . [With commodities] it is the definite social relation between men themselves which takes on for them the phantasmagorial form of a relation between things. In order to find an analogy to this, we must flee to the nebulous realm of the religious world. Here, the products of men's heads seem endowed with a life of their own, as independent forms entering into relation with each other and with humans. So it is in the commodity world with the product of men's hands. This I call the fetishism that adheres to the products of labor, as soon as they are produced as commodities and which is accordingly inseparable from the production of commodities. (Marx 1867, 1:38–39)

While Charles de Brosses constructed fetishism as a primitive and primordial religion and Auguste Comte recharacterized fetishism as a primitive mentality, Marx used the term to analyze modern capitalism as a form of "primitive accumulation" (Pietz 1993, 151). On the one hand, Marx accomplished this by returning to the original meaning of the word *fetisso:* man-made. Marx emphasized that commodities are "the products of men's hands" and therefore human artifacts part of a social exchange. Marx's conception of "commodity fetishism" thus soldered together religion and economics in a seemingly novel fashion, but as we have seen, the ethnological literature on the fetish already involved concerns about trade and economics.

Renaissance merchants exploring the west African coast felt that the natives engaged in irrational trade practices: certain trinkets were personified and invested with religious and social powers that gave them values beyond their (European) instrumental market value (Pietz 1987, 24). To the Europeans' delighted consternation, the savages would trade gold articles for European rubbish in an exchange that seemed foolish and infantile. As anthropologist Marcel Mauss pointed out, the problem of the fetish could only arise as an "immense misunderstanding" emerging at the interface between two cultures "with no other foundation than the blind obedience to colonial custom and the *lingua franca* spoken by the Europeans" (1968–1969, 2:244–45). More profoundly, such a "misunderstanding" could only arise because of definite power inequities, for the label of fetishism was (and would continue to be) derogatory: a marker not just of a different value system but of an irrational, delusional one. Whether it was Europeans identifying African fetishes as "in fact" worthless rubbish or Calvinist explorers equating African fetishes with superfluous

Catholic idols, *fetishism* was deployed as a disparaging term to *unmask* or *interpret* a conceptual delusion of a society considered inferior (Pietz 1985, 14).

Marx similarly deployed the term *fetishism* to disparage capitalist mentality and "vulgar economics" (Geras 1971). Marx read the German translation of de Brosses's *The Cult of the Fetish Gods* and other works on the history of religions in 1842. At that time he noted in an article that Cuban savages had interpreted gold to be the Spaniards' fetish (Iacono 1992, 79). Later, in *Capital,* he developed his analysis of the capitalist commodity as fetish. In the capitalist mode of production, according to Marx, where the laborer is alienated from the product of his or her labor as well as from other laborers, manufactured products take on a life of their own. Instead of being related to the human activity of their production and use, the value of products is determined at moments of exchange when value seems natural and intrinsic to the product. This transformation of products into commodities disguises their *artifice*—their "real" nature as products of human labor and of social exchanges (Marx 1867, 1:38–39). Scientific (that is, Marxist) economics "destroyed this false appearance and illusion . . . this personification of things and conversion of production relations into entities, this religion of everyday life."[13] Marx and Marxist economics thus claimed hermeneutic superiority: the power to unmask the religion of capitalism as the cult of commodity fetishes.

Marx and Marxists were not alone in unmasking the "fetishization" of commodities in capitalist consumer culture.[14] French political conservatives of the time were also worried about the ill effects of rapid modernization, industrialization, and the concomitant explosion of mass consumer culture, particularly in Paris. As already suggested from the opening case of Marie D——, the department stores were a major site for focusing these anxieties. The *grands magasins* or *bazars* (so called because they sold a variety of merchandise) sprung up during the Second Empire with Baron Haussmann's reconstruction of the heart of Paris. As historian Michael Miller points out (1981, 3), the new department stores were monuments to the emerging bourgeois culture of consumption—they staged in spectacular, novel ways "the culture's identification with appearances and material possessions" and the abundance of industrial production.[15] They emerged as a result of a constellation of factors during the Second Empire: industrialization (particularly of textile manufacture), urbanization, railroad expansion, improvements in banking, and overall economic prosperity. These social and economic developments, like the department stores, were also perceived as a threat to traditional familial and economic institutions. Unlike the old, family-run stores and exclusive boutiques, the department stores were vast, urban, democratic institutions. Despite their luxurious appearance, they were open to the public, and people of all classes mingled promiscuously on the sales floor and in the public reading rooms. An article on the *grands bazars* in the conservative newspaper *Le Figaro* concluded on an ominous note: "Is it therefore written in stone that materialist and ultra-modern democratic society will smother forever our old [Christian] society?" (Ignotus 1881).

Historian Rosalind Williams (1982, 13) suggests that the new department stores superimposed two conflicting consumer lifestyles that reflected a fundamental tension in post-Revolutionary French society: elitist consumption (the aristocrat's pursuit of the unique and exclusive) versus democratic consumption (the purchase of popular, inexpensive mass-produced commodities). Emile Zola, always with his finger on the pulse of the body politic, represented the social problems of the *grands magasins* in his novel *Au Bonheur des Dames* (alluding to the name of an actual store, the Paradis des Dames.) Zola was partly inspired by the *Figaro* article, and he highlighted the following paragraph in his clipping of it:

> These great bazaars are the fatal and immediate consequence of a materialist and democratic epoch. Nothing will make me say that I like them—but none can prevent me from seeing in them one of the most striking products of the fin de siècle. Fins de siècle are always interesting like the ends of chapters! (Ignotus 1881)

Zola also turned to medical writers for their critiques of the stores' commodity temptations and flashy merchandise displays. These willfully stimulated the imagination and prompted an "epidemic" of kleptomania.[16]

Although the diagnosis of *klopémanie* was first coined in 1816 and later theorized by Marc as a monomania,[17] the disorder received enormous publicity and was declared a "social problem" only with the birth of the department stores.[18] "In the interest of their commerce, [businessmen] have practiced the art of seduction, of temptation, in a truly brilliant fashion," wrote Paul Dubuisson, chief physician of the Sainte-Anne Asylum(1902, 41). Allowed to see and touch the wealth of merchandise at their will (a pleasure never permitted in traditional stores), women at the great *bazars* felt a powerful attraction much like that of church, Dubuisson warned (42). Marie D——, the silk fetishist, had blamed these merchandising techniques for her kleptomania: "All they have to do is not expose their silks so and I wouldn't take anything" (Clérambault 1910, 585). Dubuisson shared these concerns about the deviously imposed compulsion to consume: "[Shopping] no longer is a fantasy, it is a need; it is not just a distraction, it is a cult. Truly, the manner in which temptation is organized in the great department stores is beyond all praise, Satan could not have done better" (43). These ideas were also voiced by Zola's character Mr. Mouret, the owner of Le Bonheur des Dames. Mouret excitedly tells a friend how the dazzling sales displays—lit by newly invented electric lamps—drew out a whole variety of thieves:

> First, [Mouret] cited the professional female thieves who caused the least damage since the police knew them all. Then came the thieves due to mania, a *perversion of desire, a new neurosis that alienists had classified,* recognizing the sharp temptation exerted by the department stores. Finally, there were the pregnant women, *whose thefts were specialized:* thus, the police commissioner had discovered in one of these women's homes two-hundred-forty-eight pink gloves stolen from all the sales counters of Paris. (*Bonheur,* 632; emphasis added)[19]

Those women whose theft was not specialized earned the label *collectioneuses,* for—much like Felicity—they filled up their homes with small items of little value. It was usually reported that the articles remained unused, with the price tags still attached. Take for example Mme. G——, in whose home the police discovered, among other items, 5 pairs of boots, 22 pieces of silk and wool material, 24 handkerchiefs, 56 pairs of black stockings, and 33 pairs of socks, all with prices still affixed (Dubuisson 1902, 71). This was not a pure monomania, Dubuisson explained, but a degenerate indulgence in a primitive animal instinct to stockpile. Pregnancy especially increased this desire to amass, which was the root of all varieties of useless, childish collecting for the sheer pleasure of possession. Some could satisfy themselves with the pleasant "tipsiness" (*magasinite*) provided by a visit to a store (188). For others (mostly *héréditaires* and neurotics, pregnant and menstruating women), their moral sense could not resist this degenerate, primitive instinct or their female physiological weakness: theft became "an incomparable voluptuousness" (208).

While Zola relied on medical theories to inform his fiction, doctors reciprocated by turning to Zola's novels for the most dramatic illustrations of the passion of the *voleuses des magasins.*[20] Dr. Lacassagne, speaking at the Fourth International Criminal Anthropology Conference, warned that, "these department stores are always 'Le Bonheur des Dames' and constitute a serious danger to sickly and weak people" (1896, 82). In his 1904 thesis on kleptomania, Dr. Soubourou quoted Zola frequently. The best example of the disorder is found at the end of *Au Bonheur des Dames* with the arrest of the Countess de

Boves, caught red-handed with 14,000 francs'-worth of lace stuffed into every
nook of her ample dress. Zola's description has all the flavor of medical acuity:

> For a year now, Mme. de Boves had robbed thus, ravaged by a furious, irre-
> sistible need. The crises had worsened, growing to the point of being a *volup-
> tuousness* necessary for her existence, sweeping away all thought of prudence,
> satisfied by an even sharper pleasure since, in full view of the masses, she
> risked her name, her pride, the high status of her husband. . . . [S]he stole al-
> though her pockets were full of money, she stole to steal, as one loves for the
> sake of loving, under the whip of desire, with the neurotic derangement that
> her unquenched appetite for luxury had whetted, formerly, through the enor-
> mous and brutal temptation of the department stores. (*Bonheur,* 793; empha-
> sis added)

We are again reminded of Marie D—— who masturbated in the middle of the
stores with purloined silk. Marie, like many other working-class shoplifters, was
usually less fortunate in her dealings with the authorities than the Countess,
who was discreetly dismissed after signing a simple confession. It was precisely
high social standing and the ability to pay that encouraged doctors and courts
to diagnose kleptomania rather than condemn wealthy shoplifters for vulgar,
utilitarian theft. Zola expressed another diagnostic subtlety: audacity and the
fear of disgrace further kindled her desire. Although Zola did not explicitly
claim that Mme. de Boves engaged in public masturbation and orgasm, the imperative, irrational voluptuousness of her lace theft alluded to the intimate connections between kleptomania and fetishism.

Dr. Dupouy described these irrepressible pleasures quite explicitly in the
case of Hélène M——, who stole silk corsages exclusively from two department
stores. "Once the act is committed," he observed, "it is an enormous relief, a
sensation of immense well-being, a very special state of satisfaction, with, as
with fetishists, *sensations of voluptuousness* followed by ejaculations" (1905,
419). Dupouy noted, however, that the patient experienced a "sensation of
ejaculation without nonetheless experiencing orgasm" (423). Despite this,
Dr. Dupouy diagnosed Hélène M—— as a fetishist. Although in M——'s case
the fetishism was secondary to the kleptomania, Dupouy insisted that in many
other cases of kleptomania, fetishism or some other perverse sexual irritation
was the primary spur to theft.

The new cult of material objects that was so craftily staged in the Second
Empire's temples of commodities inflamed new pleasures of consumption, of
female public visibility, and of social commingling fuelling much concern.

Some conservatives blamed these modernist developments of capitalist consumer culture for the deterioration of traditional social institutions: family, church, home, and business. What if these provoked, false pleasures of modernity were so commonplace that they had become the norm? Alfred Binet's novel theory of amorous fetishism provocatively suggested that an irrational, primitive psychology might lurk at the core of even the most normal love.

## Binet's Family of Perverts

By the time Alfred Binet first employed the notion of fetishism to designate patients whose sexuality revolved around night bonnets, boot nails, and aprons, he could rely on ethnologists who had already drawn connections between religion, eroticism, and primitivism.[21] Binet thus formulated a rather complex network of associations in one sentence: "These patients' adoration of inert objects such as night bonnets or boot nails resembles in all ways the adoration of the savage or the negro for fish bones or shiny stones, with the fundamental difference that, in our patient's cult, religious adoration is replaced by a sexual appetite" (1887a, 144).

Binet is probably better known today for the psychological tool he developed with his colleague Théodore Simon: the Binet-Simon I.Q. test.[22] His development of the notion of an "intelligence quotient" was just one product of a long life of diverse research projects earning him the reputation as a founder of the French school of experimental psychology. He trained in both law and medicine, and in 1883 he was introduced to Charcot at the Salpêtrière. An association with Charcot allowed Binet to employ hysterical patients in his studies of hypnotism, hallucination, and animal magnetism. Relying on his experience with the mentally alienated, Binet also wrote several realist dramas.[23] While he was familiar with the numerous articles on sexual perversion published in the early 1880s during his time at the Salpêtrière,[24] his essay on "amorous fetishism" singled out Charcot and Magnan's work as his greatest inspiration. Indeed, Binet fully agreed with his mentors' hypothesis that all "sexual perversions" (inversion and erotic attraction to objects or body parts) belonged to a single nosological entity: they were simply the variable symptoms of one class of neurological degeneration. In this he followed along national lines, opposing the Germans who isolated sexual inversion as a distinct disorder.[25] Even inversion, Binet explained, is "a perversion entirely of the same order [as attraction to inanimate objects] . . . and a man who today only loves men might, in a different milieu, have only loved night caps or boot nails" (1887a, 165).

Rather than undermine Charcot and Magnan's theory of the neuropathology of sexual perversion, Binet proposed to explain the genesis of its diverse psychological manifestations. "For the psychologist," Binet explained, "the important fact is elsewhere; it is to be found in the direct study of the symptom, in the analysis of its formation and its mechanism, in the light that these disease cases shine upon the psychology of love" (146). The psychology of love followed a single set of laws; therefore, the pathological cases could be used to illuminate the normal cases. Conversely, this implied that "everyone is more or less fetishistic in love; there is a constant dose of fetishism in even the most regular love" (144). Binet's contribution to sexology was to claim perversity as a natural mechanism of the psychology of love: "The true fetishists are those lovers of boot nails or white aprons; but if we stretch the terms, then we are in the presence of a natural family of perversions, and there is a major interest in giving this family a unique name" (145). It was this "natural family of perversions" that Binet baptized *fetishism*. By setting aside the matter of the neuropathology of perversions, Binet could instead theorize their psychology in three ways: classifying the normal versus the pathological and the typology of fetishisms; hypothesizing the childhood implantation of the specific fetish; and speculating about the psychic activity and pleasure of the fetishist.

Binet destigmatized the distinction between normal and pathological forms of fetishism by renaming them *grand fétichisme* and *petit fétichisme*. *Petit fétichisme*—the normal fetishism of ordinary love—was "easily dissimulated" because it appeared as part of the search for beauty in the loved one (260). But we should not be fooled: "The attraction that the lover experiences for all the parts of a person's body are not the product of a platonic admiration or a purely aesthetic sentiment; this attraction is sexual, and female beauty is a cause of genital excitement in men" (272). Comparing it to Darwin's description of avian "artistic combat" over beautiful plumage or song, Binet forthrightly unmasked aesthetic competition as just another manifestation of sexual selection—a matter of sexual instinct rather than aesthetic choice. In cases of socially inappropriate matches, Binet suggested, we should suspect a fetishistic motive: "A rich, distinguished, intelligent man marries a woman without youth, nor beauty, nor wit, nor anything that attracts most men; there is perhaps in these unions a sympathy of odor or something analogous; it is *petit fétichisme*" (145). As with the savage trading gold for trinkets, the fetishist sometimes made socially unwise amorous transactions.

*Grand fétichisme* "one simply could not fail to recognize," Binet initially claimed rather unrigorously (144). It betrayed itself by thefts and violent acts. Later on he was more circumspect: "The line of demarcation [between the normal state and its deviations] is very difficult to trace; often, in the world, one takes as a lover's pure extravagances what is really a sexual perversion" (261). Ultimately, it came down to social criteria: fetishism is "the adoration of things inappropriate to directly satisfying the ends of reproduction" (261). Following Binet's principles, the suspicion of fetishism hovers around all amorous liasons marked by their sterility or contravention of social standards.

He distinguished three broad classes of fetishism: love of a body part, love for inanimate objects, and attraction to a psychic quality. In the first category, he discussed fetishism of the eyes, hand, hair (the infamous "braid cutters"), and odor.[26] Under the second category, he examined clothing, handkerchief, nightcap, and boot-nail fetishists, as well as sexual inverts. The third class included the erotic attraction to punishment, flagellation, and "exhibitionism" (named in 1877 by Lasègue).[27]

All these varieties of fetishism were triggered by a childhood association. Given Binet's early attachment to associationist psychology, he turned first to the authority of Condillac. In chapter 1 we noted Condillac's warnings about the impact of lascivious images and texts on the imagination and the importance of the association of ideas in the establishment of likes and dislikes. Binet echoed Condillac's observations, particularly that of Descartes's lifelong attraction to cross-eyed women. Descartes thus became Binet's first example of a fetishist. Furthermore, Binet relied on Descartes's *Treatise on Passions* to explain how these peculiar attractions and aversions are acquired: some powerful, childhood experience or trauma remains implanted in the mind, creating a permanent affective association that persists even after the original event is forgotten. Binet underscored this final element: "Here is the important point, and Descartes did not fail to recognize it. The acquired aversion for certain objects becomes independent of the memory of the fact that gave birth to that aversion" (147 n.1). The choice of the term *fetishism* (bearing associations with "primitive" cults) aptly embellished Binet's formulation of the condition as a primitive and infantile mechanism of the psychology of love: fetishism is established in infancy, persists in the unconscious and easily risks becoming unreasonable, irrational, and countersocial (traits also linked to primitives and children.)

Finally, Binet mused over the psychic mechanisms for ingraining and enjoying the fetish. He emphasized the role played by the "resonance box" of precocious masturbation—it amplified and fixated the fetish in the erotic imagination by dint of repeated association (163). His best example of this is a case we know well, a man Binet identified as a fetishist of punishment, clothing, and self-exhibition: Jean-Jacques Rousseau. Binet quoted extensively all the piquant scenes from the *Confessions,* notably the spanking by Mlle. de Lambercier and Rousseau's masochistic fantasies. Rousseau's confessions supported Binet's claim that erotic tastes are established in childhood by accidental association and that the conjunction of masturbation and the repeated "work of the imagination" firmly implanted the fetishistic desire. This imaginative work or "erotic rumination of the fetishist" (253) focused on some small part or quality of the loved one: "The part is substituted for the whole, the accessory becomes the principal" (274). Normal love, on the other hand, is a "harmonious" complex of fetishistic attractions to the whole body of the beloved with whom one coupled (Binet assumed this is a woman and the fetishist a man.) Pathological fetishism was a matter of erotic synecdoche or metonymy: substitution of a part for the whole, or for something related or contiguous.[28] Completely inverting the historical association of religious fetishism with primitive polytheism, Binet suggested that "in normal love, fetishism is polytheistic" while perverse fetishism is monotheistic in its cult of a single attribute (274). Indulging in some imaginative work of his own, Binet offered yet another analogy: "The love of the pervert is a theater piece where a simple bit player advances to center stage and takes the leading role" (274). Being an amateur playwright himself, Binet undoubtedly had an especially keen sense of the danger of such theatrical chaos.

The monotonous drama of the *grand fétichiste* consisted of the "erotic rumination of the continent": "[They] thus managed to satisfy their genital needs by constructing love novels in their heads" (269). Like the idolatrous savage, "erotic ruminants" secretly engaged in a private, useless mental cult of an erotic image. Beyond the mere images came whole fetishistic scenarios. In addition to Rousseau's fantasies, Binet referred to the erotic tales scripted by the boot-nail fetishist. Mr. X—— concocted all variety of stories with young girls visiting a cobbler to have nails placed in their shoes and feet, or worse, have their feet cut off:

> One of the aforementioned fantastical stories returned involuntarily to [Mr. X——'s] mind phrase by phrase; and at the same time, erection occurred, which soon resulted in ejaculation without even putting hand to penis; he wished, on the contrary, that the ejaculation not occur since it prevented him from continuing his story, and he much preferred the pleasure experienced through the story to that procured by ejaculation. (Charcot & Magnan 1882, 309)

Although, as Rousseau also suggested, the erotic "furors of the imagination" might be satisfying enough to produce continence or impotence, they often wore thin (Binet 1887a, 266, 269). "Ruminants, who understand very well this inferiority of the imagination, seek with a remarkable sagacity the means to force the mental image to render all the pleasure it can give" (269). Thus they seek to "dynamogenize the image" by exteriorizing it through speaking and writing.[29]

Binet thereby identified the two critical elements that have occupied us in our examination of the erotic imagination: the confession of erotic fantasies performed by "patients," and the writing of them as performed by doctors, their patients, and novelists. By 1887 sexual perversions had captured the popular imagination, and Binet recognized that "we find them mentioned, and at times rather well analyzed, in some contemporary novels" (144).[30] In his article, medical and literary cases alternate with one another to such a degree that one loses track of any distinction. With the notion of "dynamogenization," Binet rendered into psychological terms the connections between oral or literary confession, the erotic imagination, and pleasure. Dynamogenization through writing obliges the writer to analyze his or her image, to strengthen, define, and give it contour:

> This necessity must equally contribute to excite the imagination of the subject when it is lazy. Perhaps we should search in similar psychological facts the reason for which so many mystics, Suso, Saint Theresa, Rousseau, etc., wrote their own biography in which they describe, with countless details, their mystical exaltations. (270)[31]

Given the recurrent association of mysticism and eroticism throughout the century, Binet's suggestion is hardly scandalous. He had already explained young priests' devotion to statues of the Virgin Mary as fetishistic (161). More interesting is the fact that Binet explicitly connected the erotic imagination to literary production, yet he was careful not to simplistically label the many novelists he cited as "fetishists" themselves. Take for example Adolphe Belot, whose novel *The Mouth of Madame X*. . . Binet "dissects." The hero, Binet concluded, is indubitably a fetishist of the mouth, and Belot confirmed that it was based on a real person. The book presented a clear case of mental pathology, Binet concluded, so he was perplexed by the fact that critics had decried the novel as licentious rather than recognizing it as a "description of a case of mental pathology" (272). Other medical analysts would be far less discerning in their diagnosis of the sexual perversity of novels, authors, and society—further blurring the boundaries between fiction and medical cases, the normal and the erotic. An especially good example of this is the medical treatment of J. K.

Huysmans and his novel *A Rebours*. The supposed olfactory fetishism of the novel and of Naturalist authors in general provoked acerbic cultural criticism and particularly florid erotic dynamogenizing among medical authors.

## The Stench of Decadence

> Little by little, the arcana of [the art of perfumery], the most neglected of all, opened themselves before des Esseintes who deciphered its complex language—as subtle as literature—with a style of unprecedented precision under its floating and vague appearance.
>
> To do this, he had been obliged to study its grammar, understand the syntax of odors, deeply penetrate the rules that govern them, and, once familiar with this dialect, compare the creations of the masters [of perfumery] . . . , disassemble the construction of their phrases, weigh the proportion of their words and the disposition of their periods. (Huysmans, *A Rebours*, 153–4)

Like a medieval monk or hermetic alchemist, the Duke Jean de Floressas des Esseintes collects, classifies, ruminates, and revels in the "language" of odors. Like a Dr. Frankenstein of perfumery, he concocts courtesans out of essential oils and excites himself into a "nervous crisis." He exhausts himself in sensuous debaucheries not only of perfume but also of flowers, books, engravings, music, gems, liqueurs, etc. Joris-Karl Huysmans's hysterical, effeminate hero is a classic, if ever-so-refined, *collectioniste-fétichiste*. To borrow Binet's term, we could say des Esseintes is supremely skilled at dynamogenizing sensations. Throughout *A Rebours,* des Esseintes indulges in the pleasure of an aesthete, analyzing the language of the senses and admiring the refined erotism of his sensuous "compositions." Des Esseintes's particular affinity for odors further qualifies his diagnosis: "The lover of odor" Binet explained, "is of especially great interest to the psychologist, because this genre of fetishist is intimately associated with the existence of a sensorial type: the olfactor [*l'olfactif*]" (1887a, 157). The olfactor (or more conventionally, the olfactory fetishist) was the object of intense medical and artistic scrutiny because the analysis of olfaction concentrated scientific, cultural, and literary concerns about the primitive, the artificial, the unconscious, and the erotic.

Classical authors, such as Aristotle and Theophrastus, long ago described an association between the period of rut and pungent smells (*osphrésis*) in animals.[32] However, during the Enlightenment, natural scientists, public hygienists, and the French *philosophes* examined odors and the sense of smell with new interest. Generally, the study of the senses was critical to materialist, sensualist savants such as Condillac and Cabanis. In his *Treatise on Sensations* (1754), Condillac went so far as to give olfaction primacy among the human senses. Cabanis reasoned that there had to be some "sympathy" (or neurological association) between the nose and the other internal organs—especially those of the digestive tract, to which taste and smell were most closely linked. Not least amongst these sympathetic links was that between olfaction and the genital organs (Cabanis 1802, 526–28). Thanks to the direction and funding of Cabanis, Hippolyte Cloquet (whom we first encountered as a close friend of the gourmand Brillat-Savarin) studied the many scientific and philosophical writings and empirical/folk preconceptions of odors and olfaction. He published his research in *Osphresiology, A Treatise on Odors, of the Sense and Organ of Olfaction* in 1821, and it remained the reference text on olfaction throughout the nineteenth century.[33]

For Cloquet, "osphresiology" (the science of smell) was central to the sensualists' "science of man." They were confident that an understanding of "bodily economy" or physiology would then clarify the "laws of social association," in other words, a code of natural morality for the ethical satisfaction of human needs.[34] A taxonomy of olfactory sensations was just the first step in this broader analysis of the laws of association between sensations, thoughts, and actions—at the level of both the individual and the social bodies. Cloquet believed that olfaction was the primary instinctual organ for self-preservation in subhuman species because of its extensive sympathy with the digestive and reproductive systems (1821, 20).[35] Although sight and hearing had grown to predominate in the sensory life of humans, odors continued to produce sneezing, lacrymation, sleep and wakefulness, nausea, strong affective reactions, and genital excitation. The importance of olfaction in reproduction was quite apparent in both animals and humans, Cloquet noted. Many animals exude strongly odorous substances from their sex organs (such as females' *smegma vulvæ*) to facilitate male-female recognition and coitus (126). He added that "civilized" women continued to exploit the seductive power of smell through the use of perfume.[36] Conversely, he suggested that female "genital neuroses" (such as hysteria) could be excited or calmed by particular odors (126). Indeed, reports of "genital and nasal reflex neuroses" (such as "rose fever") proliferated in the late nineteenth century, linking parosmia (olfactory perversion) to genital disorders.[37]

The stigmatization of olfaction as a primitive, bestial sensation was given a neurological and anthropological foundation thanks to Pierre-Paul Broca's contributions to comparative anatomy and evolutionary thinking. A physician,

politician, and founder in 1859 of the Society of Anthropology, Broca is especially remembered for his work on the neuropathology of aphasia, particularly
the cerebral cortical area and the corresponding expressive aphasia that bear
his name. His research on the "great limbic lobe" of the cerebral cortex was the
last in a series of projects in comparative anatomy. Through it, he hoped to
demonstrate the transformation of species and the continuity of the so-called
phylogenetic series up from simple animals, to mammals, to "primitives," to
(white, French) men (Broca 1869, 1870, 1871). He could thus confirm his
preconceived hierarchy of the human races through objective neuroanatomical
features.[38]

The "limbic system" connected the olfactory cortex of the forebrain with
hypothalamic areas supposedly responsible for autonomic functions (including
fight, flight, and sexual behaviors). Broca noticed striking changes in the size
and location of the olfactory cortex of animals occupying successively higher
positions on the evolutionary ladder. He interpreted these anatomical findings
as proof that olfaction had played a major role in the intellectual development
of the animal series but its importance had waned in the primate series. These
evolutionary forces had led to the diminished olfactory lobes of humans.[39] His
ethological claims were supported by his discovery of the "limbic sulcus": a
small groove in the cerebral cortex (see Figure 7). He proclaimed the limbic
sulcus a "trait of inferiority" and an "index of incomplete evolution arrested at
the simian stage" (1879b, 449). The limbic sulcus was present in all primates
and "inferior races" of humans, but absent from Europeans (except for some
"idiots and imbeciles").[40] Broca attributed the absence of the limbic sulcus in
normal "civilized people" to the "influence of the social state, education, and
disuse" of the sense of smell among the civilized (1879b, 451). Anthropologists
had frequently reported that "primitives" depended on their olfactory powers
to track down game, enemies, and runaway concubines (1879b, 450). Unlike
these "inferior races," civilized people did not rely on olfaction for survival but
for refined luxury and discrimination.

Although Broca and other anthropologists of his time helped to lend scientific credence to such parallels between phyletic and social evolution, these
schemes were not novel. They follow in the tradition of French transformism,
which traced the chain of beings from "lower" animals to the primates, then to
the human "primitives," and finally to "civilized" Europeans. As we saw in the
discussion of Morelian degeneration theory, these Lamarckian mechanisms of
evolution also served to explain the reverse process of *atavism:* the regression
from the civilized to the primitive bestial state (often equated with "imbecility"

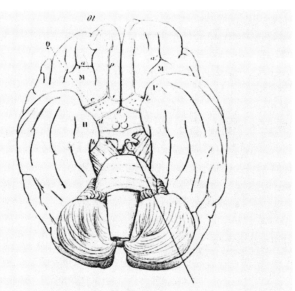

Fig. 14. — Face inférieure du cerveau d'un homme mort de la paralysie générale des aliénés (1/2 grandeur).

Pour montrer la bandelette diagonale on a détaché et attiré en arrière avec un crochet le chiasma et les bandelettes optiques, qui se trouvent ainsi reportés en arrière des tubercules mamillaires.

O*l*, le renflement olfactif; *p*, son pédoncule; *i*, racine olfactive interne; *e*, l'externe, disparaissent dans la vallée de Sylvius, sous la pointe du lobe temporal; Q. l'espace quadrilatère perforé; *dd'*, la *bandelette diagonale*; son extrémité externe et postérieure *d* se jette sur la face profonde du lobule de l'hippocampe H; son extrémité antérieure et interne atteint le bord interne de l'hémisphère en avant de la racine grise du chiasma, et se jette sur la face interne, où elle se perd dans le carrefour.

P, le pôle temporal; *l*, dépression représentant le sillon limbique des singes.

M, M', le centre olfactif antérieur ou orbitaire, limité antérieurement par l'incisure en H, qui à droite *aa*, la forme d'une H, et qui présente à gauche, *a'*, une forme un peu différente.

Figure 7. The olfactory nervous system. Inferior surface of a human brain from a patient who died of general paralysis of the insane. From Paul Broca's "Research on the Olfactory Centers" (1879, 429). The letter *l* indicates the "depression representing the limbic sulcus in monkeys."

or "idiocy"). Although all systems and surfaces of the body might exhibit stigmata of degeneration, the nervous system was particularly susceptible to degenerative action and demonstrated its pathology as various symptoms of *névrose* (neurosis) or neurasthenia (nervous weakening), and eventually more serious nervous degeneration.[41]

In addition to being affiliated with the most "primitive" of the senses, odor was also associated with putrescence, filth, and disease. The theory that contagious diseases were spread by miasmas (noxious effluvia of swamps and corrupt matter) was gradually discredited in the late nineteenth century with the microbiological discoveries of scientists such as Louis Pasteur.[42] The concern over the noxiousness of foul odors, particularly in the great cities such as Paris, nevertheless persisted even as Pasteurian germ theory was accepted.[43] As historian Alain Corbin (1982) has shown, nineteenth-century doctors and public hygienists further connected these associations between fetid odors, primitivism, and disease to the stench of the urban lower classes. Closely related to the preoccupation with physical odors was the metaphorical use of odor to represent moral and cultural corruption. Louis Veuillot, editor of the conservative Catholic daily *L'Univers,* in his polemical *The Odors of Paris* (1867) lambasted the Second Empire and the Hausmanization of Paris, which he claimed together served to further the circulation of journalistic, literary, and theatrical sewage. He also reiterated the elitist critiques of that other product of Hausmanization, the department stores. The whole book is a vicious diatribe against the fetor of the "vile multitudes," democracy, republicanism, and modernization.[44]

Given this rich network of nineteenth-century associations concerning odor, it is not surprising that Binet singled out "the lover of odor" as a particularly interesting object of study. A psychological understanding of the *olfactif* promised to explain many contemporary social mysteries. Binet echoed reports of the savages' reliance on odors and women's exploitation of perfumes. For him, pathological olfactory fetishism was just the extreme form of this natural eroticism of odors: "For certain men, what is essential in a woman, is not beauty, wit, goodness, or refinement of character,—it is odor; the pursuit of the cherished odor determines them to seek an old, ugly, vice-ridden, degraded woman" (156). He predicted that countless inappropriate matches and peculiar, socially disruptive behavior were due to *olfactifs:* for example, "a married man, head of a family, who cannot smell a certain female odor without following that woman in the street, to the theater, or anywhere" (156). Olfactory fetishism could also be suspected as the real obsession for many object fetishists: for example, the man with a collection of over three hundred stolen handkerchiefs, who "inhales their aroma and retires, stumbling like a drunkard" (162).

Degeneration to this sensory predominance of the nose was to descend woefully low on the social and evolutionary ladders. Max Nordau said it quite plainly: to privilege those senses that human evolution had specifically quelled was to "suppress one's frontal lobe and substitute in its place the olfactory lobe of a dog."

The sniffers [*flaireurs*] among degenerates represent an atavism that steps back not just to the earliest times of man, but infinitely further back to the era before man. Their atavism marches back to the animals among which, just like musk-bearers today, sexual activity was directly excited by odorous materials. (Nordau 1893, 2:463)

While Magnan and Lombroso applied Morelian degeneration theory to neurology and criminology respectively, Dr. Max Nordau sought to catalogue new signs of degeneration by exposing its cultural stigmata.[45] These, he argued, were particularly evident in French fin-de-siècle artistic styles, which infected civilization globally.[46] A physician, novelist, playwright, and literary critic, this German Jeremiah of degeneration dedicated his immensely popular book *Degeneration* to Cesare Lombroso. Nordau set out to apply Lombroso's positivist science of society and criminality to the analysis of art and artists. "Degenerates are not always criminals, prostitutes, anarchists or outright lunatics," Nordau warned, "they are often writers and artists. But these present the same intellectual—and often also somatic—traits as the members of the single anthropological family who satisfy their morbid instincts with the assassin's dagger or the dynamiter's explosives, rather than satisfying them with the pen or brush" (1893, 1:v–vi). Like Binet, Nordau set out to uncover a vast "family" of degenerates—in his case, linking the overtly insane or monomaniacal to the politically, artistically, and sexually deviant. He was in line with leading medical figures of his day. Valentin Magnan, the main proponent of neurodegeneration theory, had declared at a meeting of the Medico-Psychological Society:

> A *héréditaire* can be a savant, a distinguished magistrate, a great artist, a mathematician, a politician, an able administrator, and exhibit profound defects from the psychological perspective: strange eccentricities, surprising behavioral abnormalities, . . . morbid instincts, appetites and sentiments, which thanks to weaknesses of the will, push them to the most extravagant and often dangerous acts. (1886, 99)

Nordau freely mixed the degenerationist ideas of Magnan, Morel, and Lombroso with the notion of neurasthenia. Mystical, symbolist, and decadent art, Nordau declared, were the effect of degeneration and hysteria, or at least, early neurasthenia (1:31). In addition to physical stigmata, there were to be found the mental stigmata of Magnan's "superior degenerate" class who display the characteristics of moral insanity: unbounded egoism, impulsiveness and emotionalism, mental weakness and despondency, powerlessness, inane reverie, an excessive "delectation in the imagination," mysticism (or religious mania), imitation, and impressionability (1:39–48). These authors—with more or less pronounced moral insanity, imbecility, and dementia—produced "pathological art" and "exercise[d] a powerful suggestion on the masses," especially the impressionable youth hungry for novelty (1:vi). Thus the public, infected by the cultural elite, delighted in the artificial and contrary-to-nature: "Elegant titillation only began where normal sexuality ceased" (1:26). This fin-de-siècle public was impressionable, fadish, fetishistic, and "oniomanic" (that is, they suffered from "purchasing mania") (1:50). To this material consumerism corresponded an aesthetic consumption of ever more sensational, spectacular, and bizarre stimulations.

One of these new and degenerate neuro-aesthetic excitements was odor. "The pioneers [in art]," Nordau wrote sarcastically, "address themselves to the sense of smell, unjustly disdained till now by the fine arts, and they invite it to take part in the aesthetic pleasure" (1:28). Fin-de-siècle books stank of incense and manure. The cultural avant-garde pinch their nose and dive into the "mobile cesspool of unattenuated Naturalism" (1:26). Given the stigmatized history of olfaction, it is not surprising that a "diagnosis" of olfactory decadence was accompanied by the suspicion of sexual perversion. Nordau mounted an especially virulent attack against the Naturalist school and its father, Emile Zola. In the previous chapter I mentioned Nordau's disdain for Zola's "scientific novels." Nordau went far beyond deriding Zola's intellect and art, however. He read that art as a symptom of Zola's "advanced degeneracy": "The fact that he is a sexual psychopath is betrayed in every page of his novels" (2:456). Nordau refined his diagnosis further: "Accompanying M. Zola's sexual psychopathia is the role olfactory sensations play in his work. The predominance of the sense of smell and its relationship to the sexual sphere is striking in many degenerates. In their work as well, odor acquires a great importance" (2:458). Nordau was already familiar with a monograph, *Odors in the Novels of Zola,* written by Leopold Bernard, a philosophy teacher and Inspecteur de l'Académie from Montpellier. Zola was a "symphonist of odors," Bernard proclaimed;

> He is the novelist with the quivering nostrils, a subtle sense of smell, always tickled by the mysterious effluvia of the air; he is the man who has most lived by the nose, who has most suffered and most delighted by the odor of things . . . ; his imagination, a rare thing, has preserved the lively impression, and he can, when he wishes, refresh it to the point of affording himself the illusion of the original experience; he also excels in noting odors, in describing them, analyzing, classing, seizing their secret harmonies, their mysterious correspondences with sentiments and ideas, their deaf but nonetheless irresistible influence on decisions and conduct. (1889, 7)

Bernard passed in review the most odorous scenes in Zola's novels, thoroughly documenting his claim that smell plays an unprecedented role in Zola's novelistic world. This is most striking in *Le Ventre de Paris* [The belly of Paris] (1873), the third installment of the Rougon-Macquart cycle, and a novel where the odors of the market, the aromas of the charcuterie, the stench of filth and poverty rise thick and fulsome from every page. The "symphony of cheeses"—one of the most memorable passages in French literature—sates the reader with three pages of pungent and frankly nauseating aromas from twenty-three cheeses. Zola leaves no doubt about the toxicity of odors:

> The warm afternoon had softened the cheeses; the mold on the rinds melted, varnishing them in rich copper red and gray-green tones, like ill fermented wounds; . . . a flood of life had bored through a livarot, birthing through that gash a crowd of worms. And behind the scales, in its narrow case, an anise flavored géromé exuded such an infection that the flies had collapsed all around the box. (*Ventre*, 828)

These odors were all carefully documented in Zola's preparatory dossier. Zola even made notes to himself to write "a page on dung" and to describe the "strong odor of fowl."[47] Bernard rightly claimed that the omnipresence of odors in Zola's novels was carefully premeditated. The reason, Bernard explained, was to inform the reader about the milieu and the individual characters: "Each character exudes a particular odor depending on their age, sex, state of health or illness, their secret vices, the hereditary composition, their status" (14). In other words, Zola attempted to exploit odor as a diagnostic attribute, as an index of "hereditary composition," just as Broca, Lombroso, and other anthropometrists had done with so many other physical traits.

An association between certain odors and "sexual appetite" was also an important element in Zola's literary use of odors (Bernard 1889, 22). One example of "voluptuous, aphrodisiacal, erotical odors" (22) in Zola's novels is a fleeting moment between Florent, the largely gynophobic hero of *Le Ventre de Paris,* and the fishmonger, Louise ("La Belle Normande") Méhudin: "When her camisole gaped open, [Florent] imagined he saw rising, between two white masses, the smoke of life, a steamy breath of health that smacked his face, as if stirred up from a malodorous focus of the Halles [market], by the sweltering evenings of July" (*Ventre*, 738). It was this raw brutality, this materialist primacy of the gut over the brain, that delighted Bernard. Furthermore, it was because Zola "wanted to evoke the beast which always sleeps in the depths of human nature" that he made odor and taste—the "animal senses"—the equals of the intellectual and aesthetic senses (21). It was *precisely* this animality that Nordau most feared in the work of Zola and other Naturalist and Decadent authors who idealized the cycle of excess consumption, sensory exhaustion, and unorthodox, artificial stimulation (1:28). These decadent obsessions, Nordau insisted, were to blame for the spread of neurasthenia, sexual deviance, and degeneration.

Nowhere is this cycle of degeneration and decadence more exhaustively portrayed than in Huysmans's *A Rebours* (which in one English translation is appropriately rendered as *Against Nature*). Nordau described its hero, des Esseintes, as "an anemic and nervous weakling, the inheritor of all the vices and degeneration of an exhausted race" (2:108). (Here, as throughout *Degeneration*, the nationalist subtext is quite thick.) Since 1876, Huysmans had been a member of Zola's circle of Naturalist authors committed to a scientific, realist representation of the material rigors of life and the biological decay of French society. In *A Rebours*, his last novel before breaking with Zola, Huysmans explicitly diagnosed des Esseintes as "degenerate." The venerable ancestors of the Floressas des Esseintes line had been large, athletic men, we are told, but the more recent descendants all showed the signs of degeneration: "The decadence of this ancient house had, undoubtedly, followed its regular course; the effemination of the males had continued accentuating itself; as if to complete the labor of ages, the des Esseintes had intermarried their children for two centuries, wearing down the remains of their vigor in consanguineous unions" (*Rebours*, 61). Jean des Esseintes was the last "runt" of this family and the initial description of him echoes a century of medical portraits of hystericoneurasthenic onanists. He was

> a skinny young man of thirty, anemic and nervous, with hollow cheeks, icy steel-blue eyes, an up-turned yet straight nose, and skinny, spidery hands. By a singular phenomenon of atavism, the last descendant resembled the ancient patriarch, the mignon, whose extraordinarily blond, pointy beard and ambiguously languid and cunning expression des Esseintes had revived. (61–2).

To complete this medical history of atavism and effeminacy, we are told that his mother suffered from nervous breakdowns if exposed to too much light or noise, and that he had had a solitary, monkish education among the Jesuits. He becomes a misanthropic recluse, and after having sated himself on all forms of excessive carnal repasts, his sexual drive was just as weak as his nerves. In an act of refined cynicism, he hosts a black-themed dinner party as a wake for his defunct virility.

Des Esseintes was also the fashion plate of the dandy: "He acquired the reputation of an eccentric which he completed by dressing in white velour costumes, gold-embroidered vests, planting, in the guise of a cravat, a bouquet of Parma violets in the cleavage of a collarless shirt" (70). This was, in fact, one of the outlandish outfits of one of the best known dandies of Huysmans's circle, Robert Count of Montesquiou, widely believed at the time to be the model for des Esseintes as well as Proust's homosexual character in *Remembrance of Things Past,* the Baron de Charlus.[48] As we saw in the previous chapter, des Esseintes's style also had a profound influence on Oscar Wilde and his British circle of aesthete dandies.

Throughout *A Rebours,* des Esseintes is cloistered away from the world he abhors in a bizarre house of his own design. There he systematically exhausts one appetite after another in a compulsively encyclopedic fashion. His custom-built "mouth organ" (*orgue à bouche*)—a contraption for blending liqueurs—allows him to experiment with the gamut of gustatory stimuli and compose pieces of music for the palate. Like the *collectionomanes* described by Dr. Codet (1921), des Esseintes goes on feverish buying sprees of exotic plants and orchids, rare books, manuscripts, and engravings.

His dominant, we might say obsessive, aesthetic quest for the artificial, unnatural, and factitious is repeatedly associated with his religious aspirations: "Thus, his tendencies towards artifice, his need for eccentricity," he wonders, "were they not ultimately the result of specious studies, of otherworldly refinements, of quasi-theological speculations; they were fundamentally transports, aspirations towards an ideal, towards an unknown universe, a distant beatitude, desirable as that which the Scriptures promised" (126). As in the construction of religious fetishism itself, a delusional cult of material objects is the basis of des Esseintes's feverish religiosity. Nevertheless, he tires of each series of purchases and sensations and must turn to a new one. With each cycle, his nervous crises become more and more severe.

Midway through the novel he is stricken with olfactory hallucinations, "perversions of smell" or "parosmia," to use the official medical term (Collet 1904, 83). After ascertaining that his manservant can smell nothing out of the ordinary, des Esseintes realizes that "the neurosis was returning, once again, with the appearance of a new illusion of the senses" (152). For therapy he turns to experimenting with perfumes, a sort of "nasal homeopathy" (152). Through this early aromatherapy he becomes thoroughly familiar with all the essences of the perfume industry, hoping to create a "grammar of perfume" (154). In addition to this episode, there are countless other odorous events, so numerous that Havelock Ellis was struck by the "olfactory hyperaesthesia" of the novel (1931, xx).[49] As another expression of his obsession with the artificial, des Esseintes's experimentations in odors allow him to develop a "precision of *fiction*"—a "science of smell" (153).[50] Huysmans portrayes his hero as a hybrid between a philologist, a psychologist, and an alchemist: both analyzing the

"soul" of perfumes and composing odorous mixtures to imitate natural perfumes. The culmination of his labors is the creation of a "human essence" that

> smelled of skirts, announcing the powdered and painted woman, stephanotis,
> ayapana, opoponax, chypre, champaka, sarcanthus, over which he layered a
> touch of seringa in order to suggest with the *factitious* life of make-up which
> they released, a *natural* flower of sweaty laughter, of joys which toss about in
> the open sun. (157; emphasis added)

In this ultimate refinement of olfactory perversity, des Esseintes concocts a
wholly artificial perfume woman. Inevitably, he is overwhelmed by his aromatic
alchemy and tormented by a storm of olfactory hallucinations. These "assailed
his exhausted nose, overwhelming once again his shattered nerves, prostrating
him to such a degree, that he collapsed swooning, almost dead, at his window
sill" (161–62).

Havelock Ellis, who was fascinated by Huysmans and his hero, called this
particular form of sexual metonymy (replacement of "normal" sex for odorous
excitation) "olfactory fetichism," perhaps the first use of the term (1905, 74).
Although Ellis praised the Decadent aesthetic, he also noted an association between "neurasthenic sensitivity to odors" and the loss of sexual vigor. Even
more specifically, Ellis pointed out that "olfactory attractions are especially
marked" in inverts (75). This is confirmed in chapter 9 by a series of des Esseintes's actual sexual experimentations—unlike the sensually suggestive but
asexual sensory overindulgences of the other chapters. In his stereotyped fashion, des Esseintes follows a pathway to increasingly artificial, "unnatural" sub-
stitutions. In the case of sex, the nadir is sexual inversion and the three sexual
reminiscences are evoked by the taste and smell of candies. The progression of
love affairs in chapter 9—from the American circus performer, to the female
ventriloquist, and finally to an effeminate young man—is representative of a
chronic descent into sexual "degeneration" and loss of virility. As we saw in the
previous chapter, this was a matter of great concern in France at the time.[51]
This descent and fetishization is also evident in the very first liaison with the
American acrobat, Miss Urania. The latent homosexual nature of this affair is
suggested by her name, since *uranism*, as discussed earlier, was a common term
for sexual inversion. Des Esseintes's infatuation with Miss Urania grows as he
increasingly imagines that this athletic trapeze artist is a man, and that he is correspondingly being feminized. When he finally arranges for a rendezvous, he is
totally disappointed by her *lack* of the "stupid bestiality of a carnival wrestler,"
about which he had fantasized (146). His most satisfactory love affair is with a

pale, effeminate schoolboy he encounters by chance in the street. It seems logical to him that this most "unnatural" of loves should be the natural one for him, predisposed to it as he is through a sodomitic ancestor and a religious training that had "stirred up the illegitimate ideal of voluptuousness; libertine and mystical obsessions confusedly haunted his brain twisted by a stubborn desire to escape the vulgarities of the world, to ruin himself, far from venerable practices" (151). Effeminacy, inversion, and pederasty become the natural outcome of degeneracy and a revolt against the commonplace. Huysmans later described his hero as too effeminate and degenerate even to be a proper sodomite. He admitted in a letter to Marc-André Raffalovich: "Des Esseintes is an exceptional being, in that vice [sodomy], as in the others; he is, in sum, an almost unlikely sodomite given his constitution."[52]

*A Rebours* and its hero were thus the epitome of fin-de-siècle decadence and all its sensual perversities.[53] Huysmans's literary imagination as well as his person were equally accused of participating in and fomenting the fetishistic aesthetic of the period. In Dr. Nordau's cultural and literary diagnosis of the social ills of *entartente Kunst* (degenerate art), he made little distinction between fiction and reality or des Esseintes and Huysmans. The fictional character was diagnosed as seriously as a "real" patient and, likewise, Huysmans's stories were taken as symptoms of the authorial pathology of the *olfactif. Là-Bas* (a novel of 1891) "furnishes Mr. Huysmans the occasion to wallow and snort in the most atrocious filth with a porcine satisfaction," Nordau exclaimed (2:119). Even Huysmans's contemporary biographer perpetuates the aura of Huysmans as an olfactory fetishist, one who "loved sniffing those female bodies [of prostitutes] . . . [and ] needed odors, gestures, novel situations to reanimate him, otherwise a woman alone provoked no feeling" (Vircondelet 1990, 65). Was Huysmans the novelist as much of an impotent fetishist as his hero des Esseintes? Was Huysmans a novelist and, eventually, a celibate Benedictine monk precisely *because* he was a fetishist? This tradeoff between "normal" sexual potency and literary potency had been hypothesized by Binet when he explained that the coital impotence of the fetishist was replaced by "imaginative work" and "erotic rumination."

If the essence of fetishism lay in secret, imaginative work rather than overt acts, it demanded new hermeneutic or interpretative work on the part of doctors if they were to successfully unmask and diagnose the *érotisme* of a growing number of people whose "antisocial" behavior was suspected of having perverse erotic roots. So, although we now find Max Nordau's work to be literary interpretation rather than medical diagnosis, his "pathophilology" was not so different from the diagnostic approaches of his medical colleagues. Confronting the seeming proliferation of sexual perverts, physicians debated the best means of understanding and classifying these manifestations of erotic behaviors and, more elusively, erotic pleasures. While Binet had proposed the primitive fetishistic cult as a model for unmasking all perverse practices, other medical writers insisted that perversions of fantasy were variations of sadism or masochism.

## S & M and the Hermeneutics of Desire

With my knees bent, dressed in the pink silk bloomers I bought much earlier, I placed a Vaseline lubricated billiard ball in my anus. I had taken care to place a little piece of old linen beneath so as not to soil my bloomers. Now, while holding the ball with my left hand, I pushed on it as if to *swallow it with my anus*. With my right hand I held my bloomers. At that moment I was only half erect. Once the ball is in my anus, the preparatory work is over; the real joy is about to begin. While masturbating with my right hand, I struggled to *pass the ball*. When I had managed that, I shoved it back in with the left hand, repeating this six, eight, ten, twelve times. . . .

I have described the facts. Now these are my sensations during the act. They were extremely complex and much less clear than during my masturbations of earlier years. I always experienced a double pleasure: 1st. In part, the entrance and exit of the billiard ball in my anus gave me the sensation of a virile member accomplishing the same work of entering and exiting, and, in my imagination, I attached that virile member to the body and the face of young men 20 to 25 years old that I had encountered recently and who had most charmed me by their face, their dress, their male appearance and *their patent leather boots*.

Their images appeared successively, four, five, six in number, but I was careful to reserve one of the most seductive to finish my thrust, at the moment of ejaculation. 2nd. *It seemed that these young men with patent leather boots engaged in pederasty with me and were masturbating me at the same time.* (Garnier 1895, 398–99)

These exquisitely detailed and candidly self-reflective confessions by Louis X——, like the Italian invert's "novel," clearly betray the author's tremendous pleasure in the very act of relating them. Unlike the Italian, Louis was not writing independently and freely but was compelled to do so in his medicolegal defense. A twenty-six-year-old "man of letters" from a good family, Louis was arrested on charges of "outrages to public decency" for masturbating openly in the Vincennes Park. He underwent mental evaluation by

Drs. Legras and Paul-Emile Garnier of the Special Infirmary of the Police Prefecture of Paris. Garnier was a student and colleague of Magnan, Lasègue, and Legrand du Saulle, and in 1886 became physician-in-chief of the Special Infirmary and one of the leaders in forensic medicine.[54] As we might predict, the doctors discovered that the family medical history was rich in degenerate disorders, particularly on the more dangerous maternal side (including suicide, alcoholism, convulsions, and eccentricity). Louis was, nevertheless, highly intelligent and educated; he even had a law degree. But he really yearned to be an author. He bore all the marks of the dandy: he was tall, thin and well-dressed, wore a monocle, had an effeminate voice, literary pretensions, and manicured, feminine hands. "The nails," the doctors noted, "are the object of quite a particular cult and maintained at an extraordinary length that would be incompatible with any manual labor" (394). Most significant for diagnostic purposes was that he wore brilliantly shiny, patent leather shoes.

His lengthy memoir-confession painted the classic picture of the onanist-invert. He had been a lonely, sad, effeminate youth who had begun solitary and mutual masturbation at age thirteen. From that time forth, he could only accomplish the "voluptuous spasm" by contemplating patent leather shoes—"a contemplation towards which he was instinctively impelled even as a child" (395). After reading of "sexual aberrations" in the Greek classics at the age of twenty-two, he developed "vague desires for passive pederasty" (396). However, his first ideal was to meet an educated, sensitive young man with whom to talk of literature, exchange caresses, and masturbate. His early literary efforts "enjoyed a complete lack of success" (397). As his sodomitic desires and patent leather shoe fetishism evolved, the doctors noted, "there began an uninterrupted succession of incidents in which the culture of letters and a morbid search for the strangest ideal marched side by side" (397).

As Louis's confessions revealed, he developed elaborate rituals for satisfying in his body and through his imagination his desires for sodomy with particular young men with patent leather boots. To use Rousseau's phrase, Louis could enlist these young men and put them to use in his own fashion in carefully choreographed erotic performances. In parallel with these bedroom rituals, he began inscribing a stereotyped graffito with "absolute regularity" in the public urinals of the Vincennes Park: "The phrase began thus: *I lend my ass to handsome men who have patent leather shoes*' and ended with repugnant promises" (400). As he wrote these words, Louis would stare at his patent leather boots and enjoy an erection. He had finally acquired these boots after years of resisting the temptation. He devoted himself to their care and the mere glint off their brilliant surface excited him to a voluptuous spasm. Their odor was also highly exciting: "He sniffs them; their perfume is highly agreeable" (402). Their feel "procure[d] exquisite sensations" as well, and he would squeeze them between his thighs, "taking care to modulate his ardor, as if he were afraid to harm them" (402). Garnier and Legras reported that Louis X— was involved in a "relationship with his boots" and "traces the following sketch, whose obscenity, however revolting in itself, must not let us forget that we are in the presence of a pathological obsession":

> I put on my pink bloomers and my boots. I climb on two chairs, my legs spread, and I slightly open the door of my mirrored armoir to see myself from behind thanks to the reflection in the mantle mirror. While masturbating myself, I obstinately maintain my gaze on my buttocks, my thighs and above all my boots. At that moment I would like to be able to make love to myself, to abandon myself to caresses all over my body, whose image I see in the mirror. The sight of my boots excites me enough that, usually, I can dispense with the introduction of the billiard ball in my anus. My goal is to project the jet of sperm into the opening of one of the two boots, and when I manage that, it is the paroxysm of pleasure. Other times, at the point of ejaculation, I rub my buttocks, my thighs, my anus with one of my boots while I tenaciously contemplate the light reflected off the other boot. . . . This operation, in the excessive pleasure it procures, gives me a sensation of triumph, of victory, when the seminal liqueur strikes my boots. (402–3)

One day Louis spots a handsome young bicyclist who seems to glance at Louis's patent leather boots. "No further doubt, [the bicyclist] desires him as much as he himself yearns for his caresses: in a paroxysm of excitement he exhibits his genitals" (403). What disappointment when the young man turns away with indifference, and what a shock when Louis finds himself arrested for public indecency.

Garnier and Legras confronted an increasingly common medicolegal dilemma. They noted that it was incontestable that this defendant's *conduct* argued against him, but "must one consider him a vulgar sodomist unworthy of pity"? (404). No, they were of a different opinion, for they felt it their medical duty to "analyze what is found in reality under such appearances" (404). In digging under Louis X——'s overt, public, criminal behavior, by exploring his imaginative practices and their history, Garnier and Legras concluded that he suffered from "hereditary mental degeneration with sexual inversion, obsessions, and very active morbid impulses" (405). The court followed the doctors' recommendations by dismissing the criminal case against Louis X—— and instead placing him in a mental asylum.

Aside from the technical issues involved in this particular case, Garnier reproduced the entire medicolegal evaluation in the *Annals of Public Hygiene* in order to demonstrate that inversion and fetishism were innate, not acquired by accidental mental association as Binet had proposed. Garnier emphasized that even the patient's attraction to shiny boots was "instinctive." Furthermore, Binet's theory considered inversion itself as a variety of fetishism: the delusional devotion to men as fetishes and substitutes for women. This fetish theory could not account for Louis's case of *homosexual* fetishism—except as double fetishism. Binet's theory also suggested the continuity between "normal" and pathological fetishism, if only in their psychological mechanisms. Garnier, on the other hand, made it clear that homosexuality was a distinct and most serious form of degenerate sexual perversion. However irrational the erotic tastes of the heterosexual perverts, at least they did not confuse genders Garnier explained: "This total, teratological error is the lot of the *invert*" (385). The diverse sexual perversions were matters of teratology (that is, birth defects), not acquired psychological deviation.

Binet had emphasized the role of masturbation in firmly implanting fetishism in rituals of hypersexual dynamogenization. Garnier instead argued that true perverts engaged in a delusional form of fetishism and sterile fantasy. Louis X—— was no "vulgar masturbator" who utilized material procedures and some erotic mental representations to provoke an orgasm, Garnier explained (404). X——'s obsession with patent leather boots degenerated to such a point that he "engaged in sexual relations with them." His exalted imagination so anthropomorphized his patent leather boots into his "homosexual ideal" that he feared hurting them by squeezing them too much (406). X—— was rather like Esquirol's platonic, frigid erotomaniac obsessed with an ideal love. The fetish was not a supplement to coitus, but fully satisfied any coital needs through a "psychic onanism, if we may call it thus, a psychic onanism which only doubles and supports the real or material onanism to which all these deviants abandon themselves with passion" (351).

His literary pretensions and his graffiti practices were an integral part of this psychic eroticism: "pederasty, onanism, and literature constitute a *trilogy* without which X—— cannot see complete happiness!" (405). Garnier concluded that, contrary to what had previously been thought, "the fetishist, far from being hypersexual from the point of view of venereal pleasures, is rather an insufficient person which nothing usually attracts to the union of the sexes. Genitally, he sins by absence rather than excess" (351). Therefore Garnier reserved the designation of "imaginatives" or "psychics" for those who were the most disinterested in coitus (whether homo- or heterosexual) and the most genitally "insufficient."

Another classic case of the imaginative sexual pervert was that of Auguste C——, the white-apron fetishist first described by Charcot and Magnan (1882, 317). Garnier presented the case to the Society of Forensic Medicine of Paris in March 1887 after C—— was arrested for stealing a white *matinée* (morning negligee) which, in a state of drunkenness, he had mistaken for the "apron of his dreams" (Garnier 1887, 275). Despite several intervening arrests, three stays at the Sainte-Anne Asylum, and an internment at the police infirmary in 1885, C—— had not been able to restrain his obsession with aprons. A police search of C——'s apartment revealed a large collection of sperm-soiled aprons. The forty-three-year-old day-laborer was a man "upon whom a morbid heredity weighs heavily": he had a drunken father, an insane uncle, a "mentally feeble" brother, and a nervous, melancholic mother and sister (269). Garnier reclassified C—— as an "impulsive onanist": a degenerate who experiences genital excitement simply and almost exclusively by sight or mere mental representation of a certain object (268).

> At night he dreams of white aprons; during the day he thinks of them unceasingly. If he does not manage to procure the sight or the possession of the desired object, at the right moment, he experiences a profound malaise; he is depressed, but then he calls his imagination to the rescue. He concentrates, closes his eyes and before him floats the white apron, just as it appeared the first time. . . . The liveliness of this mental representation is great enough to provoke, without the aid of masturbatory maneuvers, an erection and even succeeds in ejaculation. (271–72)

This genital hyperesthesia and the potency of the imagination over actual sexual potency was a critical element in the pathology of "sexual perversions" as far as Garnier was concerned.[55] He focused attention on a dominant theme in fin-de-siècle medicine and society that we have noted before: male impotence or asexuality and its concomitant effects, infertility and depopulation.

The same core anxiety emerged in the case of V——, a young book clerk and ex-seminarian with an "obsessive appetite" for silk who, Garnier explained, in every way shared the timidity, melancholia, solitariness, and religiosity of C—— (the apron fetishist). Arrested for rubbing against ladies in silk dresses, V—— had written in his confession, "I have to admit that a woman only pleases me for the silk that covers her" (Garnier 1893, 463). He had just as much pleasure with a silk dress alone. Like other impulsive onanists, Garnier explained, V—— could experience orgasm merely by imagining the beloved material, but was otherwise impotent with women. Garnier's initial classification system of sexual perversions, therefore, presented a spectrum of growing sexual inadequacy (relative to reproduction) from the psychic onanism of the heterosexual fetishist to the total *horror feminæ* of the invert. Along this spectrum of perversity, aside from the inescapable degenerate inheritance, the imagination was the major aggravator. Because of his vantage point in the police prefecture, Garnier mainly came in contact with people detained for theft, violent crimes, rape, or public indecency. As first suggested in his book on *Apparent and Hidden Sexual Anomalies* (1889), he increasingly suspected that some perverse erotic element lay at the root of many apparently unmotivated crimes (just as Binet had believed that fetishism was the cause of inappropriate marriages). In particular, Garnier theorized that sadism (or, as he coined it in 1900, "sadi-fetishism") was the paradigmatic perversity.

Medical discussions of sadism and masochism per se had sprung up only in the last decade of the nineteenth century. As noted earlier, Binet had included an extensive analysis of Rousseau's "voluptuousness in pain" and his attraction to punitive women. But Binet had diagnosed Rousseau's sexual perversion as a form of "psychic fetishism": an attraction to a tyrannical character trait. During the November 28, 1888 session of the Juridical Society of Moscow, Dimitry Stefanowsky, the substitute Attorney General of Cracow, named this condition *passivism* and its pendant *tyrannism*. Utilizing Rousseau's case, Stefanowsky explained passivism as the "complete and absolute abdication of one person's will in favor of another's, with an erotic aim"; the male passivist and female tyrannist formed a couple, sharing the voluptuousness of the martyr and the executioner (1892a, 294). In an attempt to theorize passivism as the master perversity, he also suggested that fetishists and inverts who found pleasure in odors, bodily secretions, oral sex, or sodomy were all really passivists seeking humiliation (1892a, 295; 1894, 742).[56]

The terms *sadism* and *masochism* were popularized by Krafft-Ebing in a publication of 1890 where he acknowledged that fiction writers had been the first to examine the voluptuousness of cruelty. He therefore used terms based on the names of two authors: the Marquis de Sade and Leopold von Sacher-Masoch.[57] In his hugely popular catalogue of perversities, *Psychopathia Sexualis,* Krafft-Ebing categorically rejected Binet's chance association theory of the genesis of pathological fetishism. Instead, he viewed sadism, masochism, and fetishism as congenital psychopathic conditions often exacerbated by sexual and masturbatory "excess" in youth (1895, 122).[58] He did, however, credit Binet for explaining the "physiological" fetishism that bonded happy, monogamous couples (23). Just as fetishism had been the model perversion for Binet, sadism and masochism were Krafft-Ebing's paradigmatic perversions. He explained sadism as the exaggeration of natural male aggressiveness, especially in the conquest of females. Correspondingly, masochism was the pathological extreme of "natural" female passivity and submissiveness (179). Male sadism might therefore be atavistic (83 n.1), while male masochism (the only type he knew of in 1895) represented "a morbid overgrowth of the female psyche" in men (183). There was therefore an undercurrent of sexual inversion in the male masochist.

Garnier presented a rather skewed population in his 1900 article on sadi-fetishishism; these were not just the petty thieves and exhibitionists who shamefully admitted their erotic obsession, these were more serious, violent criminals who refused to admit a sexual motivation for their often "bizarre" and cruel activities. A certain analytic flair—a suspicion of eroticism—was necessary on the part of the medical expert to extract a confession and explain the "true" erotic nature of the crimes.

"Voluptuousness in cruelty," Garnier recognized, had been frequently described in literature (1900a, 97), particularly Sade's novels. In the 1880s the works of Sade, which had circulated in a limited way underground, enjoyed renewed popularity and public discussion. Decadent artists especially prized Sade's stories for their elitist rebellion against conventional manners and, of course, for their sensual excesses. These resonated with the spirit of the times; one writer went so far as to exclaim, "We are all more or less sadists!" It was typical of periods of decadence, he continued, and of "all periods whose nervous systems are worn out and overwrought."[59] The usage of *sadism* in the French press was so common that when Krafft-Ebing first used the term in medicine he observed that it was already a *"mot courant"* in French literature (1895, 79 n.1). A central text of Decadent sadism was Huysmans's *Là-Bas* (1891), a novelistic (albeit rather autobiographical) account of a writer's descent into the world of demonism as he prepares a history of Gilles de Rais, the infamous French military office executed in 1440 for murdering and sodomizing hundreds of children.[60] The case had been cited in the medical discussions of Sergeant Bertrand's necrophilia, but by the end of the century it was regularly classified as an example of sadism. Huysmans's account draws a parallel between the mystical sensuality of Gilles de Rais and that of Joan of Arc, alongside whom de Rais fought in 1427. An even more terrifying vision of the voluptuousness of cruelty was painted by Octave Mirbeau in *Le Jardin des supplices* [The garden of tortures] (1899), where the heroine revels hysterically in Oriental tortures. Nordau, as we have already seen, condemned decadent artists' fascination with sadism (2:119).

Garnier believed that such destructive and angry voluptuousness was a natural element of the animalistic sexual instinct, but it became pathological when the "spectacle of inflicted pain" was required for orgasm (1900a, 98). As with all sexual perversions, the medicolegal question was the determination of responsibility. Garnier deemed that Sade was certainly abnormal but not sick: he was not the least bit contrite and was therefore fully responsible for his sexual crimes. The "true" sadist, like the invert, was the slave of a degenerate condition producing impulsive obsessions that the sadist loathed but could not resist. Garnier attempted to demonstrate that sadism and fetishism were closely tied together, not because they shared the same psychological origins (as Binet had claimed), but because the sadist usually focused his erotic cruelty on a particular body part. Flagellators, such as the one described by Régis in 1899, usually were simultaneously buttock fetishists (Garnier 1900a, 108). The same was true of the *piqueur de filles*, who periodically terrorized neighborhoods by stabbing women in the buttocks with a penknife or scissors. Further distilling the sexual perversions, Garnier proposed that patients/criminals who primarily appeared to be fetishists of other body elements (such as hair braids or pubic hair) were actually sadists, since their ultimate pleasure was in cutting or biting off the fetish. Sadism was also intertwined with object fetishism, Garnier proposed, since the true erotic pleasure was in cutting, burning, or shredding fetishized silk, handkerchiefs, or aprons (236–37).

Sadi-fetishism should also be suspected in cases of senseless, violent crimes, Garnier suggested. For example, François Maire had captured the public attention in 1898 for having cut off the ear lobes of a fifteen-year-old boy. Maire was a fairly well-educated man who fashioned himself as a "lecturer in natural sciences" but actually exercised the profession of enameler. Associates testified that he was eccentric and had a "monomania for earlobes." He repeatedly tried to convince his young coworkers to pierce their ears to prevent facial pimples, and he regularly accosted boys in parks with the same proposition while manipulating their earlobes. Despite much evidence of his guilt, Maire obstinately proclaimed his innocence. In his "Discourse on the Detailed Summary of My Life," an autobiography written while in detention, he admitted that he recommended ear-piercing for scientific reasons and had even invented an instrument for doing this efficiently, but this did not mean that he was interested in cutting ear lobes (Garner 1900a, 217).

The examining doctors repeatedly urged him to confess the erotic nature of his crime, but he insisted on his complete innocence, writing that *"he will never reveal his secret,* since no one has the right to penetrate into the mystery of his consciousness and that no one has the right to interrogate his soul" (216). Garnier concluded that in the absence of a candid confession, Maire's strange act could be explained only as a result of either sadi-fetishism or delusional "surgical dilettantism" (218). Lacking any clear evidence of an erotic obsession, the court judged Maire responsible for his acts and condemned him to two years in prison.

When examining bizarre, violent criminals such as Maire, Jack-the-Ripper, or Vacher L'Éventreur (a French "ripper" case that preoccupied the country in 1899), Garnier suggested a sadi-fetishistic motive be carefully sought.[61] Garnier also resurrected the case of Sergeant Bertrand as an extreme example of sadi-fetishism. The medicolegal expert's duty in such cases was to determine whether the defendant suffered from degenerate pathology and deserved medical treatment rather than criminal punishment (246). Garnier complained that this task was complicated by the enormous popular fascination with such cases: "The public opinion, overexcited by the horror of the details, revealed far too willingly by the press, creates such a current of indignant reprobation and vengeful wrath that the emotion is even felt by those who are entrusted with the delicate mission of judging, as impassive observers, free of the passion of the mob, with science as sole guide" (244). The suspicion of erotism was clearly not just the privilege of the medical expert.

With a new palette of perversities and erotic psychologies to choose from, the public, as well as the medical profession, was urged to uncover the "true" erotic motive of almost any peculiar, socially reprovable or criminal behavior. The master perversity might be fetishism, passivism, or sadism (as Binet, Stefanowsky, and Garnier proposed respectively), but with any of these possibilities, the erotic substitution of the pervert was mirrored by the hermeneutic substitution of the analysts who, claiming to "penetrate the mystery of consciousness," read a hidden erotic master narrative in a whole variety of texts and confessions. It became increasingly necessary to interpret patients' stories to get beyond the superficial level of behaviors to the underlying erotic mechanisms. Or, as Charcot reportedly advised, "Il faut chercher la chose génitale" (one has to look for the genital motives). The realm of the imagination—of erotic dreams, fantasies, and pleasures—revealed more of a subject's "true" sexual nature than his or her actions, whether overtly sexual or not.

## Normal Love and Other Erotic Fictions

Even as the last decade of the nineteenth century witnessed the birth of sexology and the invention of new "perversities," the old categories of onanism, erotomania, and inversion remained ever present. As we have seen in this chapter, however, their significance and even their meaning underwent important reevaluations as they were associated with new phenomena such as fetishism, sadism, and masochism. While doctors of the time did not fail to note the masturbatory history of a patient, their interest had thoroughly shifted from the morbidity of the mechanical act of seminal waste to the psychic effects of solitary "erotic rumination" over sexual narratives. As they further explored the subterranean workings of the erotic imagination and vastly expanded the range of its "perverse" manifestations, doctors edged closer to the inevitable question posed by one psychologist: Is love a pathological state? (Danville 1893). In a book review of Emile Laurent's work on the pathology of love (1891), the prominent sociologist and criminologist Gabriel Tarde declared:

> Morbid love! But, perhaps one will ask, is there any love that isn't an illness? Is not love always a fever that alters the pulse, disturbs or accelerates respiration, troubles the mind? It blinds us to the defects of the loved object and highlights its imaginary beauties; and by this double hallucination, negative and positive, through this complex delirium of the senses and the brain, pushes us to despair, to ruin, to crime, to death. However normal it might be . . . it is but a voracious hunger for live human flesh, a form of anthropophagy that develops along with civilization; and its grip halts all work, extinguishes all curiosity, stifles all noble passion, nourishes a monstrous mutual egoism. The lover, like the sick person, is necessarily lazy, uninquisitive, inactive, indifferent to anything but his illness; and isn't it the worst of diseases, the one that fears nothing more than its own cure? (Tarde 1891, 585)

So *all* lovers were obsessive, irrational, bestial necrophiles like Sergeant Bertrand? No—Tarde was being facetious. He believed that Laurent's book on fetishism and sexual perversity amply demonstrated the "distance that separates ordinary love from its extraordinary aberrations" (586). The territory between these ideal extremes was, however, vast and troublesome, obliging Tarde to be on the defensive. He was willing to include class-transgressive marriages and the love of prostitutes in the realm of the pathological, but the tragic love of Romeo and Juliet had to be salvaged as normal. Normal and pathological love had to be distinguishable by nature and not just degree. Tarde rejected Laurent's suggestion that normal love was characterized by harmonious physical and moral attractions between lovers. That would force one to accept as normal the lascivious but consensual perversities of assassins and their mistresses (588). Tarde concluded that a distinction based on social utility was necessary. "Truly normal love (thereby very rare, I admit, at least in the state of perfect *normality*) is that through which are pursued jointly not only the vital ends of generation and the purity of races, but also the social goals of patriotic greatness, family preservation, and the purity of manners" (589). Previously, "normal" love could be presumed to be the dominant, "natural" variety. By the end of the nineteenth century, "perfectly normal" love appeared to be a rarity instead of the norm. In Tarde's estimation, it was an uncommon sentiment that enriched the family and the nation.

Other psychologists described love as the satisfaction of physiological or evolutionary imperatives, and a primeval chemotaxic drive: the attraction of sperm for ova (Delboeuf 1891). Tarde described the object of normal love as socially uniform, whereas "morbid love is provoked by the most diverse objects" (1891, 590). Similarly, Danville (1893) explained that the normal love instinct was aimed indifferently to a large class of appropriate and interchangeable mates, while pathological, "passional love" was specialized to an individual and was obsessive, neurotic, and degenerate. He relied on Pierre Janet's description of passional love as a viral infection that only afflicted a man if he was weak, depressed, or mentally ill (1889, 436). In order to preserve the "normality" of love in the face of proliferating evidence of its antisocial "deviations," it was stripped of its passion, excitement, individuality, and imaginativeness—all of which became symptoms of love's pathology.

What was the cure for the epidemic of "morbid love" produced by the multiplication of modern incitements to desires that went unsatisfied? Tarde suggested that if religious faith could no longer offer salvation, then the only thing that could "tear away the crowd from the cult of pleasure" was the consolation of maternity and paternity: "Because there is no other manner of surviving than by being reborn in one's children, men should ceaselessly multiply their number, out of self-interest as much as patriotism" (595).

Tarde's expression of depopulation anxieties is typical for the French fin de siècle,[62] but also uncannily echoes the contemporary American rhetoric of "family values." Like the late-nineteenth-century defense of "normal love," the late twentieth-century phantasm of family values has been so loaded with social, patriotic, racial, religious, and economic demands that few, if any, of its champions actually exemplify it. The ideological utopian fiction of "family values" enshrines cultural conformity and rationalist social utility as the only form of "normality" that will protect the nation against the decay and decadence of individualist, irrational, and immoral "cults of pleasure."

The public had no interest in such "pathological passion," Tarde claimed, only the "normal type of love. . . . No erotic aberration has inspired a novel, nor a painting, nor a theatrical work, nor even a comedy" (592). This was clearly a misrepresentation of popular cultural tastes at the time. Even if writers such as Zola, Mirbeau, and Dubarry had not been writing passionally perverse novels, the public could (and did) turn to medical texts for tales of the erotic imagination. In turn, these medical erotic narratives were influenced by broader social interests and concerns: consumer culture, anticlericalism, industrialization, depopulation, the conflict between elitism and democracy, the weakening of traditional family structures, and even novelistic styles.

The interdependence between physicians and novelists in the exploration of erotic narratives is particularly remarkable. Each borrowed material from the other as they interpreted the hidden world of the erotic imagination. Doctors had once simply reported patients' stories and usually taken them at face value. By the end of the nineteenth century, sexologists were scrutinizing these confessions not only to classify sexuality but to understand the psychic mechanisms of erotic pleasure. Sexual practices that first seemed singular and insane were now being interpreted as phenomena of more generalizable psychologies: of masculinity, femininity, love, passion, consumerism, religiosity, artistic creativity, collectionism, and so on. As doctors and novelists charted new erotic territory, the boundaries between normal eros and pathological erotism became ever more unclear.

All it took to reveal the perverse underside of the normal was a careful reading of either patient narratives or literary narratives. In fact, a characteristic of the medical texts we have been examining is their constant re-reading and reinterpretation of erotic narratives. Rousseau's *Confessions* is the best example of this. Nineteenth century doctors sequentially diagnosed Rousseau with almost every sexual perversion save necrophilia. Similarly, many other stories resurfaced from one medical article to another—for example, those of Sergeant Bertrand, the shepherd who divided his penis, the nightcap fetishist, and the white-apron fetishist. As these stories were collected and circulated from doctor to doctor, they took on new color and significance with each re-reading and retelling.[63] The "collectionomania" and analytic "erotic rumination" of the nineteenth-century physicians themselves was clearly quite productive of new scientific theories of sexuality.

Doctors' scientific, erotic rumination was intimately tied to their historical rumination. In fabricating theories of erotism, doctors wove and rewove a network of histories: the patient's "degenerate" family history, the history of religion, phylogenesis and transformism, the history of the human race, the narrative of atavism. In addition to being blamed for all varieties of perverse literary and artistic productions, the erotic imagination was also blamed for perverse historical productions. Take, for example, the "Archives of Spanking": a "Sadian's" extensive documentation of whipping and spanking throughout history, collected for his personal erotic rumination (Régis 1899). Doctors' own "archives of erotism" swelled through their own labors as physicians urged their subjects to reveal all. The new perverts filled thousands of pages of medical books and records with true erotic confessions, and in the process crystallized new sexual identities and histories for themselves. These autobiographical productions informed and, increasingly, relied on medical terms, metanarratives, and histories. Although stigmatized as deviant, pathological, and insane, perverts often found solace in this medicalization and even found pleasure and self-affirmation in these new nosological formations. Furthermore, the medical reach was so broad and its cultural currency so great that erotism in general took on the colors of perverse pleasure. Finally, we cannot overlook the element of pleasure in doctors' scientific production as they pored over their archives of erotism. Nor can I deny feeling a similar element of pleasure as I have ruminated over the same archives during the writing of this book, which, like the many other scholarly works on sexuality, represents just one bloom in the historical efflorescence of erotic literature. Twentieth-century "perverts"—an ever growing and apparently dominant population—are finding new, nonmedical outlets for the pleasurable confession of erotic imaginings, obeying the modernist impulse to make sex speak in all possible contexts, from analysts' couches to television studios to cyberspace.

# CONCLUSION

# *From the Talking Sex to Sex Talk*

**O**ne day Mangogul, the Sultan of the Congo, was royally bored with his life and his favorite consort, Mirzoza. Having exhausted her store of scandalous tales, Mirzoza suggests that fresh stories of the court's gallant adventures would certainly entertain His Highness. Since ladies would never freely volunteer such revelations, Mirzoza wisely suggests that the court genie, Cucufa, be consulted. "I want a very simple thing," Mangogul tells Cucufa, "to procure some pleasure at the expense of the women of my court." After some initial resistance, Cucufa accedes to his sultan's wishes and presents Mangogul a marvelous ring. If the monarch directs it at any woman, she will recount her intrigues in a loud, clear voice. They will not speak through their mouth, Cucufa warns, but "through the most frank organ in them, and the most knowledgeable of the things you wish to know: their jewels." Armed with this powerful instrument for confession, Mangogul embarks on a thorough investigation of the venality, hypocrisy, treachery, and virtuousness of his court and empire. As candid, new voices emerge from under ladies' skirts, women and men alike are struck with terror and shame.[1]

*The Indiscreet Jewels* (1748) is Diderot's only known licentious tale. Like similar contemporaneous works, the story is set in an exotic, oriental locale that served as a cover for both libertinism and political censure.[2] Some literary scholars have argued that the work is a roman à clef satirizing the court of Louis XV, much as the later *Zoloë and Her Two Acolytes* (attributed to Sade) ridiculed Napoleon's circle, and Joe Klein's anonymously published *Primary Colors* makes fun of the 1992 Clinton campaign.[3] Sultan Mangogul is Louis himself, who delighted in the matinal recounting of the court's scandal chronicles gathered by police spies. As further inducement to read the novel as disguised truth, Diderot repeatedly identifies its scribe as an African historian extremely conscientious of his duty to posterity.

Whether or not elements in the novel correspond to real people and events in Louis XV's court, Diderot uses this fantastical conceit to satirize the manners, ideologies, and institutions of his time. Academies of science, medicine, and barber-surgery, as well as the worlds of theater, music, and philosophy are all scrutinized in this voyeuristic narrative of sexual policing. As the true sex lives of aristocrats, nuns, courtesans, and artists are exposed by *le sexe* (the genitals), so are the intimate connections between social institutions and sexual affairs. The political crisis instigated by these revelations stimulates the attention of the learned societies which frantically try to silence the chatty labia.

After the first jewel speaks, one of the listeners immediately interprets the phenomenon medically as a product of "hysterical vapors" (15). Soon the Academy of Sciences of Banza dedicates itself to investigating the marvel. The historian-narrator tells us that "the chatter of jewels produced an infinity of excellent works; and the important subject swelled the bulletins of the academies with many memoirs that can be considered the finest efforts of the human intellect" (23). Diderot's naughty wit pokes fun at the language and manners of savants as well as their doctrinaire *esprit de système*. In so doing, he sides with *philosophe* friends and collaborators, such as Condillac, in condemning Cartesianism and Newtonianism. Whichever their philosophical affiliation, the savants agree that it must be a natural, material phenomenon.

In a claim that Tardieu echoes a century later, Doctor Orcotome boasts to having personally witnessed many jewels "in the paroxysm," and declares that female genitalia are like vocal cords (25). They had always spoken, but in such a low voice that even their owners had not heard them. It was not surprising that they were now speaking more loudly, Orcotome explains, "in these days when we have pushed freedom of conversation to the point that we can speak of the most intimate matters without impropriety or indiscretion" (27). Eventually they would all speak, he predicts: "If they remain silent, it is because they have nothing to say, or that they are deformed, or they lack the ideas or the terms" (27).

Oddly enough, it seems that Orcotome's prediction has proven correct. Throughout the previous chapters we turned the magical ring of historical analysis on diverse cultural documents to extract a growing volume and variety of talking sexes since the mid-eighteenth century. Like modern day equivalents of Orcotome and the academicians of Banza, we have been the inquisitive and perplexed auditors of a parade of talking sexes from the first confessions of shameful onanists to the purple prose of elite inverts and the scientific sex talk of medical experts. But are the indiscreet jewels of Diderot's time telling us the same kinds of stories as the patent leather boot fetishist of the late nineteenth century? Clearly not. *Un sexe qui parle* (a talking sex) is quite different from talking sex.[4]

The genital confessions recorded by the fictional African historian focus on acts of copulation and on the identity and genital prowess of those men, women, or animals visiting the speaker's jewel. Like other libertine literature of its time, *The Indiscreet Jewels* seems cold and ironically aloof in tone. These texts are more concerned with political satire and social commentary than with sensual arousal, or at least it appears that way to today's readers.[5] Even Sade's works seem like conventional picaresque tales interrupted by brief sexual tableaux and lengthy philosophical disquisitions.[6] Nevertheless, these clearly were popular texts and were—to use Rousseau's coy phrase—"dangerous books" read with "one hand." In them, mechanical acts and visual titillation monopolized sexual arousal.

Similarly, early medical writers on onanism worried about the mechanics of humoral loss and nervous exhaustion. Later physicians, however, were more concerned with the psychology of sexual excitement. Medical preoccupation with the erotic imagination mounted throughout the nineteenth century, incorporating (rather than displacing) material issues such as somatic physiology or hereditary degeneration. Patients' first confessions (like those of the indiscreet jewels) were unwillingly extracted from them in medicolegal inquisitions. But as time went on, they increasingly explored their sensations, passions, and fantasies of their own accord. Ironically, it was in the ostensibly cold and un-friendly setting of the medical examination room that people began to develop "the ideas and the terms" for the erotic.

By the end of the century, some "perverts" (like the Italian invert) were exploiting the medical press not only to learn about their "disorder," but also to expose their erotic inner life. These growing refinements of erotism touched on so many aspects of sexual arousal that the only sexuality *not* labeled "perverse" was conjugal reproductive copulation.[7] The transition from the mechanics to the erotics of sex is epitomized by the confession of the patent leather

boot fetishist. Recall that after his elaborate description of his sexual perfor-
mance with billiard balls, silk bloomers, and the boots, he tells us, "I have just
described the facts. Now, here are my sensations during the act. They were very
complex and much less clear than during my masturbations of preceding
years" (Garnier 1895, 398).

Medical and cultural representations of sexuality had also become much
more complex, no longer merely depicting copulation and seminal loss as in
the eighteenth-century.[8] On the one hand, *The Indiscreet Jewels* and other Enlightenment political pornography used sex (including "unnatural" sex) to satirize powerful political institutions. By contrast, the evolving medical and fictional literature of the erotic implicated all classes, ages, and sexes in a wide
network of meanings of self and society. Furthermore, the erotic imagination
was entangled in a variety of social anxieties: political instability, national enfeeblement, colonial unrest, European racial rivalries, depopulation, degeneration, decadence, women's enfranchisement.

Foucault suggests that the "truth of the sex" has been a major (perhaps *the*
major) development of modernity (1976, 92–93). But the nature of that truth,
the reasons for its extraction, and the aims for its confession have varied enormously over the past three centuries. Diderot's talking sex had a mind of its
own: its clear, truthful voice was distinct from the civilized, rational speech of
the "superior mouth." Contrast this with the uncertain phrasings of patients,
doctors, and novelists straining to hear the voice of the erotic imagination and
incorporate its "truths" with the workings of the "civilized" mind. It was precisely because this passional, truthful voice seemed integral, perhaps even essential, to the rational "normal" voice that it was feared.

Another important reason the voice of the erotic seemed unprecedented
and threatening was that it had a distinctly feminine tone. Diderot's chattering
jewels have a huge impact because they tell the absolute truth, even to the cha-
grin of their owners. A courtesan swears: "As long as they are prudent enough
to speak only of that which they understand, I will believe them as oracles"
(20). Dr. Orcotome similarly refers to the female genitalia, women's "inferior
mouth," as the *delphus* (25)—alluding to the Delphic oracle. Diderot's Delphic genitals reveal the true activities and motivations of people. But against
what falsity is this truth of the sex contrasted? In each hilarious episode, jewels
loudly contradict the modest, prudish, or virtuous assertions of their mistresses.
Diderot presents a world in which women have far greater libidinal desires and
activities than they could ever confess, and have far more influence in society
than men would ever admit. It is only the magic ring that bypasses the artifice
and deception of women's superior mouth and compels their inferior mouth to

speak. The truth of the sex and its otherwise discreet social role is thus revealed, at Mangogul's command, "at the expense of the women of [his] court."

Diderot was far more liberal on sexual matters than Rousseau, but the *encyclopédiste*'s vision of women's sensual drive in the imaginary Congo is similar to Rousseau's views of "natural" female sexuality.[9] Rousseau believed that women had unlimited desire and that it was their sensuous artifices and camouflaging modesty that gave them psychological and political power over men in the state of civilization (*Emile*, 447). The "humor" of *The Indiscreet Jewels*, therefore, lies in unmasking this female desire and thus shattering women's erotic dominion over men. The strategy would be used most famously in the 1793 trial of Marie-Antoinette, who was accused of a variety of sexual perversities as well as having used sex as a means of inducing Louis XVI to deceive and betray the French people.[10] Female seductions and deceptions had also been attacked and satirized under Louis XV, whose mistresses had been feared as powerful court intriguers.[11]

This obsession with extracting confessions from women's hyperactive yet double-dealing sex contrasts with the preponderance of male cases in the medical literature on the erotic. While Tissot and other anti-onanism campaigners always warned that girls could suffer the same ills as boys and even worse, and while there were even a few monographs dedicated to female "secret habits," antimasturbatory tracts principally concerned male seminal emissions. The erotomania literature presents only a few female cases. In the French medical material on inversion, "tribadism" was unproblematically recognized and dismissed as an age-old vice of little new scientific interest. From the beginning, case reports of fetishism described women with cloth or dress fetishes, yet Clérambault insisted as late as 1908 that true fetishism had only been described in men and might reflect an aspect of specifically male psychology (452). Even Brillat-Savarin, after first relying on a female informant, marginalized her erotic anecdote and turned to men for their wisdom on the "genesic" power of truffles. Confronted with the dismissal or erasure of women from this medical literature, we must ask: Were women really not speaking, or were doctors not listening? Did nineteenth-century male doctors share Orcotome's antipathy to women's inferior mouth, as when he explained, "And besides, it is not simply in speaking that one is heard: so how could women, who already have difficulties being heard with one mouth, be heard speaking with two?" (*Bijoux*, 27).

Although women's voices are under-represented in this scientific literature, that does not mean that medical and cultural views of female erotism were lacking. Indeed, in many ways they were preponderant. Rousseau and Tissot faulted onanism, like civilization, for softening the body and the nervous system. They opposed this effeminate physiology to the robust, virile body of savages or peasants. "In becoming social and a Slave," Rousseau explained, "[man] becomes weak, fearful, groveling, and his soft, effeminate manner of living ends up sapping his force and courage" (1755, 139).[12] A soft nervous system and imaginative impressionability were intrinsically female characteristics. Therefore, the imagination itself was a problem of effeminate civilization. Rousseau put it quite bluntly, "The imagination, which wreaks havoc among us, does not speak to savage hearts" (1755, 158). The reason for this was the absence, in the state of nature, of female deceptions or male sexual deferral. Onanism was the inevitable product of this effeminate state of civilization, where men took morbid refuge in the imagination because women did not satisfy them on demand.

Tissot and Rousseau contrasted the childlike innocence of the Arcadian savage with the effeminate perversions of civilized man. But as we have seen, a reversal of metaphors occurred in the early nineteenth century. The primitive, the child, and the laborer were no longer the ideal but the problem. With the advent of degeneracy theory, these three figures were lowered to the level of women. They were consigned to the inferior rungs of the evolutionary ladder and associated with caudal, primitive regions of the nervous system. Once Esquirol's medieval notion of lovesickness had been cast aside, alienists perceived the erotomaniac as a victim of imperative primitive sexual drives related to the hypersexual cerebellar impulses lying repressed in women.

Doctors explained the pathology of male inverts as a form of hysterical effeminacy due to neuropsychic atavism. Like courtesans, the sodomitic prostitute and the poetic invert excelled in the subterfuges of makeup and language. The sodomite, however, exploited factitiousness, whereas the invert embodied it psychically: his very desire was artificial and self-deluded. As in the anti-onanism literature, the erotic imagination was the dangerous locus of these "unnatural" self-conceptions and liaisons. The invert's predilection for pleasures of the imagination—whether sensual or novelistic—was a symptom of a neurasthenic exhaustion that would eventually pervert the "genesic sense" as well. The late-nineteenth-century cultural preoccupations with elitist decadence and democratic mediocrity (which haunted Huysmans's des Esseintes) conflated sexual inversion with effeminacy, impotence, and imaginary delirium.

Erotic fetishism from its inception in the work of Binet was characterized as a primitive erotic delusion. Although most of the cases described were men, doctors linked fetishism to stereotypically female imaginative malleability and commodity covetousness. At a time of deep political anticlericalism in the

Third Republic, physicians also construed female religiosity—exaggerated in hysteria and religious-erotomania—as a primitive theological practice.

Thus although the literature we have reviewed mostly presented men talking sex, doctors and novelists were hearing a female voice. Or more precisely, they were listening to a vetriloquized female sex that spoke through doctors' imagination with threats of irrationality, disorder, and primitivism.

This human beast was terrifying represented in Zola's novel of that title, *La Bête humaine* (1889). Zola's entire Rougon-Macquart novel cycle traces its psychopathic genealogy to a woman: Tante Dide, whose original act of adultery with the insane, alcoholic Macquart spawned the degenerate family tree. Although she was "ardent, passionately amorous, moved to fits" for the first eighty-three years of her life, she was reduced to a state of mute, hysterical catatonia throughout her final two decades (*Docteur Pascal*, 973). In the system of Zola's experimental novels, she was the first bad seed, the original sinner in the Adamic Fall narrative that also preoccupied Morel in his theory of degeneration.[13] *La Bête humaine* "experiments" with her great-grandson, Jacques Lantier, who suffers from a monomania driving him to seek erotic fulfillment in slashing women's throats. As he struggles to resist this impulse, he perceives his degeneration as a form of hereditary pollution with prehistoric roots:

> The family was not very stable, many had a chink. At certain moments he felt it acutely, this hereditary chink. . . . [I]t was like sudden losses of equilibrium in his being, like cracks, holes through which his self escaped amidst a great smoke that deformed everything. . . .
> Each time it was like a sudden crisis of blind rage, a continually reborn thirst to avenge very ancient offenses, whose precise memory he had forgotten. Did it come from so far back, from the evil that women had done to his race, from the grudge amassed from male to male since the first deception in the depths of the caves? (*Bête humaine*, 1043)

This hereditary conceit (alluding to spermatorrhea) was not Zola's invention. He simply novelized a dominant theme of nineteenth-century medical and fictional literature evoking the erotic: *la bête humaine* crouching in the dark recesses of the individual and collective psyche was the primitive, pathological, deadly erotic imagination, and its sex was female.

Gender was a major specter haunting the cultural imagination of the erotic in France, but it was not the only one. A new territory of the erotic was mapped out for battling a variety of social and cultural preoccupations: class, race, nationalism, civilization, progress, and professional and philosophical disputes. The medical and cultural imagination of the erotic, however, did not simply squeeze subjects into rigid labels. These labels or identities mutated constantly as individuals struggled to clarify, treat, or celebrate their sexual yearnings. They refined their sexual identity as they learned to narrate their *érotique* and fabricate its history.

The erotic imagination had many closely interwoven histories. Personal sexual histories are entangled with medical tales of sexuality. Fictional erotic stories, in turn, relied on the new ideas and words of medicine even as medical writers drew upon fiction to illustrate their theoretical fabrications. Enmeshed in these narratives are traces of the changing social and political situation of France: the revolutions (governmental and industrial), the rise of the bourgeoisie, urbanization, feminism, consumer culture, the wavering fortunes of the church, foreign wars and domestic class wars, colonization. Thus the erotic seemed ever more intrinsic to the preservation of the species, the nation, the bourgeoisie, and the patriarchy.

The many factors I have traced here are particularly French; however, one could similarly examine the narratives of the erotic arising in other national contexts. These would probably have their own peculiarities, but as we have glimpsed in the cases of Germany and Britain, these were also interwoven into the French story. We might well expect this to be generally the case since so many of the "words and ideas" for speaking the erotic arose in France. Indeed, the importance of the erotic in today's psyches, politics, and society resonates significantly with the construction of the erotic imagination in nineteenth-century France even as the narration of the erotic continues to be a territory for discovery and contention.

In the United States, for example, the politics, merchandising, and publicizing of the erotic is a national obsession that takes myriad forms. These attest to the growing importance of the erotic not just to private pleasures, but also to group identities, consumption habits, public health, and all aspects of popular culture. Conversely, new forms of erotic pleasure have emerged and gone public thanks to these social pressures. In order to tackle these controversies thoughtfully and productively we must listen attentively to entangled individual, professional, and social narratives as we, in turn, spin our intimate and our collective *histoires érotiques*.

# A Psychoanalytic Supplement: From French Auto-Erotography to Freudian Auto-Ergography

> I always find it uncanny when I can't understand someone in terms of myself.
>
> Sigmund Freud[1]

**R**eaders familiar with psychoanalysis have no doubt been struck by the uncanny similarities between the preceding eighteenth- and nineteenth-century medical ideas and the theories that Sigmund Freud began to develop at the turn of the century. Notions of infantile eroticism, psychosexual development, childhood trauma or seduction, original bisexuality, primitive erotic drives, and the psychogenesis of fetishism, for example, seem to belong to the domain of psychoanalysis. Obscure issues such as the noxiousness of masturbation or the role of olfaction in the evolution of civilization were also preoccupations of Freud's. I have assiduously kept Freud out of the picture in order to avoid what historian Mark Micale (1995, 125) calls "Freudian histor-ical teleology": the tendency to present the history of psychiatry as the gradual anticipation of, or failure to perceive, Freud's ultimate verities. Aside from being ahistorical, such an approach fails to cast any critical light on Freud's hy-potheses since these are taken as natural facts.[2] In the case of the present study, almost all the preceding material antedates Freud's psychoanalytic theorizing begun in the 1890s. French doctors first ignored psychoanalytic works and then received them with hostility in the 1910s because of nationalist and profes-sional rivalries.[3] Thereafter, psychoanalysis took root slowly because French psychoanalytic institutions were riven by professional and personal infighting. Nevertheless, psychoanalysis ultimately achieved broad cultural appeal after 1968 through its political deployment.[4]

Although Freud was unknown in France until the turn of the century, there is no denying that psychoanalysis has had a tremendous impact on psychiatry, the academy, and culture since then. In this concluding supplement I wish to historically contextualize Freud in relation to the French literature on the erotic. He was a genius, but also a man of his time. Part of his brilliance was in syn-thesizing, professionalizing, and institutionalizing disparate scientific ideas and social concerns of his age. Ironically, he also recapitulated some of the processes we have seen here: sexual confession and anamnesis transformed into scientific knowledge and stimulus for fiction. In the final section, I consider how Freud collapsed the roles of doctor, patient, and novelist into one as he transcribed his life into a professional auto-fiction: his *Autobiographical Study*.

## Nervous Energy and Biogenetic Histories

Throughout the nineteenth century the French were committed to organicist and neurogenital theories of sexuality. To a certain extent they remain attached to such biological conceptualizations of gender and sexuality.[5] Historian Frank Sulloway (1983) argues that one of the most important Freudian "myths" is that Freud cast aside such biologism in favor of a purely psychological model of psychosexual development. In fact, it was with much regret that Freud abandoned an active research career in neurobiology and turned to clinical medicine in 1882 because of his poor prospects as a Jew in Austrian academe. Sulloway's careful reading of Freud's work shows that many of the common-place tenets of Victorian biology—degeneration theory, biophysics, psycho-Lamarckianism, and Haeckel's "biogenetic law" (that ontogeny recapitulates phylogeny)—profoundly shaped Freud's theories. They provided the hidden foundations that allowed Freud to believe psychoanalysis was a science and not just a metaphysical system as some French doctors claimed.[6].

As we have seen in the preceding chapters, hereditary degeneration theory dominated late-nineteenth-century pathology. Freud has been represented as the slayer of this dogma. He did state, for example, that *most* inverts could not be considered degenerates (1905a, 138). Generally, however, Freud accommodated his theory of psychoneuroses to hereditarianism.[7] Freud (like Binet before him) wished to explain the specific manifestation of a neurosis through acquired, psychological mechanisms involving the childhood experiences of those with "hereditary predispositions" (Sulloway, 92–93).

Perhaps the most important aspect of Freud's "crypto-biology" was his electroeconomic theory of neurophysiology and pathology as epitomized in his "Project for a Scientific Psychology" (written in 1895 but only published posthumously). It would be too large a task to explain Freud's elaborate and fantastical theory of nerve energies, cathexis, discharge, and repression.[8] Suffice it to say that the "Project" utilized purely neurophysical mechanisms to model psychological principles that were significant in his later work: primary and secondary processes, the identification of dreams as wish fulfillment, hysteria as a product of pathological repression, and other theories. The "Project" also betrays Freud's peculiar, reactionary belief in the pathology of onanism. Hysteria, he wrote, was due to the premature loss of nervous energy through masturbation (1950, 357).

Freud and his intimate friend and collaborator Wilhelm Fliess were certain of the neurotoxicity of masturbation and coitus interruptus.[9] Throughout their correspondence, Freud identified these as the cause of melancholia, neurasthenia, and nasal disorders.[10] Freud explained the pathology of masturbation—what he called the "primary addiction" (1985, 287)—in mechanical terms: "It can be further assumed that excessive masturbation—which according to the theory leads to too great an unloading of E. (the end organ) [i.e., the genitals] and thus to a low level of stimulus in E.—excessive masturbation extends to the production of s. S. [somatic sexual excitation] and brings about a lasting reduction in the s. S., thus a weakening of the p. S. [psychic sexual group of neurons]" (1985, 99). As I pointed out in chapter 1, the belief in the pathogenicity of masturbation had died out in France by the end of the nineteenth century; however, doctors continued to view onanism as a symptom of degeneracy. Freud, nevertheless, held on to views that seem to echo Tissot's hydraulic mechanism.[11]

Freud constructed upon this mechanist biologism a vast psychology of the unconscious, of repression, and of sexuality. The synthesis of these issues was not a major concern of fin-de-siècle French psychologists with the significant exceptions of Alfred Binet and Pierre Janet. These two contemporaries had been close colleagues, but later became academic and intellectual rivals. Janet developed a complex, novel system of "psychological analysis" of the "subconscious"—a term he coined. He also pioneered the interpretation of dreams, the cathartic cure of neuroses, and other psychotherapeutic techniques that Freud, to Janet's consternation, claimed as his own innovations. However, Janet never especially focused on erotism. In fact, he objected to what he viewed as Freud's "dogma of pansexuality."[12]

Binet, as we have seen, was quite interested in sexuality and proposed an associationist psychology of erotic attachment. In the *Three Essays on the Theory of Sexuality,* Freud approvingly cited Binet as having been "the first to maintain (what has since been confirmed by a quantity of evidence) that the choice of a fetish is an after-effect of some sexual impression, received as a rule in early childhood" (1905a, 154).[13] Although Binet did not develop a general theory of the unconscious, his theories of childhood erotic associations and of psychological automatism (1886) were consonant with Freud's dynamic theory of the unconscious. Binet, quite uniquely in late-nineteenth-century France, also proposed that infantile associations were a universal mechanism for the acquisition of erotic predilections. Furthermore, he suggested that not all erotism was perverse, but that *petit fétichisme* was a normal form of erotism on a continuum with pathological *grand fétichisme.* Nevertheless, Binet and his colleagues saw the "sexual perversities" as distinctly pathological and neurodegenerate.[14] Freud, on the other hand, universalized perversity. His theory of infantile "polymorphous perversity" suggested that perversity was not only on a continuum with normal sexuality but was the primordial erotic soup from which "normal," heterosexual, reproductive sex evolved.[15] As Freud put it (after his laudatory mention of Binet): "The conclusion now presents itself to us that there is indeed something innate lying behind the perversions but that it is something innate in *everyone,* though as a disposition it may vary in its intensity and may be increased by the influences of actual life" (1905a, 171).

To arrive at this conclusion, however, Freud relied on commonplace nineteenth-century analogies between the evolution of the human species, the progress of races and civilizations, the hierarchy of economic classes, and the development of children. For Freud, the individual's sexual evolution paralleled the sexual stages in phyletic evolution from monads, to bisexual creatures, to unisexual ones (Sulloway, 199). Haeckel had hypothesized this in 1891;

Binet (1887b) had developed the idea into a full psychology of microorganisms; and Delbœuf (1891) had proposed that civilized love was just a behavioral elaboration of the spermatozoa's primeval drive to unite with the ovum.[16] We have also seen that nineteenth-century doctors drew parallels between individual psychosexual development and the evolution of eroticism from "primitive" to "civilized" man. Freud employed this model in explaining the genesis of civilized, adult sexual shame, disgust, and morality (1985, 279). He also hinted that the lower rung of civilization was analogous to that of peasants and the lower classes (1985, 163). These ideas persisted in Freud's thinking beyond the period of his interactions with Fliess in the 1890s. In the preface to Bourke's *Scatological Rites of all Nations,* Freud wrote of defecation: "[T]he chief finding from psycho-analytic research had been the fact that the human infant is obliged to recapitulate during the early part of his development the changes in attitude of the human race towards excremental matters which probably had their start when *homo sapiens* first raised himself off Mother Earth" (1913, 336). His use of "Mother Earth" is significant since he believed a prehistoric male human's first adoption of upright posture liberated him from the sexual periodicity determined by female menstrual odors. Thus, bipedalism not only prompted menstruation taboos, but also the development of shame, morality, and the "organic repression" of anal and olfactory eroticism (as suggested earlier by Broca). This was the first step, Freud argued, towards civilization (and its discontents) (1930, 100n.). Freud's prehistoric narrative had more profound implications: "With the assumption of an erect posture by man and with the depreciation of his sense of smell, it was not only his anal eroticism which threatened to fall victim to organic repression, but the whole of his sexuality; so that since this, the sexual function has been accompanied by a repugnance which cannot further be accounted for" (1930, 106n.).

Freud's history of "normal," civilized heterosexuality is, therefore, a tale of prehistoric neurological repression of erotism recapitulated in contemporary child-rearing practices. Although Freud and his French predecessors relied on similar neurobiological principles and interwoven historical narratives of erotism, they arrived at somewhat different conclusions in their psychiatrization of the erotic imagination. For Freud, the erotic imagination revealed a forgotten or repressed childhood history, and it was a sphere for accomplishing therapy. For the French, the erotic was a (perhaps widespread) taint of hereditary degeneracy and was largely irreparable.

Why did Freud and the French arrive at such divergent therapeutic conclusions? One reason is that the two had different patient populations. As we have seen, French doctors often wrote about individuals arrested on "public immorality" charges who had been explicitly diagnosed with some variety of sexual perversion. It is no wonder that these patients' medical histories splay out their sexual preoccupations on the surface. When Freud erected the foundations of his theory of sexuality in 1905, he had not treated any "inverts" or indeed any adults who engaged in "perverse" sexual behavior.[17] He admitted that the information for his essay on "The Sexual Aberrations" was derived second hand from the "well-known writings" of German sexologists and Havelock Ellis (Freud 1905a, 135n.). (Of his French colleagues, he only mentioned Binet, Féré, and Magnan.) Freud's early analysis patients were apparently sexually "normal." Perversity, if it existed, was not on the surface of their stories (as in the French cases). Freud developed the technique of psychoanalysis to expose the erotic imagination under the skin of patients' narratives. Therefore, the psychoanalyst's interpretation took precedence over the patient's original, first-person history. One index of this is the relative dearth of patient voices in Freudian texts compared to the abundance of first-person patient confessions in nineteenth-century French medical literature on erotism.

While Freud lacked bona fide "sexual perverts" for his analysis of the erotic imagination, he did not lack his own imagination, and he struggled to examine its perversities. Like Rousseau, Freud used his autoanalysis as a universal index case. He went further by turning self-analysis into a system of psychology, psychosocial analysis, and professional development (psychoanalysts must still undergo personal analysis as part of their training). In this process, the subject's erotic narrative is displaced by the scientized, professional retelling of Freud's autobiography.

## Freudian History or Self-Representation?

Freud never wrote a formal autobiography; therefore, his *Autobiographical Study* of 1925 is the closest we get to the form. In the introduction to this short work, James Strachey noted the difficulty of translating the original German title, *Selbstdarstellung*.[18] More accurate terms would be *self-portrait* or *self-representation*. Strachey therefore coined a term to classify the essay: *auto-ergography* (from the Greek *ergon*, work or activity).[19] He did not define this neologism, but we might gloss it as "an account of one's work or career." Freud's *Autobiographical Study* is the logical text for examining the relationship of self-representation to the erotic imagination, medical knowledge, and historical narratives. The semantic ambiguity we explored in the "dangerous supplement" of erotism recurs in this concluding section: Was the Freudian erotic narrative an addition to or a substitution for other narratives, particularly the history of his professional development through his self-representation?

Freud began his *Autobiographical Study* by noting that he had already written a *History of the Psychoanalytic Movement* "which contains the essence of all I have to say on the present occasion" (1925, 7). The current article, therefore, had to be more than a professional history. Echoing Rousseau, Freud acknowledged the difficulty of the literary task before him: "I must endeavor to construct a narrative in which subjective and objective attitudes, biographical and historical interests, are combined in a new production" (7). Constructing such a biographicohistorical narrative should have come easily to Freud. He had used literary and (pre)historic narratives as the backbone of psychoanalysis, and his personal experience, particularly his auto-analysis of 1894–1899, had provided his fundamental psychoanalytic insights.

We have seen in the previous chapters that French physicians had freely dipped into fiction for case material. Freud, like his French colleagues, had praised authors and artists for their intuitive understanding of the human mind and nature (1907a, 8). Yet Freud made use of literature in a drastically different way. In his postscript to Wilhelm Jensen's novella, *Gravida*, Freud wrote: "[Psychoanalysis] no longer merely seeks in [novels] for confirmations of the findings it has made from unpoetic, neurotic human beings; it also demands to know the material of impressions and memories from which the author has built the work, and the methods and processes by which he has converted this material into a work of art" (1907a, 94). Freud first published analyses of literary works in *The Interpretation of Dreams* (1900), which included interpretations of *Oedipus Rex* and *Hamlet*. The former was the basis for his notion of the "Oedipal complex." He had already described it in a letter of 1897 to Fliess as a widespread experience: "I have found, in my own case too, [the phenomenon of] being in love with my mother and jealous of my father, and I now consider it a *universal event* in early childhood" (1985, 272; emphasis added).

Freud produced this and other fundamental insights of psychoanalysis in 1894–1899, a period when he engaged in intense self-analysis and suffered peculiar neuroses (neurasthenia, headaches, nasal and other disorders, anxiety dreams, railroad phobia, etc.). He also recalled during this period that as a small child he had slept with his mother, seen her naked, and become attached to an ugly, clever, old nanny (1985, 268–71). Biographers and students of Freud have mythologized this period, describing it as an interval when he accomplished a "heroic feat," made all his discoveries, and was in a state of shamanistic "creative illness."[20] One analyst declared that the Freud-Fliess correspondence of the 1890s reveals how "Freud had no doubt that he had through an act of heroic and unique courage undertaken to understand in himself, and others, what humans had always sought to repress, mythologise, or rationalise in terms other than the truth of experience itself."[21]

The theoretical conclusions of this self-analysis were publicized in *The Interpretation of Dreams,* which relied on Freud's interpretation of several dozens of his own dreams. We need not speculate on the mystical nature of Freud's nasal and other neuroses, but we can safely say that Freud arrived at the central tenets of psychoanalysis in the late 1890s, and that he himself believed that his self-analysis and "little hysteria" were essential to these conceptual discoveries (1985, 261). (One is reminded of Flaubert's and Baudelaire's similar comments on creative hysteria). In the introduction to *The Interpretation of Dreams,* Freud confessed: "For this book has a further subjective significance for me personally—a significance which I only grasped after I had completed it. It was, I found, a portion of my own self-analysis, my reaction to my father's death [on October 23, 1896]—that is to say, to the most important event, the most poignant loss, of a man's life" (1900, xxvi).

The statement reflects one of the central beliefs of psychoanalysis, that there is a latent, "true" meaning below the apparent manifestations of the psychic life. The pivotal moment in Freud's recognition of the deceptive mechanisms of the psyche was his abandonment in 1897 of the "seduction theory" (that patients had been actually sexually traumatized in youth) in favor of the Oedipal drama, which reinterpreted these memories as phantasies. This radical move was prompted by his abandonment of the conviction that his own father was a "pervert" who was responsible for the hysteria of his children, including Freud (1985, 230, 264, 268). In the *Autobiographical Study* Freud simply explains that he made a "mistake" in believing patients' stories were "historical truth" (35).[22]

From that point forward, psychoanalysis was defined by an attitude of skepticism, even distrust, toward the patient, for "the work of analysis involves an *art of interpretation.* . . ."

> The analyst, who listens composedly but without any constrained effort to the stream of associations, and who, *from his experience, has a general notion of what to expect,* can make use of the material brought to light by the patient according to two possibilities. If the resistance is slight he will be able from the patient's allusions to infer the unconscious material itself; or if the resistance

is stronger he will be able to recognize its character from the associations, as they seem to become more remote from the subject, and *will explain it to the patient*. (1925, 41; emphasis added)

Not only is the analyst presumed to have interpretative superiority over patients, but the psychiatrist enters the analytic struggle equipped with anticipated stories. What were these tales behind the "manifest" content of patient stories other than Freud's own erotic phantasies elevated to the level of universal master narratives. Freud himself was sensitive to this criticism that "interpretation" might really be "suggestion," and he felt obliged to deny it concerning the Oedipal complex: "I do not believe even now that I forced the seduction-phantasies upon my patients, that I 'suggested' them" (1925, 34).

Dream interpretation was a model of the psychoanalytic "art of interpretation": stripping away the manifest "façade" and "make-believe" to reveal the true meaning, that is, the Freudian narrative (1925, 43). As a powerful art of interpretation—of unmasking the artifices of the manifest—psychoanalysis would later be applied to normal psychology and to religious beliefs.[23] Given that Freud became such a master at stripping away the artificial, superficial stories of life to reveal the disguised Freudian, erotic narrative beneath, it is remarkable that his *Autobiographical Study* makes no mention of his personal erotic life or the self-analysis of the late 1890s that was so essential to the foundations of psychoanalysis. Why did Freud erase his own erotic memoirs? Four years before his death, Freud wrote in the postscript to the *Autobiographical Study*, "Two themes run through these pages: the story of my life and the history of psychoanalysis. They are intimately interwoven. This *Autobiographical Study* shows how psychoanalysis becomes the whole content of my life and rightly assumes that no personal experiences of mine are of any interest in comparison to my relations with that science."[24] The central phrase of this statement—"psychoanalysis becomes the whole content of my life"—can be understood in two ways: (1) Freud dedicated his life to psychoanalysis; (2) literally, psychoanalysis is entirely about Freud's life. The two interpretations are not mutually exclusive.

Perhaps more than any of Freud's other works, the *Autobiographical Study* is dedicated to erecting the heroic myth of Freud as the solitary, embattled, misunderstood genius who single-handedly created psychoanalysis. He systematically downplayed the early influence of colleagues and denigrated their work.[25] In this history of the seventeen-year gestation period of psychoanalysis, Freud makes no mention whatsoever of his relationship with Wilhelm Fliess (which

Jones [1953, 287] awkwardly described as an "extraordinary experience" but "a passionate friendship for someone intellectually [Freud's] inferior"). Freud erased his "dearest in truth" who was so critical to his self-analysis, theoretical cogitations, and recovery from neuroses in the 1890s.[26] The passionate friendship and the erotic recollections that spawned psychoanalysis were suppressed in favor of an official, professional personal history—an auto-ergography—to cloak Freud's seminal auto-erotography.

Freud's transformation of erotography into ergography mirrors and condenses the activity I have documented throughout this book. Individuals' struggles to elucidate and voice their erotic experiences were woven into a network of broader scientific and cultural narratives. In being received, processed, and diffused by biomedical and novelistic writers, these erotic imaginations adopted new narrative forms that would shape the sexual identities of future individuals. In Freud's case, not only was this erotic self-examination conducted in interaction with the commonplace biomedical ideas of the time, but it founded a system of psychiatry that has had major responsibility for molding the sexual subjectivities of individuals in the twentieth century. Even Freud's own sexual subjectivity and erotic history was not immune to the interpretations and revisions of his science of psychoanalysis.

The erotic became a dynamic palimpsest of constant inscription and erasure, blurring the boundaries between reality and fiction, truth and deception. It is a slate on which no one—neither doctors, patients, novelists, nor historians—can read the "true" text. Each reader becomes as active a writer of their own narrative as those authors whose auto-graphies are being analyzed.

I will close with one final citation from Freud's postscript to the *Autobiographical Study* to illustrate the inadequacy of any one attempt to fathom the erotic. First, recall Rousseau's challenge and his proud claim of having painted a human portrait "exactly after nature and in all its truth" and "a unique and useful work which may serve as the first point of comparison for the study of men" (*Confessions*, 3). In contrast, at the end of his life Freud seems disillusioned in the power of confession, or at least in his power to control the retelling of his own confessions. Even after portraying his life story as indistinguishable from the history of a "science" uniquely dedicated to extracting and interpreting intimate erotic histories, Freud trails off into silence:

> And here I may be allowed to break off these autobiographical notes. The public has no claim to learn any more of my private affairs—of my struggles, my disappointments and successes. I have in any case been more open and

frank in some of my writings (such as *The Interpretation of Dreams* and *The Psychopathology of Everyday Life*) than people usually are who describe their lives for their contemporaries or for posterity. I have had small thanks for it, and from my experience I cannot recommend anyone to follow my example. (1925, 73) Fortunately for psychoanalysts, millions of people have ignored Freud's final warning. Instead they have followed the example of Rousseau and many nineteenth-century "sexual psychopaths," placing the erotic at the heart of contemporary Euro-American culture.

# *Timeline of Sexual Perversions**

1640    J. Ferrand's *De la maladie d'amour* (1610) translated as *Erotomania.*

1710?   *Onania* condemns masturbation and advertises quack cures.

1758    Masturbation authoritatively medicalized by S. A. A. D. Tissot.

1782    Posthumous publication of Rousseau's *Confessions* (Part 1).

1791    Constituent Assembly eliminates French antisodomy laws.

1810    J. Esquirol develops the notion of "monomania," including "erotic monomania" and "theomania."

1819    A. Matthey coins the term *klopémanie,* which C. Marc renders as *kleptomanie* in 1840.

1857    B. Morel publishes his *Treatise on Degeneration.* A. Tardieu publishes his *Medicolegal Study of Assaults on Decency.*

   C. Baudelaire's *Les Fleurs du mal* and G. Flaubert's *Madame Bovary* accused of violating good morals.

1861    E. Monneret describes *nécrophilie* in his *Treatise on General Pathology.*

   Guy de Maupassant uses *nécrophile* in 1884 in his short story "La Chevelure."

*Several terms (such as *voyeur* and *frotteur*) have earlier, non-erotic denotations.

| | |
|---|---|
| 1864 | K. H. Ulrichs calls himself and others with a "female psyche confined in a male body" Urnings. |
| 1868 | First German usage of *homosexual* and *heterosexual,* in a letter from K. M. Kertbeny to Ulrichs. |
| 1869 | C. Westphal introduces the diagnosis of "Contrary sexual sensation." |
| 1877 | E. Lasègue coins *exhibitionnisme.* |
| 1878 | A. Tamassia renders Westphal's term into Italian as *inversione dell'istinto sessuale.* |
| 1881 | J. Krueg employs the English term "perverted sexual instinct." |
| 1882 | J. M. Charcot and V. Magnan translate Westphal's term as *inversion du sens génital* and discuss other *perversions sexuels.* |
| 1883 | J. Richepin first uses *voyeur* in a prose work, *Le Pavé.* |
| 1884 | J. Péladan mentions coprophagia in his historical novel, *Le vice suprême.* |
| 1886 | The first edition of R. Krafft-Ebing's *Psychopathia Sexualis* coins no new terms; these appear in subsequent editions: e.g., coprolangnia, frottage, *zoophilia erotica* (sensual excitement with animals), and zooerastia (copulation with animals). |
| 1887 | Binet theorizes "amorous fetishism." |
| | G. Macé describes the *frotteur* in his criminological text, *Un joli monde.* |
| 1888 | D. Stefanowski lectures on "tyrannism" (pathological cruelty) and "passivism" (erotism in humiliation). |
| 1890 | R. Krafft-Ebing employs the terms *Sadismus* and *Masochismus.* |
| 1892 | J. Kiernan uses *heterosexual* in English to refer to those with "inclinations to both sexes." |
| | In Memphis, Alice Mitchell murders Freda Ward in a widely publicized lesbian love crime. |
| 1895 | Oscar Wilde trials. |
| 1896 | M. A. Raffalovich coins the term *unisexual* for people with same-sex attraction. |
| | Krafft-Ebing first describes erotic paedophilia as a perverse attraction to children. |
| 1898 | George Bedborough put on trial for selling H. Ellis's *Sexual Inversion.* |
| 1910 | M. Hirschfeld describes the "transvestite" in a monograph by that title. |
| | H. Ellis in 1928 coins the terms *sexo-aesthetic inversion* and *eonism* to refer to transvestitism. |
| 1924 | The English translation of W. Stekel's *Peculiarities of Behavior* introduces the terms *voyeurism* and *paraphilia* (interest in perversions). |
| 1949 | D. O. Cauldwell first describes "psychopathic transexualism." |

1952    The first edition of the *Diagnostic and Statistical Manual of Mental Disorders (DSM)* groups the "sexual deviations" (including homosexuality) under the category of "sociopathic personality disorders."

1966    J. Money develops the notion of gender identity disorder.

1968    *DSM-II* reclassifies the sexual deviations as a separate category of personality disorders.

1973    The American Psychiatric Association votes to remove homosexuality from *DSM-II* and replace it with "sexual orientation disturbance."

1980    *DSM-III* creates a new class, the "psychosexual disorders," including psychosexual dysfunction, paraphilias (the fetishisms), gender identity disorder (transsexualism), and "ego-dystonic homosexuality."

1984    J. Money and M. Lamacz coin *gynemimesis* to describe men who live as women without sex reassignment surgery. Men attracted to them are "gynemimetophilics."

1986    In *Bowers v. Hardwick*, the U. S. Supreme Court upholds the state of Georgia's antisodomy law.

1987    *DSM-III-R* deletes the diagnosis of homosexuality entirely, leaving the paraphilias and sexual dysfunctions as the two main classes of "sexual disorders."

1993    R. Blanchard and P. Collins invent the term *gynandromorphophiles* to describe all men erotically attracted to cross-dressed or anatomically feminized men.

1994    *DSM-IV* collects sexual dysfunction, the paraphilias, and gender identity disorder under the heading "sexual and gender identity disorders."

# NOTES

## Introduction

1. See "Secret CIA report reveals Saddam Hussein's bizarre sex life," *The National Examiner,* 12 March 1991. The tabloid press is an inextinguishable fountain of these spurious or real sex scandals.

2. Ernest-Armand Dubarry served as a corresponding journalist in Italy early in his career and was one of the most active writers on the question of Napoleon III's Italian policy. He returned to France to cover the Franco-Prussian campaign and then served as editor of *Le Pays* (1871) and *Le Figaro* (1875), political director of *La Gazette* (1876), and collaborator on *Le Ralliement* (1877). He then succeeded Jules Verne as popular science writer for the periodical *Le Musée des familles.* He wrote in a variety of genres: poetry, history, geography, novels, short stories, and travelogues. He planned to include twenty novellas in his series *Les Déséquilibrés de l'amour.* Although hugely popular, only eleven volumes were actually published from 1896 to 1902 (Micale 1995, 192). These covered fetishism (1896a, 1898b), homosexuality (1896b), incest (1902a), hermaphroditism (1897a), sadism (1898a, 1901), and other sexual perversions (1898c, 1899, 1902b), as well as hysteria (1897b).

3. Dubarry (1896b, 8) citing Tardieu (1857, 2).

4. It is due to these historical roots that psychoanalysts such as Robert Stoller (1985, vii), can conclude that the "perverse" and the "nonperverse" share the same dynamics of erotic excitement: hatred and the desire to humiliate. Also see psychologist Louise Kaplan's study of *Female Perversions* (1991a) which argues that femininity itself is a perverse gender script that functions as a defense mechanism. More broadly, she argues that "socially normalized gender stereotypes are the crucibles of perversion" (1991b, 128). Emulating Freud's original approach, psychoanalyst Gerald Fogel asks, in the introduction to his anthology *Perversions and Near-Perversions in Clinical Practice,* "What can perverse sexuality teach us about the normal" (1991, 4). Can distinctions between the "normal" (or the "near-perverse") and the "perverse" be logically maintained when perversity is found to be at the origins of the so-called normal? The *New York Times* recently took note of this "perversification" of the normal (Goleman 1991). French psychoanalysts tend to maintain sharper distinctions between normal and perverse sexuality. Analyst Gérard Bonnet, for example, declares that "perversity is

situated closer to eroticism or pornography than sexuality strictly speaking" (1993, 12). For him, true "sexuality" is "complete union or procreation." See Rosario (1992) for a discussion of contemporary French sexology.

5. For example, Dr. Allan Hamilton in an article on the "civil responsibility of sexual perverts" (1896, 503), blamed French writers for opening American eyes to sexual perversion. Duggan (1993, 795) also discusses the impact of French novels on American sexology and popular culture. De Grazia (1992, 6) notes that the early prosecution of "obscene" novels in England was directed at French works.

6. See the *Trésor de la langue française*. Previously, the word *erotic* denoted amorous poetry or dispositions. There will be a detailed discussion of the etymology of *erotic* and *erotism* in chapter 2.

7. One is reminded of Condillac's *Traité des sensations* (1754) and Cabanis's *Rapports du physique et du morale de l'homme* (1802). The later "physiologies" were small, humorous texts on students, porters, creditors, debtors, etc. Honoré Daumier illustrated one: *Les physiologies parisiennes* (1850). One of Honoré de Balzac's earliest works was *Physiologie du mariage* (1829). Bourget (1902) returned to the form to criticize "modern love."

8. I discuss Cloquet's "physiology of smell," *Osphresiologie* (1821), in chapter 4.

9. Cf. Foucault (1976, 25).

10. On the way clinical histories are shaped and used by the doctors for their own professional purposes, see Hunter (1991). Epstein (1995) provides an excellent review and analysis of the role of narrative in medical practice and diagnosis. Both of these works, however, focus on doctors' storytelling rather than the patients'.

11. Anthropologist Arthur Kleinman (1988) explores how "illness narratives" help subjects make sense of their suffering.

12. Compare with de Lauretis (1984, 159) who favors a more social reductionist understanding of subjectivity.

13. There was, of course, no psychoanalysis in the nineteenth century, nor anything like the various talk therapies common today. It was not until the 1890s that the term *psychiatry* was even used regularly in France, and not until this century that "physician-alienists" regularly adopted the label *psychiatrist*. On the use of the term *psychiatrist*, see Goldstein (1987, 6–7). On the Golden Era of French psychiatry, see Castel (1976).

14. See Foucault on the "birth of the clinic" (1963) and the development of the human sciences (1966); also see Coleman (1982) on the growth of the public hygiene profession.

15. Today some of these pathologies fall under the rubric of "sexual dysfunctions, paraphilias, and gender identity disorder" according to the official nosology of the American Psychiatric Association (1994). But these taxonomies have gone through much contentious modification, as Bayer (1987) demonstrates in the case of homosexuality.

16. In two small books, Foucault introduced the public to the rich documentation printed in medical journals. The two works, *Herculine Barbin* (1978) and *Moi, Pierre Rivière . . .* (1973), are built around dossiers originally published in a nineteenth-century medical journal, the *Annales d'hygiène publique*.

## Chapter 1 Onanists

1. *Les Confessions* (108–9; emphasis added). I cite Rousseau's work by title.

2. The Littré dictionary (1873) only refers to the seminal and theological denotations which the *Trésor de la langue française* (1988) lists as "literary and archaic." The English usage of *pollution* in reference to environmental contamination (rather than ritual profanation) dates back to at least 1420. Nevertheless, the earliest usage denotes seminal emission apart from coition (*Oxford English Dictionary*, 2d ed.).

3. Derrida productively exploits the double, almost conflicting, connotations of "supplement" (1967, 207–9). First, it can refer to a complement or extension of an existing corpus, e.g., the supplement to a dictionary. Second, it can refer to an exterior addition or surplus, e.g., a supplementary fee for an express train. Derrida mainly explores the supplementary nature of symbols to real things (i.e., signifiers to signifieds), and of writing to speech.

4. Robert Nye (1984, 1993a) has especially developed the theme of fin-de-siècle medical and sociological anxieties over French national decay. It is a compelling historical argument that I will refer to frequently.

5. I rely on Stengers and Van Neck (1984) for their extensive intellectual history of masturbation from the Middle Ages to the nineteenth century. Their valuable documentary work, however, ventures no historical interpretations of the causes and social meaning of the *"grande peur de la masturbation." Mollicies* was also a common medieval term for effeminacy or sodomy, which led to an easy association between what today appear as clearly distinct "sins" (see Bullough & Voght 1976).

6. St. Paul's first epistle to the Corinthians (6:9–10) was a frequently cited passage, which declares that the *malthakoi* (Greek for "soft") would not inherit the heavenly Kingdom. See Boswell (1980, 106–7) and Halperin (1990, 22–24).

7. On the history of *semen* (seed), see Gerlach (1938), Héritier-Auger (1989), and Sissa (1989).

8. Thomasset and Jacquart (1985, 236) discuss the "disease of continence" in the works of Galen, Constantine the African, and Avicenna.

9. MacDonald (1967, 431) errs, therefore, when he equates Boorde's term *gomorrea passio* with masturbation.

10. Stenghers and Van Neck (1984, 44) identify only two pre-eighteenth-century medical texts that contain unequivocal, if fleeting, condemnations of masturbation. The German physician Enttmüller explained in 1670 that gonorrhea might be due to "nefarious *manstuprationem.*" In 1706, the British doctor Edward Baynard vaunted the use of cold baths to treat impotence which he claimed was caused by "that cursed school wickedness of masturbation."

11. There is no extant first edition of *Onania*. The British Library catalog dates a now destroyed first edition as "1710?" Stengers and Van Neck (207n.1) date it 1715. MacDonald (424n.4) dates it around 1708.

12. See Neuman (1975, 2) on the publication history of *Onania*.

13. For more on early eighteenth-century anti-onanism literature, see Stengers and Van Neck (1984) and Tarczylo (1983, pt. 2, ch. 2).

14. For example, Spitz's (1953) whiggish history presents the theory of onanistic pathology as a transient aberration of medical science, while Szasz's (1970, 180–206) antipsychiatric critique of the antimasturbation campaign portrays it as a sadistic, Victorian medical witch-hunt. Focusing on a selection of particularly lurid cases, Barker-Benfield (1976) and Masson (1986) have depicted these same doctors as wholesale practitioners of medical atrocities against women.

15. Relying on a Freudian "repressive hypothesis," Duffy (1963) proposes that the anti-onanism campaign was a product of a so-called Victorian Age "synonymous with prudery." From the functionalist sociological perspective of Talcott Parson's "sick role," Hare (1962) and Gilbert (1975) suggest that masturbation represented a silent compact between doctors and patients: a positive diagnosis of "onanism" allowed doctors to overcome their therapeutic inefficacy, while patients' acceptance of the onanist sick role represented a secular, medicalized form of penance. Neuman naturalizes the masturbatory phenomenon by suggesting that the earlier onset of puberty and the bourgeois delay of marriage led to an actual increase in the practice of masturbation precisely at a time when bourgeois values prescribed economic and sexual thrift. Similarly, Hare posits an actual increase in masturbatory behavior which he attributes to heightened fears of venereal diseases. Rejecting both Freudo-Marxist and functionalist explanations, Tarczylo (1983) proposes instead that the anti-onanism campaign arose, paradoxically, as an intrinsic part of progressive Enlightenment ideology and a growing fear of declining fertility in France. Laqueur (1989) echoes Tarczylo's critique, adding the suggestion that suppression of the "solitary vice" was associated with the regulation of antisociality and a rampant imagination (1992). See Engelhardt (1985) on masturbation in Victorian America.

16. The sentence in italics originally appeared in Latin. I am grateful to David Halperin for assisting me with this English translation.

17. As Ludmilla Jordanova has noted on the eighteenth-century popularization of medicine: "Notions of sin, evil, crime and punishment are all incorporated into a larger vision, which sets improper sexual activity in the context of class relations, family dynamics, responsibility and dependency" (1987, 77).

18. Portmann (1980) portrays Tissot as a politically conservative "representative of the Ancien Régime" and an opponent of the French Revolution who was faithful to the sovereign of Bern and his patrician caste. Emch-Dériaz (1984), on the other hand, argues that Tissot's works reflect his ideological commitment to Enlightenment concepts of public health and welfare.

19. Tissot to Dr. J. G. Zimmermann, 3 February 1761 (Leigh 1970, no. 1257n.).

20. See letter from Tissot to Rousseau, 3 July 1762 (Leigh 1970, no. 1946).

21. *Emile* went on sale in Paris at the end of May 1762. It was condemned by the Sorbonne on June 7, the Paris Parliament two days later, and the Archbishop of Paris on August 28, and then burned in the streets. Tissot defended *Emile* and its author to medical friends such as Albrecht von Haller and Johann Casper Hirzel (Leigh 1970, nos. 2052 and 1994).

22. Rousseau to Tissot, 1 April 1765 (Leigh 1970, no. 4227); also letter nos. 1980, 2006, 2525, 2566 in Dufour (1930).

23. Elosu (1929) describes Rousseau's chronic ailments and his longstanding animosity towards doctors.

24. Tissot to Rousseau, 8 July 1762 (Leigh 1970, no. 1966).

25. The editor of Rousseau's correspondence notes that "Rousseau could have countersigned many of the pages of [Tissot's *Advice*], for example those where Tissot decries rural depopulation, unhealthy city life, the overworking of common people, etc." (Leigh 1970, no. 1966n.a).

26. Rousseau to Tissot, 22 July 1762 (Leigh 1970, no. 2022).

27. As Ariès (1960) describes it, the "discovery of childhood" as a distinctive stage of life began only at the end of the seventeenth century and was marked by the rise of children's schools, the changing iconographic representation of children, and the evolution of children's clothes.

28. Barker-Benfield (1972) describes the anti-onanism campaign as an expression of an American preoccupation with spermatic economy: the self-managed accumulation and wise investment of male energies. Similar concerns are expressed in French anti-onanism texts regarding both men's and women's reproductive economies. See Elizabeth Williams (1994) on the *philosophes'* conception of *le physique et le morale*. The latter should not be simply understood in the current English sense of "morality."

29. See Bloch (1974) on Rousseau's impact on Enlightenment pedagogy.

30. For other critiques of Rousseau's misogyny and antifeminism, see Kofman (1982), Okin (1979), and Zerilli (1994).

31. For further analysis of Rousseau's sexual and gender politics, see Schwartz (1984).

32. Laqueur (1992) suggests that the concerns with the imagination outweighed the inadequate and often contradictory worries about the somatic pathophysiology of onanism. I argue that these went hand in hand.

33. On the rise of literacy and pornography see Dawson (1987). The word *pornography* (as exemplified by Restif de la Bretonne's *Le Pornographe,* 1779) originally referred to writings about prostitution rather than sexually explicit fiction. The latter was known as "licentious literature" in the eighteenth century (Kendricks 1988). The history of pornography at this time—its "golden age" (Alexandrian 1989)—has been the object of much recent scholarship. Aristocratic licentiousness inspired substantial pornographic political satire, especially during the Revolutionary period (see Hunt 1991, 1993; de Baecque 1991). Growing secularism and anti-Catholic sentiment also created a favorable climate for anticlerical pornography depicting libertinism in convents and seminaries (Wagner 1991). On the wide circulation of "clandestine literature" more generally and its political functions, see Darnton (1991).

34. Also see Goulemot (1991, 10).

35. See Goldstein (1987, 90–91) on Condillac's influence on Pinel.

36. Bienville's *Nymphomanie* was evidently quite popular in its time since it was republished in seven French editions and translated into English, Dutch, German and Italian. For what little is known of its obscure author, see G. Rousseau (1982). Also see Goulemot (1980).

37. Here Bienville prefigured the later therapeutic recommendations on hysteria by Robert Brudenell Carter (1853).

38. Rather than mention the word *lesbienne* himself, Tissot quotes Sappho: "Lesbides infamem quae me fecistis, amatae" (beloved lesbians who made me infamous) (1760, 65). I am grateful to Katherine Park for this translation.

39. On political pornography featuring Marie-Antoinette, see Hunt (1991).

40. In fact, the diagnostic labels *masochism* and *sadism* were not coined until the late nineteenth century by Richard von Krafft-Ebing in the sixth edition of his *Psychopathia sexualis* (1891).

41. For a psychoanalytic interpretation of the spanking scene, see Jury (1947). Lejeune (1975, 49–85) provides a detailed narratological analysis of it.

42. I use the phrase "psycho-sexual genetic narrative" to refer, as Butler (1990) does, to stories that attempt to explain the emergence of erotic desires. Freudian psychoanalysis is of course founded on such personal genetic erotic narratives, and also *prehistoric* ones, i.e., the Oedipal and totemic stories. I will return to these in the concluding supplement.

43. The terms *mastupratiomanie* and *mastupratiomane* seem to have been coined by Dr. Debourge (1852), a member of the Conseil d'hygiène publique et de salubrité of Montdidier, France.

44. Misch (1907, 1) claims that philological interest in autobiography was a product of the "European Enlightenment spirit," and that the very word *autobiography* is of late-eighteenth-century coinage. Lejeune (1975, 340) attributes the rise of the genre itself to Enlightenment bourgeois values and the cult of the self. On the importance given to Rousseau as the father of the genre, see Frye (1957, 308). Huntington Williams (1983) more specifically credits Rousseau with founding the Romantic autobiographical form which actualizes the virtual self through new techniques of autofictionalizing.

45. The scathing review in the *Journal des gens du monde* (1782) found the *Confessions* boring, insipid, egotistical, and abusive of its readers' indulgence. For other reactions to the first part of the *Confessions* see Lejeune (1975, 49–50).

46. Starobinski (1957) discusses Rousseau's fascination with his own virtue. Blum (1986) examines Rousseau's frequent invocation of "virtue" and the way the image of the virtuous Rousseau was evoked for a variety of political purposes throughout the French Revolution.

47. Also see Laqueur's analysis of masturbation and prostitution as antisocial acts (1989).

48. See Weiner (1970, 1993) on the rise of socialized medicine and the construction of the "citizen-patient" in Revolutionary France. See Ackerknecht (1948) on Napoleonic public hygiene. Coleman (1982, 21) discusses Restoration hygienists' metaphors of the social body and its pathologies.

49. Virey (1828, 79).

50. Foucault suggests that this preoccupation with heredity represented a shift from the aristocratic cult of "blood" to the bourgeois cult of "heredity" (1976, 164). But as we see here, the latter was also a concern with blood—a genetic blood that was malleable to environmental and behavioral manipulations, unlike "blue blood."

51. See Coleman (1982, 34–35) on French hygienists' concerns over fertility. Depopulation anxieties (probably ill-founded) had troubled the country throughout the eighteenth century too as France saw rival nations outstrip it in industrial and military manpower.

52. See Fairchild (1961) on the political uses of the "noble savage" ideal. As English politician and paleohistorian, Sir John Lubbock (1834–1913), put it in his *Prehistoric Times* (1865), "The true savage is neither free nor noble; he is a slave to his own wants, his own passions; . . . ignorant of agriculture, living by the chase, and improvident in success, hunger always stares him in the face and often drives him to the dreadful alternative of cannibalism or death" (qtd. in Stocking 1968, 41). I turn to nineteenth-century anthropology in chapter 4.

53. See Nye (1975) and Pick (1989) on the mounting concerns during the late nineteenth century over the urban poor and the working classes.

54. Also see P. Moreau (1882).

55. See Staum (1980, 292–97) on the disappointment of radical, materialist *Idéologues* (such as Cabanis) with the rise of Bonaparte.

## Chapter 2   Erotomaniacs

1. A peculiarly nineteenth-century diagnosis, "chlorosis" was a disease predominantly of adolescent girls who were chronically exhausted and had a pale, greenish tint. Some historians have reduced it to a form of anemia (Hudson 1977; Siddall 1982); Brumberg (1984) and Figlio (1978) provide more complex social analyses.

2. Baillarger's observation is in a long scientific tradition: locating "femininity" or female illnesses, particularly mental illness, in the female body (especially the sexual organs). See Smith-Rosenberg (1986, 182–96), Smith-Rosenberg and Rosenberg (1973), Shuttleworth (1990), Showalter (1985), Barker-Benfield (1976), Schiebinger (1989), Laqueur (1990), and Russett (1989).

3. We can also guess that her and others' erotolalia provided a definite titillation for medical and lay readers of erotomania cases.

4. Erotomania was reintroduced in the American Psychiatric Association's *Diagnostic and Statistical Manual-III-Revised* (1987, 199–203) as a type of "delusional (paranoid) disorder" distinct from schizophrenia. According to the *DSM-III-R* the defining erotic delusion is of being loved by another, usually a person of higher status, a famous person, or a superior. "The delusion usually concerns idealized romantic love and spiritual union rather than sexual attraction." Often the subject makes insistent, even threatening, attempts to contact the object of the delusion. Most clinical cases are female, while most forensic cases are males who "come into conflict with the law in their efforts to pursue the object of their delusion, or in a misguided effort to rescue him or her from some imagined danger. The prevalence of erotic delusions is such as to be a significant source of harassment to public figures" (199). Prior to the publication of the *DSM-III-R*, psychiatrists debated the clinical autonomy of the diagnosis, with some arguing that "erotomania" is usually a symptom of schizophrenia or an organic psychosis (Ellis & Mellsop 1985). Segal (1989) defends the validity of the diagnosis and the

*DSM-III-R*'s characterization of it, which he believes echoes that of Emil Kraepelin (1921) and Clérambault (1942). The *DSM-IV* (1994) retains the condition largely unchanged as diagnosis 297.1: "Delusional disorder, erotomanic type." For more on male erotomania, see Taylor, Mahendra, and Gunn (1983), and Gagné and Desparois (1995).

5. See Segal (1989). G. G. de Clérambault resurrected the phenomenon of erotomania in 1913 to describe a passing episode in a case of *délire de persécution*. He would later classify it under the general rubric of *psychoses passionelles*. Clérambault's erotomaniac syndrome (or "pure erotomania") consists of the delusion of being in amorous communication with a person of a higher social standing who was the first to fall in love and make advances (1942, 346). Despite vehement assurances to the contrary by the object of love, the subject remains convinced of this love; however, hallucinations are absent. Clérambault noted a regular progress on the part of the subject from optimism, persecutional feelings, to querulousness (1942, 331–32). He also believed that although platonic love (*Platonisme*) predominated in many cases, it was only superficial. Nevertheless, he felt that Platonism was more common in erotomaniacs than in the "normal man" because the erotomaniac's passion was a matter of pride more than love (335). For a more extensive discussion of Clérambault's syndrome, see Signer (1991). For more on Clérambault, see Papetti (1980). I return to him in chapter 4.

6. Taylor, Mahendra, and Gunn (1983), for example, erroneously credit Esquirol (1815) with the first psychiatric description and then overlook a century of writings on "erotomania" until the work of Clérambault in the 1920s. Segal (1989, 1262) also dismisses this nineteenth-century research. Also see Enoch, Trethowan, and Barker (1967).

7. *Trésor de la langue française*, s.v. "érotique" (B.1.a and B.3.b).

8. Dr. D. Jeanroi (1730–1816) in the *Encyclopédie* offered the two traditional denotations of *érotique*.

"*Chanson, poésie*, espèce d'ode anacréontique, dont l'amour et la galanterie fournissent la matière. . . .

"*Médecine*, . . . c'est une épithète qui s'applique à tout ce qui a rapport à l'amour des sexes: on l'employe particulièrement pour caractériser le délire, qui est causé par le dérèglement, l'excès de l'appétit corporel à cet égard, qui fait regarder l'objet de cette passion comme le souverain bien, et fait souhaiter ardemment de s'unir à lui; c'est une espece d'affection mélancolique, une véritable maladie, c'est celle que Willis appelle *eroto-mania*, et Sennert, *amor insanus*" (12(2):912–13, s.v. "*érotique*"). It is odd that the *Encyclopédie* refers not to the Frenchman Ferrand, but to Thomas Willis, who presented the medieval, humoral view of erotomania as a form of melancholic, insane love (*amor vesanus*) with heroical actions (*gestis heroicus*) (Willis 1670, 282).

It would take an extensive digression for me to discuss the uses of the word *erôs* from the Greek classics onward. Let me note briefly that the word denoted passionate sexual desire, in contrast to *philia* (affection or love). Halperin (1990) argues that Greek *erôs* was structured around a gender polarity: feminine/passive/receptive versus masculine/active/penetrative. Even Plato's attempt in the *Symposium* to construct an ideal of reciprocal pederastic desire relied on conventional models of "feminine" reproductivity (Halperin 1990, 142–47). While *erôs* might have been represented as a malady, *érotisme* did not connote deviant or perverse sex until the nineteenth century.

9. See Jacquart (1983, 43–53). Constantine the African translated Ibn al-Jazzār's text *Zād al-musāfir* (tenth century) under the title *Viaticum peregrinantis*. One chapter of the *Viaticum* on *"amor qui et eros* [or *hereos*] *dicitur"* (love that is also called eros/heroic) is the subject of an excellent monograph by Wack (1990). The *Viaticum* was a widely recopied text and was the subject of numerous commentaries. It was a standard medical textbook in Paris by the end of the twelfth century, and in Montpellier by the early fourteenth century (Wack, 48). One of Constantine's students, Johannes Afflicius, is believed to be the author of another translation of Ibn al-Jazzār's text under the title *Liber de heros morbo* (Book of the disease of heroes). This text gives *heroicus* a new meaning: "those who suffer from the disease of heroes." The text thus gave a clearer model of the idealized, melancholic love-suffering of the chivalric hero (Wack, 46–47).

10. Wack (1990, 166–69) argues that the aristocratic predominance of the disorder resulted from the psychic tension between men's inordinate power over women versus men's ideal courtly subservience to their beloved. Wack further suggests that the medical discourse on lovesickness allowed the medical students, faculty, and literate male readers to master their anxieties over these conflicting cultural amorous conventions (173). Wack proposes that the subsequent feminization of heroic love in the Renaissance may have been due to the availability of new Classical medical texts depicting lovesick women (175).

Italian Renaissance medical authors continued decribing *amor hereos* as amorous obsession. Carnal desire was often distinguished from true love as a bestial appetite or even as demonic possession (see Beecher 1992). In all cases, love and carnal desire were represented as obeying heterosexual aims, even if for pleasure alone (Pietropaolo 1992).

11. See Wack (1990, 175).

12. The English usage of "erotic" also arises from the conflation of "erotical love" and "heroical love" in a nongendered fashion. The *Oxford English Dictionary* (2d ed., s.v. "erotic") credits Richard Burton with the first printed use of "erotical love" during his discussion of "Love, or Heroical Melancholy" in *The Anatomy of Melancholy* (1620, pt. 3, sect. 2, Memb. 2, Subs. 1). Also see Pigeaud (1992).

13. These cases appeared in the *Mémoires de la Société médicale d'émulation,* the Idéologues' medical society under the direction of Pinel (see Goldstein 1987, 49).

14. See Goldstein (1987, 153–58) for further discussion of Esquirol and monomania.

15. See E. Williams (1994, 8) on the multiple connotations of *le moral* at the time.

16. Esquirol, however, subtly shifted from neuropsychological to neuroanatomical models in his later discussion of the "seat of erotomania." The original 1815 text with the 1838 variants given in braces reads: "Il nous suffit d'avoir fait sentir que cette maladie est une véritable altération {de la sensibilité et} de la faculté pensante, pour qu'on en conclue que les fonctions de *l'organe de la pensée* {[he substitutes] l'encéphale} sont lésées. . . . L'érotomanie étant une maladie essentiellement *nerveuse* {[he substitutes] cérébrale}, doit être traité comme les autres *monomanies nerveuses* {[he substitutes] affections cérébrales}" (1815, 192 {1838, 354}). He was aware of the increasingly important neuroanatomical and neurophysiological work of colleagues

such as Leuret, Foville, and Gerdy in the same decade. This research would have lasting effects, which I examine in chapter 4.

17. Leuret (1830, 200). Unless otherwise specified, all references to Mr. D——'s case throughout this section are from Leuret's article, which contains letters and medicolegal documents by Mr. D—— and numerous physicians.

18. Marc will be discussed at greater length in the following section. Guillaume Ferrus served as a military surgeon in the Napoleonic army and became a disciple of Philippe Pinel in 1814. He worked alongside Pinel at the Salpêtrière and in 1826 became chief physician for the insane at Bicêtre (Goldstein 1987, 127–28).

19. See Goldstein (1987, 175) on Esquirol, Marc, and the *Annales d'hygiène publique*.

20. On the history of the Charité de Charenton, see Weiner (1993, 272–75).

21. Dr. A.-A. Royer-Collard to the Ministre de la Police générale de l'Empire, 2 August 1808; qtd. in Cabanès (1901, 188).

22. Préfet de Police to the Ministre de la Police, 24 Fructidor, XII; qtd. in Cabanès (1901, 183). Lever (1991, 600) notes that Sade was held at Charenton under the official designation of a "malade de police."

23. Maurice Palluy, Directeur de la Maison Royale de Charenton; qtd. in Cabanès (1901, 196).

24. See Foucault (1976) and Nye (1989).

25. Foucault (1976) sees this starting at the end of the century with the "entomologization" of perversities.

26. On C.-C.-H. Marc's earlier career and the Conseil de salubrité de Paris, see Weiner (1974).

27. On Charcot's anticlericalism, see Goldstein (1987, ch. 9). On the iconography of hysteria, see Gilman (1993).

28. This narrative is compiled from *Le Siècle* (11 July 1849), the *Gazette des Tribunaux* (11 July 1849), and Brierre de Boismont (1849).

29. It is clear from the newspaper and *Gazette des Tribunaux* articles that the Bertrand trial was highly sensational and at times melodramatic. In this aspect it can be likened to the later trials of female criminals described by Harris (1989a; 1989b, ch. 6).

30. Ambroise Tardieu reproduced a lengthy "extract" of Bertrand's manuscript confession which Tardieu claims to have received from Marchal de Calvi before his death. It is not clear what may have been excised from the original. Epaulard (1901, 57–59) reproduced lengthy sections of Bertrand's confession which may have simply been copied from Tardieu, since Epaulard did not claim to have utilized the manuscript nor did he indicate its location. Shorter selections can also be found in Dansel (1991). Dansel's account is journalistic, sensationalist, and often highly speculative.

31. The theme of necrophilia or the fetishization of female body parts was especially popular in fantastical literature, for example, Théophile Gautier's *Le Roman de la momie* and *La Morte amoureuse* (see Voisin 1981, 194–98; Todorov 1970, 57, 146; Godfrey 1984). The association between love and violence would be given its most famous literary yet "scientific" expression in Zola's *La Bête humaine* (1889), where Jacques Lantier's slasher erotomania is represented as a degenerate taint tracing back to the prehistoric enmity between the sexes (*Bête*, 99). I am grateful to Henry Majewski for bringing Gautier's stories to my attention.

32. On the legal history of mitigating circumstances in France at this time, see Moulin (1982).

33. For more on the etymology of *necrophilia*, see Epaulard (1901, 9).

34. On the development of the concept of the "normal," see Canguilhem (1966).

35. At this moment of extreme national unrest during the Second Republic, the newspapers were filled with vitriolic anticlerical and antimilitary cries prompted by Louis Napoleon's Italian campaign and the state of emergency declared in France (see *Le Siècle* and *Courrier de France* during the month of July 1849).

36. The defenders of so-called "free medical education" (*enseignement libre des sciences médicales*) wished to reintroduce clerical education at all levels including medical school (Latour 1849c). Frédéric comte de Falloux—then Minister of Public Education and head of the clerical party along with Montalembert—named commissions on higher education and on medicine charged with reviewing university admissions, courses, exams, and degree granting. In principle, the commissions were charged with putting into effect the constitutional guarantee that education be free (Guérin 1849b). The commissions contributed to the eventual passage on March 15, 1850 of the *loi Falloux*, which gave members of religious orders the right to open schools without any professional qualifications and introduced strongly clerical councils to regulate the universities.

In the summer of 1849, Republican physician Amédée Latour (the editor of the *Union Médicale*) quickly suspected that something foul was brewing, since the commission included three clergymen and Jules Guérin (the editor of the competing journal, the *Gazette médicale de Paris* and a member of the Academy of Medicine) (Latour 1849b). It was clear to Latour that "freedom" was a euphemism for deregulation and, particularly, for weakening the dominance of the materialist, secular Faculty of Medicine of Paris in favor of spiritualist and clerical teaching in the French school system in general. Clerical teaching had waxed and waned since 1789 according to each government's attitude toward the church. The rise of Louis Bonaparte to the presidency during the reactionary wave after the February Revolution of 1848 brought about greater state tolerance of and collaboration with the church. This spelled trouble for the Left. In a series of articles and rebuttals that grew increasingly polemical and inflammatory, the editors of the *Union* and the *Gazette* fought political battles that made explicit the connections between philosophical ideology and "medical authority."

37. Latour (1849a, 409) cites this from a "political journal which supposedly represents the opinions of M. de Falloux."

38. Amy Taublin (1991) in the *Village Voice* explicitly made use of the word *erotomania* in her coverage of the hearings. She also noted the mention, during the hearings, of the recent movie *Fatal Attraction*, about a spurned woman driven to insanity and murder.

## Chapter 3   Inverts

1. Foucault (1976, 59) gives the date of birth of the modern "homosexual" as 1870, when Westphal published his *conträre Sexualempfindung* article that constituted homosexuality "less by a type of sexual relations than by a certain quality of sexual sensibility." (Actually, as Féray [1981, 256] points out, the article was published in 1869.)

Chauncey (1982–1983, 116) and Halperin (1990, 15–16) are more circumspect in distinguishing the multifaceted diagnosis of "sexual inversion" (which combined elements of deviant gender behavior with physical and psychical hermaphroditism) from the diagnosis of "homosexuality" (which focused on same-sex object choice). On the importance of late-nineteenth-century medical science in constructing homosexuality in diverse European and American contexts, see Greenberg (1988), Herrn (1995), Lanteri-Laura (1979), Weeks (1976, 1977), Abelove (1993), Hansen (1989), and Davidson (1990).

2.  See Hemmings (1982, 151) on the legal persecution of Baudelaire's work.

3.  Lottman (1989, 134) and Dumesnil (1928) explain the publication history and legal entanglements of *Madame Bovary*.

4.  Aron and Kempf (1984) discuss Tardieu's career and Demeaux's campaign against onanism in boarding schools.

5.  See Copley (1989, 24) and Sibalis (1996) on French legislation concerning sodomy and "public indecency." On the persecution of eighteenth-century sodomites, see Rey (1989).

6.  On sodomitical subcultures, see Trumbach (1987) and Rey (1987). On the rise of pornographic representations of sodomy and tribadism, see Ragan (1996), Colwill (1996), and Hunt (1993).

7.  Lieutenant-General of Police Lenoir in his *Mémoires* 1:289 (qtd. in Rey 1989, 137).

8.  The semantic distinction between sodomy and pederasty had begun to erode in the eighteenth century. Police records after 1738 increasingly used the the term *sodomite* (Rey 1989, 145). Tardieu (1857, 198) was careful to define *pederasty* as "the love of young boys" and *sodomy* as the general designation for all "acts against nature," regardless of the sex of those involved. Nevertheless, he too used the terms interchangeably in his work.

9.  See, for example, a case of sodomy, delusions of persecution, and murder reported by Reignier, Lagardelle, and Legrand du Saulle (1877).

10.  While Tardieu did not comment on the predominance of fifteen- to twenty-five-year-olds in his data, I suspect that this group represents those engaged in prostitution, and that older pederasts had more private venues for congregating that afforded greater protection from police entrapment.

11.  Several of these rectal signs had been described previously. Cullier claimed a "great facility for immediately recognizing [pederasts], and he was rarely mistaken in this regard." A funnel-shaped appearance of the anus was "an almost certain sign, and one could be almost certain that those who exhibit this are stained by the vice" (qtd. in Reydellet 1819, 45).

12.  Tardieu's statements in 1857 about the specific mental characterisitics of pederasts undermines the oft-recited Foucauldian tenet that an epistemic break occured in 1870 between pederasty (as an act) and homosexuality (as a state of being) (see n. 1).

13.  On the eighteenth-century association of effeminacy and sodomy see Trumbach (1989, 134–35). On effeminacy and cross-dressing among eighteenth-century sodomitical mock-religious "orders," see Lever (1985, 318). On *molles*, see Halperin (1990, 22).

14. Sade, through the character of Dolmancé in *La Philosophie dans le boudoir* (1795, 161–62), had also declared that sodomites were naturally and constitutionally so, and that they had a distinctive, recognizable physiognomy, anatomy, and character.

15. See Rey (1987, 189) on eighteenth-century cross-dressing.

16. Newton (1972) and Garber (1992) make similar arguments concerning cross-dressing in the modern American context.

17. Article 471, § 15 of the Penal Code of June 10, 1853 criminalized transvestitism in public spaces and balls. The law was subsequently reaffirmed by police ordinances of January 1, 1927 and February 2, 1949, so that transvestitism technically continues to be an offense in France except during carnival. Transsexuals (i.e., those in any stages of sex reassignment) must regularly submit medical testimony in order to legally cross-dress in public. It is worth pointing out that earlier dress code laws existed. The decree of 8 Brumaire II (October 29, 1793) was primarily intended to give freedom of dress to male and female citizens, thus abolishing class distinctions: "Each is free to wear whatever clothes and fittings *of his sex* that please him" (Duvergier 1825, vol. 6; emphasis added). It nevertheless continued to criminalize *travestissement* in military or ecclesiastic garb, which was seen as a threat to social order.

18. Bénédict A. Morel (1809–1873) was born in Vienna and brought up in parochial boarding schools since his father travelled constantly as a supplier to the Napoleonic army. Morel was initially enrolled in a seminary before switching to medical studies; his Catholic training strongly influenced his medical work. During his medical studies in Paris he befriended Claude Bernard and was drawn into the circle of alienist J. P. Falret at the Salpêtrière. From 1848 to 1856 he was an alienist at the asylum in Maréville, and then spent the rest of his life as director of the Asyle Saint Yon (see Dowbiggin 1991, 118). Friedlander (1973) also points out the influence of Prosper Lucas's "laws of creation" (1847–1850) and of German *Naturphilosophie* on Morel's work.

19. Morel's treatise on degeneration appeared two years before Darwin's *On the Origin of Species* (1859); nevertheless, Morel's Lamarkian theory of the transmission of dysfunctional, acquired traits continued to hold sway in France throughout the nineteenth century since French biologists strongly resisted Darwin's ideas (see Buican 1984).

20. Nye (1984) and Pick (1989) carefully explore the medical and social utility of the degeneration diagnosis in Europe.

21. See Dowbiggin (1991) for a social and professional history of degeneration theory in late-nineteenth-century France, emphasizing its importance—as a credibly somatic and scientific theory—in defending psychiatric professional power in the face of the waning credibility of Esquirolian moral therapy and of growing antipsychiatric sentiment in the 1860s.

22. See Foucault (1963) and Ackerknecht (1967) on the rise of anatomico-pathological correlation in the Faculty of Medicine of Paris in the early nineteenth century. Arnold Davidson (1990) has suggested that there was a radical break between the anatomical and psychological modes of conceptualizing mental disorders, particularly "sexual perversion." Although these two perspectives were very different conceptually, I demonstrate here that there was not an epistemic break between them but a gradual

transition from the anatomical to the psychological approach. Castel (1976) documents the general ascendency of psychiatry in France.

23. The Société médico-psychologique was founded in 1852 after an abortive attempt to start it in the tumultuous year 1848. Its membership roster included the prominent alienists of the time. Its official organ, the *Annales médico-psychologiques* (which first appeared in 1843) was the first journal dedicated to psychiatry in France.

24. Goldstein (1987) traces in detail the professional history of psychiatry/ alienism in nineteenth-century France and its growing presence in the courtrooms as a means of accruing professional power.

25. In his roster of "genesic perversions," Legrand du Saulle included a necrophile as well as an eleventh-grade student who was arrested for performing "buccal masturbation" (presumably fellatio) upon a fifty-seven-year-old man under a bridge. The case appears to have grabbed the doctor's attention as a case of "reasoning insanity," not primarily because of the sexual activity but because of the fellator's youth and the fact that the adolescent performed the activity outside in the chill of winter (1876, 444).

26. Ilza Veith (1965) notes that hysteria in men was briefly reported by Aretaeus and Galen (both of the second century), but male hysteria was ignored for a millenium and a half (Veith, 22, 38). She discusses several other doctors who were significant to the male hysteria diagnosis. Charles Lepois (1563–1633) first clearly argued that hysteria was a cerebral disorder and therefore could affect both men and women, but he did not succeed in weakening the uterine theory of hysteria. Similarly, physiologist and neuroanatomist Thomas Willis (1622–1675) proposed the cerebral seat of hysteria. It was Thomas Sydenham (1624–1689), however, who most convincingly claimed that hysteria was a mental disorder due to the "faulty disposition of the animal spirits" rather than of the uterus or semen. Although this neurological etiology meant that it could affect men and women equally, Veith argues that Sydenham avoided controversy by designating the masculine version of hysteria as "hypochondriasis." William Cullen (1712–1790) repopularized the uterine theory of hysteria, broadening the pathophysiology to include disorders of menstruation and the ovaries. Although Scipion Pinel (1844, 179) propounded the neuropsychological pathology of hysteria, he still considered it a disease of women since it was a "genital neurosis" like nymphomania or *furor uterinus*. Also see the thoughtful revision of the history of hysteria by King (1993).

27. On hysteria as a caricature of femininity see Smith-Rosenberg (1986, 215) and Showalter (1993).

28. Dr. Yver, in the service of Dr. Lacassagne in 1872, reported in Klein (1880, case no. 41). Also see Stoickesco's and Henriet's cases reported by Petit (in Klein, case nos. 42 and 27); Michéa (1865b) (precocious intelligence, "little inclination for corporal exercises"). Scipion Pinel described a young man with the classical *globus hystericus* whose "genital organs were poorly developed; he had never known women, he said; he had a weak constitution, pale, feminine skin, no beard, little hair" (1844, 423).

29. Other findings described are: "caractères de féminisme" (Ledouble 1879); infantilism and effeminacy, very impressionable mother (Lancereaux 1884); "the son is hysterical like the mother" (Gschwender 1869). Also see Petit's thesis of 1875 (reported in Klein, no. 59), Couty and Arou (in Lallemand's thesis, 1877; reported in Klein, nos. 75, 71).

30. Jacques-Joseph Moreau (de Tours) (1804–1884) was born in Montrésor, Indre-et-Loire, to a father who served in Napoleon's army. He completed his medical training in Paris and did his internship under Esquirol at Charenton Asylum. He established himself at Bicêtre Hospital, where a controversy over the etiology of mental disease was raging; he sided with somaticist hereditarians. He claimed that an inherited *névrosité* (a dynamic nervous lesion) underlay mental illness. Following along Morellian lines, Moreau argued in *La Psychologie morbide* that heredity was a strong pathological element in mental illness. For more information on Moreau, see Dowbiggin (1991, ch. 3).

31. Smith-Rosenberg (1986, 206) describes the same association between hysteria and masturbation in late-nineteenth-century America.

32. From Petit's thesis (1875), reported in Klein (1880, case no. 62). See also Bouneau's thesis on hysteria (1817), reported in Briquet (1859, 15), which describes a small, thin, weak hysterical man who had abandoned himself to masturbation in childhood.

33. It should be noted that in 1881 Fabre retreated from his earlier position that effeminacy was pathognomonic for male hysteria. His change of opinion was mainly prompted by August Klein's thesis (1880), which forcefully argued that effeminacy was not a necessary or even regular feature of the disease.

34. Goldstein (1991) argues that Flaubert used his hysteria to gain a subversive, androgynous gender position from which to write of women's experience. While one can interpret hysteria to have been Flaubert's muse, Flaubert instead complained that his hysterical, feminine hypersensitivity—like masturbatory exhaustion—was the cause of his bouts of literary impotence: "Each attack . . . was a seminal loss of the picturesque faculty of the brain" (Flaubert to Colet; qtd. in Dumesnil 1905, 430).

35. Steakley (1975) examines the history of antisodomy legislation and homosexual rights in modern Germany.

36. Ulrichs derived the appellation *Urning* from Pausanias's praise of Uranian or celestial pederasty in Plato's *Symposium* (see Halperin 1990, 16). Ulrichs's works on Uranian love, originally published from 1864 to 1879, were reprinted in 1898 by Magnus Hirschfeld.

37. For more on Ulrichs's scientific basis for the "inversion" model, see Kennedy (1997). For more on the inversion model's subsequent impact on sexology, see Hekma (1994) (although this is a rather meliorist analysis critical of effeminate homosexuals).

38. For more on Ulrichs and the subsequent campaigns to overturn Paragraph 175, see Kennedy (1988), Steakley (1975), and Oosterhuis (1991).

39. The outpouring of German articles in the 1870s on contrary sexual sensation includes publications by Schminke (1872), Scholz (1873), Gock (1875), Servæs (1876), Westphal (1876), Stark (1877), and Krafft-Ebing (1877).

40. Krafft-Ebing distinguished thirteen "congenital" cases from five "temporary" cases of contrary sexual sensation. Widely admired as the founder of modern sexology, Krafft-Ebing came from a politically liberal family; his maternal grandfather had been a liberal law professor at Heidelberg University. He received his medical degree there in 1863 and took up teaching and practice in psychiatry. His interest in "inverts" began when he encountered the writings of "Numa Numantius" (Karl H. Ulrichs) in 1866. Krafft-Ebing's great encyclopedia of sexual perversions, *Psychopathia Sexualis*

(1886), grew rapidly through twelve editions and firmly established his leadership in sexology until the advent of Freud. Also see Grimm (1995).

41. Apter (1991, 17) analyzes the fin-de-siècle history of fetishism from a Freudian perspective to argue that Charcot and Magnan's article turned all fetishists into suspected homosexuals. Instead, I argue that Charcot and Magnan viewed "inversion" as just one variant of a broader "sexual perversion" diagnosis (what would later be called "fetishism").

42. Krafft-Ebing originally distinguished two categories of *Perversion des Geschlechtstriebs:* "1. Es besteht geschlechtliche Neigung zu personen des anderen Geschlechts, aber die Art der Befriedigung des Triebs ist eine perverse. a) Fälle von Mordlust als potenzirter Wollust bis zur Anthropophagie, b) von Nekrophilie. 2. Es besteht instinctiver Abscheu gegen Vermischung mit Personen des anderen Geschlechts und als Aequivalent des Defects normaler Geschlechtsempfindung geschlechtliche Empfindung gegenüber Personen desselben Geschlechts. . . . Fälle sogenannter conträrer Sexualempfindung." (1877, 301).

43. See Krafft-Ebing (1894, 14–15). For more on his efforts to repeal Paragraph 175, see Oosterhuis (1997).

44. Chevalier, however, complained in his thesis on inversion that "the French language was truly tortured before reaching the expression of inversion" (1885, 14). See his list of competing terms further on.

45. Tamassia's perceptive formulation of the problem is worth quoting in full: "Noi non possiamo con molta precisione definire l'abnorme stato psicologico, di cui ci occupiamo. La parola inversione è troppo vaga: essa include due idee: l'una che l'individuo, pur riconoscendosi di un dato sesso, psicologicamante sente tutti gli attributi del sesso opposto, ed in questa specie di dualismo tra sentimento della propria individualità e materialità dell'organismo, modella tutti i suoi pensieri, limitandosi però al puro e semplice riconoscimento di questo terribile stato; l'altra che l'individuo, posseduto egualmente da questa alterazione dell'istinto, appetisce soddisfare il proprio istinto sessuale su individui del proprio sesso." (1878, 99).

46. These points had already been stated by Klein in 1880. On Charcot's development of the diagnosis of male hysteria, see Micale (1990, 1995) and Evans (1991).

47. On French anxieties concerning national decay, infertility, and emasculation, see Nye (1984, 1989, 1993a).

48. The Italian is refering to the character of Baptiste, the groom-loving valet in Zola's *La Curée* (1871, 591). As I will explain shortly, the Italian's confession (which I cite as "Invert") was published anonymously in a medical journal in 1894–1895. Its date of composition is uncertain. Setz (1991, 82) estimates that it was written in 1887 or 1888 based on the author's references to historical events. Alternatively, the document can be approximately dated to 1889 since the Italian author wrote to Dr. Laupts upon encountering the 1896 publication of the confession, and Saint-Paul (1930, 115n.2) notes that this was seven years after the original letters were sent to Zola.

49. Undated letter from the Italian invert to Dr. Laupts; qtd. in Saint-Paul (1930, 115).

50. For the various diagnoses of Zola as a pathological writer, see Toulouse (1896) and Nordau (1893, 2:456). For more on the medical attacks of Zola, see Martineau (1907), Rolet (1907), and Pick (1989, 76–78).

51. From Zola's thank-you note of 16 April 1896 to Marc-André Raffalovich, for the gift of the latter's *L'Uranisme et l'unisexualité* (qtd. in Allen 1966, 221).

52. Critiques related by Laupts (1907, 837).

53. The italicized paragraph was censored in the original text (Invert 1895, 228), but appeared in Latin in the later versions. My thanks to David Halperin for this translation from the Latin.

54. His obscurity has persisted since most modern scholars of homosexuality cite his work without discussing his life or contributions. See for example, Lanteri-Laura (1979) and Greenberg (1988). Unfortunately, Cardon's essay (1993) suffers from factual errors and a hagiographic approach that distorts Raffalovich's writings and politics.

55. For examples of this neoconservative approach to gay rights in the United States see Kirk and Madsen (1989), and Sullivan (1995).

56. Sewell (1963, 22). Also see Ellman (1988, 282, 391–92).

57. John Gray's father had been a carpenter, but the young Gray had managed to educate himself and enter the civil service as a postal clerk and then a librarian in the Foreign Office. He was an aspiring poet—a talent which may have attracted Wilde as much as Gray's boyish looks. In any case, Wilde vaunted Gray's artistry and had promised to cover the expenses for his first collection of poems, *Silverpoints* (1892). The choice of the hero's name in Wilde's *A Portrait of Dorian Gray* was probably the main token of affection to John since the character resembles Wilde more than Gray. The young poet nevertheless took to signing himself "Dorian" in letters to Wilde (Ellman 1988, 308).

58. *The London Times*, 18 June 1894, qtd. in Sewell (1963, 20).

59. His choice of patron saint betrays a certain naughty humor. Saint Sebastian (the patron of archers, usually depicted as a seminaked, bound youth pierced by arrows) had long been an object of pederasts' veneration. The iconographically homoerotic saint was one of Wilde's favorite painted subjects and he used the name as his alias in France (Ellman 1988, 71n.).

60. For these and other details on Raffalovich, see Sewell (1963, 1968), McCormack (1991), and Ellman (1988).

61. Homosexual author and arts critic Arthur Symons met Ellis in 1888 and they became lifelong friends. They were housemates for a while and frequent travel companions. During their trip to Paris in 1890 they attended one of Charcot's public lectures at the Salpêtrière and a meeting of the Paris Anthropological Society; they also met Huysmans and Rémy de Gourmont, among other literary notables. In 1899 Symons published *The Symbolist Movement in Literature* based on his readings of and personal acquaintance with many Symbolist authors. He and Ellis published translations of Zola novels (*L'Assomoir* and *Germinal,* respectively). It was through Symons that John A. Symonds first inquired in 1892 about the possibility of Ellis commissioning a volume on sexual inversion; this would later flower into Ellis and Symonds's *Sexual Inversion* (1896). For these and other details on Symons, see Grosskurth (1980).

62. Respectively, these three points were advanced by: (1) Charcot and Magnan (1882) (2) Magnan (1885a) and Sérieux (1888); (3) Laurent (1894).

63. See Laupts's questionnaire (1894, 107) and Chevalier (1893, 39).

64. *Petit Larousse* (1985), s.v. "homosexualité."

65. Raffalovich's medicomoral apologia gained currency among twentieth-century French homosexuals, notably André Gide and Henry de Montherlant. On Gide

and his apologia for "normal," virile pederasty in *Corydon,* see Pollard (1991) and Lucey (1995). On Montherlant's archconservative nationalist politics and praise of masculinity, see Mosse (1985, ch. 8). Echos of Raffalovich are also heard in subsequent conservative, Roman Catholic, French homosexual organizations (see Rosario 1992). The conservative, rightist aspects of Raffalovich's sexual politics are completely erased by Cardon (1993).

66. A respected psychologist, philosopher, and hypnotist, Max Dessoir (1867–1947) proposed that pubescent children were in a stage of "undifferentiated" sexuality where libidinal drives could become attached to either sex or even to animals. This was all quite normal, for it was followed by a stage of "differentiation" where the libido focused on heterosexual relationships. Some children, however, never escaped these "embryonic" libidinal attachments and retained homosexual, bisexual, or other perverse orientations (1894).

Albert Moll (1862–1939) studied medicine in Berlin, Vienna, London, and Paris (with Charcot), and also learned hypnotic therapy from Hippolyte Bernheim in Nancy. He first gained a reputation for his research in hypnotism (1889). In Moll's monograph *Konträre Sexualempfindung* (1891), he pointed out the circularity of the degeneration theory of inversion, where homosexuality served as both symptom and diagnosis. He believed instead that inversion was just one of the natural variants of the sexual instinct. See Sulloway (1983, 298–305) for his discussions of Dessoir and Moll.

67. See Herdt's (1989) cross-cultural review of the coming out process.

68. On homosexual bars see Benstock (1989). On the cultural chic of homosexuality at the time, see Weber (1986, 37). On working-class lesbian culture, see Canadé Sautman (1996).

69. Hirschfeld was an early German pioneer in sexology and an active campaigner for homosexual rights. For more on Hirschfeld, see Charlotte Wolff's biography (1986). Although Raffalovich (1905, 283) bravely argued for the equitable treatment of unisexuals, he vigorously opposed Hirschfeld's Scientific and Philanthropic Committee because of the "sexual anarchy" and excessive sexual freedom he believed the Committee promoted. Steakley (1997) discusses the politics of Hirschfeld's sexology.

70. I borrow the neologism *unknowing* from Sedgwick (1988), who uses it to designate the way in which the lack of knowledge, or a willful ignorance, can be as much a source of power as any purported knowledge.

71. See Park (1997) on Renaissance concerns over clitoral hypertropy and sodomy.

72. On Enlightenment representations of "tribades," see Merrick (1996) and Colwill (1996). On the novelistic representation of lesbianism, see Aron and Kempf (1979, 148–50), and Marks (1979).

73. On the rise of popular literary images of Sappho, particularly in pseudoscientific novels, see Albert (1993).

74. In the United States—particularly since the wave of "gay liberation" and public visibility sparked by the Stonewall Riot in 1969—fictions of homosexuality especially have served the nationalist cause. During the Gulf War (1990–1991), Iraq's President Saddam Hussein was portrayed as a transvestite, sadistic, pederast (*National Examiner,* 12 March 1991). T-shirts sporting an image of a camel with Hussein's face

for an anus declared patriotically, "America Will Not be Saddam-ized" (see Goldberg 1992, 1–5). Homosexualizing the enemy and protecting the United States from homosexual invasion were a unified strategy of defense. The U.S. military, quite literally, feared a homosexual invasion in 1993 when threatened by President Bill Clinton with the open admission of gays into the armed services. U.S. television viewers were treated to grainy footage of showering enlisted men as soldiers confessed their fears of being cruised by the impending hoards of queers clamoring to enter the services. These soldiers' anxieties (or fantasies) of homosexual objectification and scopophilic feminization clearly outweighed any concerns over flashing on millions of television screens. Given the incessant mention of AIDS throughout the debate, one imagines that these soldiers feared a double contagion: both AIDS and homosexuality. Their generals' paranoid fabrications of the homosexual menace strangely mirror the very neuropsychiatric unfitness for which homosexuals were originally screened out by the Selective Service in 1940 (Medical Circular No. 1; also see Bérubé 1990, 11–5).

75. In this Platonic dialogue, Socrates tells Phaedrus the following story. Thoth (the god of numbers, geometry, letters, and games) offers Thamos, King of Egypt, letters (*grammata*) as a means of making Egyptians wiser and of improving their memory. It will be an elixir (*pharmakon*) of memory and wisdom, Thoth promises. Thamos rejects letters, predicting that they will produce forgetfulness because people will come to rely on alien marks rather than their own memory. "You have discovered an elixir not of memory," Thamos declares, "but of reminding" (*Phædrus*, 274c–275b). Writing merely produces an appearance of learning rather than true learning. Instead of a cure for forgetfulness, the *pharmakon* of writing (*logos*) is rejected as an artifice of learning: a poison of memory and knowledge.

## Chapter 4     Fetishists

1. Binet cites Max Müller for the phrase "culte des brimborions," but the French translation of Müller's *Lectures on the Origins and Growth of Religion* (1878) never uses the phrase. The translation talks about the "respect superstitieux pour de véritables brimborions" (1878a, 59), which is different in tone than the original English version of this passage: "the superstitious veneration of mere rubbish" (1878b, 65). Nevertheless, after Binet's article, the term "culte des brimborions" was cited regularly by writers on sexual fetishism. Müller's lecture will be discussed in greater detail later.

2. I cite Flaubert's fiction by the title of the work and page number in the Pléiade edition of his *Œuvres*.

3. Charles de Brosses, president of the Dijon Assembly, published a compendium of existing exploration narratives of the South Pacific, *Histoire des naviations aux terres australes* (1756). De Brosses was better known for his *Lettres familières sur l'Italie* and his *Traité sur la formation méchanique des langues* (1765). For more on de Brosses, see Iacono (1992, 59–64).

4. Adding to the etymology of the word, de Brosses explained that it was also derived from the Latin *fatum* or *fanum*, meaning enchanted, divine, or oracular. Müller (1878a, 58) argued that this etymology was false and had been invented to further de Brosses's aim of erecting the notion of fetishism as a religion. Indeed, de Brosses

claimed that savages and primitives deify the first object they encounter that "flatters their caprice" (21): pebbles, bones, shells, flowers, mountains, animals (18). He insisted, nevertheless, that fetishism was not idolatry, since the fetish was worshipped for its own sake and not because it was an image or representation of a god (20). The savage mind was supposedly too infantile to engage in symbolic activity; according to de Brosses, fetishism "corresponds to the degree zero of the human faculty of representation and symbolization" (Iacono 1992, 54). Pietz (1985, 10) points out that the fetish was first conceptualized as a material object in close relation to the body (since certain fetishes were always worn). They could control the body, its desires, health, and identity.

5. Contemporary anthropologists have rejected most of de Brosses's observations on fetishism. Some anthropologists have even questioned whether "fetishism" exists at all as a religious system anywhere. For a contemporary review of fetishism as an object of anthropological inquiry, see Augé (1988).

6. See Iacono (1992) and Canguilhem (1983) on the place of fetishism in Comte's work.

7. Of course, associations between religion and illness are to be found well before the invention of "monomania." We have already seen that medieval physicians regularly worried that the enforced sexual abstinence of priests and nuns could result in disease. Nuns had been especially singled out as a population at risk for hysteria. As we shall see further on, a connection between religious chastity and hysteria resurfaced in the nineteenth century. Louyer-Villermay (1819a, 572), for example, warned that such lengthy abstinence was a cause of "andromania": the nymphomaniacal lust for men.

8. Charles-Chrétien-Henri Marc founded, along with Esquirol, the *Annales d'hygiène publique* in 1829. They were both dedicated to the social implementation of medical knowledge and were strong promoters of the monomania diagnosis (Goldstein 1987, 175).

9. It was only because of a particular excess and mania that Dr. Guislain, for example, could diagnose insanity in a woman who repeatedly genuflected, sang religious verses, invoked the Virgin out loud, and whose entire "psalmodic conversation revolved around evangelical subjects" (1881, 155).

10. See Goldstein (1987) on medical anticlericalism during the Third Republic.

11. Dr. Santenoise's article "Religion et folie" (1900) was published in the materialist *Revue philosophique,* edited by psychologist Théodule Ribot.

12. Dr. Hospital of the Clermont-Ferrand asylum described a classic case of a "priest lover": la femme Ron—, a thirty-four year-old peasant woman, "large, robust, very ugly." Upon becoming widowed and destitute, this patient developed the imperative desire to "live with the Capuchin monks, but in the least equivocal terms and of a nature that left no doubt about the form of her insanity" (1875, 252). She was arrested for scaling the wall of what she wrongly believed to be a Capuchin monastery and insisted on leaving the asylum to go live with the Capuchins. Hospital's diagnosis of *érotisme* was definitive, confirmed by the fact that the patient's brother had been committed for depressive religious mania and the patient's autopsy revealed an evident lesion of the cerebellum (the phrenological seat of "amativeness").

13. Marx, *Capital* (London: Lawrence and Wishart, 1961–1962), 3:809; cited in Geras (1971, 69).

14. For a postmodern French critique of the contemporary culture of consumption, see Baudrillard (1979) and Baudrillard's essay on fetishism and ideology (1972). For a survey and critique of recent semiotic readings of Marx's theory of fetishism, see Pietz (1993).

15. Miller's functionalist analysis of the Bon Marché perceptively analyzes the bourgeois bureaucratic values embodied by the "total institution" of the Second Empire department store (1981). Also see Marry (1979).

16. R. Williams (1982, 12) also examines the reliance of mass consumerism on manipulations of the imagination.

17. A Swiss doctor, André Matthey, first used the word *klopémanie* to describe a "perversion of the will" driving people to useless thefts (1816). Marc first used the term *kleptomanie* to describe a "monomania of theft" particular to people of substantial means who suffered imperative, instinctive urges to steal frivolous objects they could easily afford. Although not intrinsically gendered as hysteria was, the kleptomania diagnosis was particularly reserved for bourgeois women and was associated with many supposed features of the female nervous system, temperament, and biology, especially menstrual anomalies or pregnancy (Marc 1840, 2:247–302). With the obsolescence of the monomania diagnosis, doctors sought clearer neurological and hereditary etiologies for kleptomania. Morel (1854) described kleptomania as a "pseudo-monomania" that was really an epileptiform impulsion of degenerates. Gorry (1879, 10) argued that it was never found as a pure condition but always a symptom of other serious organic degenerate disorders. For a detailed review of the medical kleptomania literature, see Seguier (1966).

18. At the Fourth International Criminal Anthropology Conference, medicolegal expert Alexandre Lacassagne declared kleptomania a "social phenomenon" (1896, 77). Antheume (1925) examines the "epidemic" of kleptomania in nineteenth-century Paris. Also see O'Brien (1983) for a feminist analysis of the prevalence of the kleptomania diagnosis at this time.

19. Citations from Zola's novels correspond to the Pléiade edition of the *Rougon-Macquart* cycle. Zola's inclusion of the pink glove robber was probably inspired by one of Legrand du Saulle's cases. In Zola's notes on the case, he jotted down: "The desire of pregnant woman especially // always the same object 600 men's black ties" (Nouvelles Acquisitions Françaises 10277, 397). Zola made extensive preparatory notes and sketches for each of his novels. These manuscript dossiers, preserved at the Bibliothèque Nationale, include not only Zola's notes to himself throughout the conception of the novels, but also relevant newspaper clippings and legal documents, research notes, correspondence from informants, and his own maps of neighborhoods and department stores. They will be cited by their "Nouvelles Acquisitions Françaises" (NAF) numbers.

20. Lunier was perhaps the only notable physician to question the female gendering of the disease when, in 1880, he objected to the label *voleuses des magasins* and substituted *voleurs aux étalages* (display counter thieves) because women were not the only kleptomaniacs and the large department stores were not the only site for such thefts. Lunier pointed out that the preponderance of female cases was due to the fact that women shop more frequently than men and the popular prejudice associating kleptomania with pregnancy, menopause, or other female "morbid dispositions" led to the systematic medicolegal evaluation of female shoplifters (1880, 241).

21. Binet mentioned, in particular, Müller (1878a) and Alfred Maury, who was an ethnologist and historian of religion. Among Maury's many works, Binet specifically cited *La Magie et l'astrologie dans l'antiquité et au moyen âge* (1860).

22. Alfred Binet was born in Nice, on July 3, 1857. His father was a physician and his mother an artist. He obtained a *licence* in law in 1878, by which time he became an adherent of Positivist criminology. He soon began medical studies and in 1883 his lycée friend Joseph Babinski introduced him to Charcot and Charles Samson Féré. Binet started frequenting Charcot's lectures and "laboratory" of hysterics (1883–1890). In the 1880s he was under the sway of English Associationism, and especially admired Mill. In 1892 he was named adjunct-director, and later sub-director, of the Laboratory of Physiological Psychology at the Sorbonne. In 1895, he and Féré founded the *Année psychologique,* which he edited until 1899. In experimental psychology Binet is known for having noted the role of the past in the present, for developing numerous research tools (esthesiometer of constant mass, dynamometer for testing intellectual fatigue, chronoscope for measuring the duration of intellectual phenomena), and for his studies on the mentally retarded. For more biographical information on Binet, see the bibliography by Wolf (1973) and the eulogies published by his colleagues Simon (1912) and Larguier de Bancels (1912). For more on Binet's work on IQ testing, see Gould (1981, 146–58).

23. Binet collaborated with André de Latour de Lorde on a number of plays (see Apter 1991, 19n.9).

24. Among his French colleagues, Binet was familiar with Ball's article on "erotic insanity" (1887) (mentioned earlier), Magnan's neurological theory of sexual perversions (1886), and the discussions of inverts by Gley (1884) and Ribot (1885, 74–76). Beyond France, Binet in 1887 was informed by Mantegazza's physiological/anthropological writings (*Fisiologia del amore* [1873] and *Gli amori dei usomini* [1885]) and the work of Tarnowsky and Lombroso on inversion. See Bleys (1995) for a detailed examination of this nineteenth-century anthropological work on sexuality. Binet criticized the theories of the Germans, particularly Westphal (1869, 1876) and Krafft-Ebing (1877). Only the previous year, Krafft-Ebing had published the first edition of his *Psychopathia sexualis* (1886). It would go through eight exponentially growing German editions before its translation into French by Emile Laurent and Sigismond Csapo in 1895. Binet did not refer to it when he described "amorous fetishism" in 1887.

25. Roudinesco (1982, 235–38) erroneously suggests that Binet opposed Krafft-Ebing's hereditary degenerationist model in favor of a psychological one emphasizing childhood sexual traumata. Roudinesco is trying to reconstruct Binet as an exemplar of a French proto-Freudian psychoanalysis.

26. On the *coupeurs de nattes,* see Voisin, Soquet, and Motet (1890), and similar cases described by Garnier (1900a, 109–10).

27. On exhibitionism, also see Magnan (1890, 1899) and Soupault (1896).

28. Also see Apter (1991, 20) on the rhetoric of fetishism.

29. Compare with Apter (1991, 22–23), who glosses *dynamogénie* as the "relationship between image making and orgasm." Binet uses the term in a much broader sense related to associationist, vibrationist notions of sensory-somatic sympathy (dis-

cussed in chapter 1): "les excitations des sens ont cette commune propriété de pro-
duire—surtout chez les hyperexcitables—une dynamogénie générale et passagère de
toutes les fonctions physiologiques" (Binet 1887a, 259).

30. Interspersed throughout Binet's article are analyses of fiction by Dumas ("La
Maison du vent") and Adolphe Belot (*La Bouche de Madame X* [1882]), as well as repeated allusions to fetishism in novels.

31. Heinrich Seuse (1295–1366) was a Swiss mystic and theologian of the Dominican order. He is the author of two mystical texts, *The Book of Eternal Wisdom* and
*The Book of Truth.* Saint Theresa of Avila (1515–1582), a Spanish Carmelite nun who
founded an ascetic branch of the order (the Discalced Carmelites), is the author of a
mystical treatise, *The Interior Castle,* and her autobiography, *The Book of Life.*

32. See pseudo-Aristotle's *Problemata* (877b20–40) and Theophrastus's *De
odoribus* (381–83).

33. Havelock Ellis, for example, cited Cloquet's *Osphresiologie* extensively in his
*Sexual Selection in Man* (1905).

34. See Staum (1980, 168) on Cabanis and the *philosophes'* political aims.

35. Also see Cabanis (1802, 1:223) on the links between odor and the intestinal
tract.

36. Cabanis also discussed the sensual powers of perfumes (1802, 1:224,
2:418). Also see the historical discussion of smells, mainly perfumes, in Classen,
Holmes, and Synnott (1994).

37. See Harrington and Rosario (1992) for a detailed account of "nasal reflex
neuroses" and the role of olfactory research in nineteenth-century anthropology, neurology, and sociology.

38. See Gould (1981) on the full range of Broca's anthropometric research and
social politics. Also see Schiller's biography of Broca (1979).

39. Two observations were particularly significant for Broca: the dramatic
"cephalization" (movement towards the frontal lobes) and amplification of the olfactory
center in mammals, and the shrinking of the olfactory centers in the primate series
(from lower monkeys to apes to humans). Broca interpreted the first trend as function-
ally signifying that olfaction had been increasingly drawn into cooperation with the forebrain and thereby had diminished its reflexive, spinal character (1878, 394–6). Furthermore, because of the primal survival value of olfaction, the cephalization of the
olfactory tubercle stimulated the exuberant development of the frontal lobes in the
mammalian series (1879b, 421). The second phenomenon (the "shrinking" of the olfactory center in primates), Broca interpreted as the "dethronement" of the "brutal cortex" (olfactory cortex) by the "intellectual cortex" (the cerebral cortex). This "frontal
predominance" in primates brought with it the repression of the instinctual, reflexive
animal functions (1878, 393–94).

40. Broca (1877, 655; 1878, 477; 1879a; 1879b, 449–51). Broca's "limbic
sulcus" was a fine cleft separating the anterior pole of the hippocampal rhinencephalon from the surrounding temporal lobe. It supposedly demonstrated the greater
functional independence of the rhinencephalon from the neocortex. The absence of
the *sillon limbique* in civilized man confirmed that for humans "the sense of smell has

lost its preponderance and autonomy" (1879b, 450). It is no longer a recognized neuroanatomical feature.

41. The diagnosis of "neurasthenia" was first popularized by American physician George M. Beard in his *Practical Treatise on Nervous Exhaustion (Neurasthenia)* (1869). He later described it as a disorder particular to Americans and their over-exhausting, energetic, ambitious lifestyles (1881). For more on neurasthenia in the United States, see Sicherman (1977) and Mumford (1992). The neurasthenia diagnosis was popularized in France in the early 1890s by Charcot, who welcomed it as a more precise entity than the old *nervosisme* (see his preface to Levillain 1891]). Also see Goldstein (1987, 335–6).

42. See Latour (1985) on the sociology and politics of the Pasteurian revolution in France.

43. The noted chemist Henri Sainte-Claire Deville, for example, delivered a short paper (1880) before the Académie des sciences on the noxious odors of Paris in which he bowed to his friend and colleague Pasteur while still fretting about the pathogenicity of excremental odors in Paris.

44. Some years later, Huysmans captured the same sense of social malaise when he had his hero des Esseintes complain about the new "aristocracy of money, . . . the caliphate of the sales counter, . . . the tyranny of money": "It was the great hell of America transported onto our continent; finally, it was the immense, profound vulgarity of the financier and the parvenu, blazing like an abject sun on the idolatrous city that ejaculated, belly up, unholy canticles before the impious tabernacle of the banks" (*A Rebours*, 239–40).

45. Max Nordau (né Südfeld) was born into a Hungarian rabbinical family. For most of his life he lived in Paris where he practiced medicine and wrote prolifically. He was a journalist for German and Austrian papers and published novels, essays, and plays. He was convinced that social progress could be achieved through strength of will, Germanic discipline, hard work, and positivist, reductionist science. He was rabidly opposed to the trends he perceived in cultural modernity: realism and naturalism in literature, Impressionism and Expressionism, and aggressive nationalism. Like other liberals, he feared that unrestrained freedom, "ego-mania," would lead to anarchy and the end of reason, culture, and order. He therefore opposed the feminist movement, which he viewed as a threat to social cohesion. Instead, he advocated strict bourgeois sexual morality. My biographical information on Nordau is from Mosse (1968). I cite the French edition of the work (1894–1895), which would have been more widely read in France than the original German edition of 1893.

46. See Silverman (1989) for the role of physicians and medical criticism in shaping art nouveau.

47. For Zola's notes on cheese odors, see NAF (10338, 288–89), and for his reminders to himself on dung and fowl, see NAF (10338).

48. See Baldick (1955, 80) on the sources for characters and places in *A Rebours*. For several of the peculiar rooms of des Esseintes's house, Huysmans utilized the descriptions of de Montesquiou's eccentric home as described to Huysmans by Stephan Mallarmé.

49. Also see Havelock Ellis (1905, 73; 1931) for further observations on odors in *A Rebours* and Huysmans's other work.

50. "Dans cet art des parfums, un côté l'avait, entre tous, séduit, celui de la précision factice" (153). One English translator has rendered this: "In this art of perfumes, one peculiarity had more than all others fascinated him, viz. the precision with which it can artificially imitate the real article" (Huysmans 1931, 106).

51. Also see Nye (1989) on the ways in which fin-de-siècle fertility concerns shaped the medicalization of homosexuality.

52. Huysmans to Raffalovich, 11 April 1896 (in Allen 1966, 215).

53. Birkett (1986, 61–97) examines in detail the Byzantine richness of *A Rebours* and its role as the foundational text of the Decadent movement .

54. Paul-Emile Garnier completed his medical studies in Paris and did an internship under Magnan at the Asile Sainte-Anne. His thesis was on delusions of grandeur in patients suffering from delusions of persecution. From 1879 to 1883 he served under Ernest Lasègue, chief physician of the Infirmerie spéciale de aliénés, and subsequently became first physician adjunct of the service (1883–1886). In 1886, Garnier succeeded Legrand Du Saule as chief physician of the Infirmerie spéciale du Dépôt à la Préfecture de police, where he examined criminal suspects and prepared medicolegal reports. He became inspector of asylums of the Seine province and was concerned with the reform of asylums, prisons, and internment houses (*Internement des aliénés* [1896]). Garnier served on the editorial board of the *Annales d'hygiène publique et de médecine légale.* Like many of his contemporaries, he was concerned with issues of potency, fertility and depopulation, and wrote numerous professional and popular works on the subject (1883, 1897, 1900b). In addition to his work on "sexual perversions," he published on the penal responsibility of morphine addicts, somnambulism, and double suicide. Some of his major monographs are: *Aphasie et folie* (1889), *La folie à Paris* (1890), and *Traité de thérapeutique des maladies mentales et nerveuses* (with Paul Cololian [1901]). For more on Garnier, see Dupré's *Hommage* (1905).

55. The doctors attending Garnier's case presentation offered differing interpretations. One likened C—— to the offenders police called *frotteurs:* men who rubbed up against women's dresses in public places. Another saw a link between these cases and exhibitionists since, after stealing aprons or handkerchiefs or rubbing against dresses, the patients immediately engaged in public masturbation. The diagnostic label *exhibitionist* had been coined in 1877 by Lasègue and would be the subject of two articles by Magnan (1890, 1899).

56. Krafft-Ebing had also hinted in this direction when he described foot fetishism as a "larval form of masochism" (1895, 160).

57. The terms *sadism* and *masochism* first appeared in 1890 in a short supplement to *Psychopathia Sexualis* (5th ed., 1890), entitled *Neue Forschungen auf dem Gebiet der Psychopathia Sexualis.* This was integrated into the sixth edition in 1891. Azar (1975, 1986) carefully traces the history of these terms and points out the compounded errors in the French medical and historical treatment of *Psychopathia Sexualis.* Azar makes it clear that, contrary to many claims, Krafft-Ebing did not coin *sadism* but that it was already part of French usage in the first third of the nineteenth century. Birkett

(1986, 19–20) confirms this. Nevertheless, the widespread medical acceptance of both terms was due to the huge success of *Psychopathia Sexualis*. Printings of Sade's works were rare and largely clandestine in the nineteenth century. The first collected edition was attempted for the first time only in 1947 and even then provoked criminal prosecution (Pauvert 1994). Stefanowsky's model of passivism and tyrannism was proposed earlier (1888) and was rather similar to Krafft-Ebing's theorization of masochism and sadism. Nevertheless, Stefanowsky (1892a, 1892b) later criticized Krafft-Ebing's nomenclature for being nonillustrative of the conditions and, in the case of masochism, an unfortunate slander of a living author. While Stefanowsky's nomenclature was used briefly in France, his priority battle against Krafft-Ebing was ultimately unsuccessful and his terms forgotten.

58. Most of my citations of *Psychopathia Sexualis* are from the 1895 French translation by Emile Laurent and Sigismond Csapo of the eighth edition, the version most accessible to the fin-de-siècle French medical and general public. Currently, the more widely available French translation (1931) is of a German version heavily edited and amended by Albert Moll in 1924.

59. *La Revue indépendante* (January 1885); cited in Birkett (1986, 19–20).

60. On Gilles de Rais, see Bataille (1972)

61. Also see Walkowitz's analysis of the uses of the Jack-the-Ripper case as both a perverse narrative and a myth for frightening "respectable" women off the streets (1982). On Vacher L'Éventreur as a case of necrosadism, see Epaulard (1901).

62. Nye (1993b) also argues that medical fetishism literature arose out of concerns over social anxieties about depopulation and health.

63. *Psychopathia Sexualis* alone is a testament to this phenomenon. Even while in the hands of Krafft-Ebing, the book grew exponentially with new observations, but even the old ones took on new interpretations from edition to edition. The work as a whole would be transformed when it was revised by Moll for its seventeeth edition in 1924.

### Conclusion

1. All quotations are from Diderot's *Les Bijoux indiscrets* (1748, 8–10). The work was published anonymously in Holland in 1748, but its authorship was immediately revealed by a bookseller acting as police informant. Like other banned literature of the time, it enjoyed enormous popularity: six reprintings and two counterfeit editions appeared within a few months, and an English translation was published the following year. Although Diderot claimed to regret this literary creation, he nevertheless composed three supplementary chapters a decade later. Adam (1968) is certain that the literary conceit is borrowed from the Comte de Caylus's *Le Nocrion* (1747). This licentious story about a man granted the magical power to make women speak in an unusual fashion was, in turn, inspired by a medieval Gallic tale: *Le Chevalier qui faisait parler les c. . . et les c. . . .*

2. In the pseudo-dedication of *Les Bijoux,* Diderot specifically cited other examples of pornographic orientalism: Crébillon's *Sopha* (1745) and *Tanzaï* (1734). These, in turn, were inspired by *The Thousand and One Nights,* which first became widely known through Antoine Galland's French translation of 1704–1717. Also see Adam (1968, 11–12) on eighteenth-century pornographic uses of the exotic.

3. On Louis XV's libertinage see Guicciardi. Adam (1968, 14), however, believes there is no consistent correspondence between historical figures and characters in *Bijoux*.

4. Foucault claims that contemporary society is still under the emblem of the talking sex. Indeed, he states that the aim of his research on sexuality is to transcribe *Les Bijoux indiscrets* into history (1976, 101–2).

5. On this point see Adam (1968, 13) and Darnton (1991). Goulemot similarly finds that "libertine" novels are dedicated to scenes of seduction and not to eliciting desire as in the "erotic" novel (1991, 62).

6. See, for example, Sade's *Les infortunes de la vertu* (written 1787, first published 1930) and *La philosophie dans le boudoir* (1795).

7. In the late-seventeenth and early-eighteenth centuries, a variety of tracts on "conjugal love" dealt forthrightly with copulative pleasure (R. Porter 1995), but these were largely replaced by works advocating passionlessness, particularly in women. Laqueur (1990, 150) attributes this to the eighteenth-century emergence of a model of two-sex incommensurability.

8. Even the "divine" Marquis de Sade's personal journal documenting his daily sexual activities reads more like a technical log than an erotic tale (see Lever 1991).

9. If the words of Dr. Bordeu in the *Suite de l'entretien entre D'Alembert et Diderot* (1830, 937) are representative of Diderot's opinions, then Diderot believed that onanism was innocuous and far better than the corruption of honorable women, rigorous continence, or the endangerment of one's health with prostitutes. He also defended pleasure with a person of the same sex by cleverly dismissing the very notion of sex "contrary to nature" (939). Rousseau, as we have seen, was only too willing to label anything he associated with "civilization" as contrary to nature. Diderot's exoticist fantasies of "natural" female sexuality in his *Supplément an Voyage de Bougainville* (1796), however, are rather similar to Rousseau's.

10. Hunt (1991) examines the ways in which the Revolutionary criminal tribunal and pornographic literature portrayed Marie-Antoinette as a lesbian, an adulteress, and the incestuous molester of the young prince.

11. On the sexual politics of Louis XV's court, see Maza (1991).

12. Landes (1988, 70–71) further examines Rousseau's critique of the civilized man as soft, effeminate, and enervated.

13. See Deleuze (1967) on the theme of the Adamic Fall and its connection to hereditary degeneration in Zola's Rougon-Macquart cycle.

## Supplement

1. Letter from Freud to his fiancée, Martha Bernays, 29 October 1982 (qtd. in Jones 1953, 320).

2. For examples of such Freudo-centrism, see some of the classics in the history of psychiatry, Zilboorg (1941) and Alexander and Selesnick (1966).

3. Turkle (1992) attributes the initial French "anti-psychoanalytic" sentiment to the self-contented state of the French bourgeoisie and to French Cartesian rationalism. However, it is also the case that Henri Bergson's intuitionist and even antirationalist

philosophy was popular at the time and that respected neurologists such as Janet had been conducting odd, neomesmeric and metaloscopic experiments (Harrington 1988). Nationalist priority disputes were certainly an issue; even Freud's earliest French supporters emphasized his (uncredited) debts to French neurologists (Regis & Hesnard 1914, 293–330). The priority disputes between Freud and Janet, the mutual mudslinging, and the misrepresentations also strongly colored Freud's reception in France. We have seen from the inversion and fetishism debates that such Franco-German rivalry was commonplace. It was not until 1922 that Freud's works began to be translated into French and have an impact—mainly in the popular press and in literature (Copley 1989, 1949). The tide of medical opinion only began turning after the Société psychanalytique de Paris (SPP) and its two journals were founded in 1926 (see Hesnard 1928, Roudinesco 1982, and Perron 1988).

4. In 1953 the SPP fragmented over theoretical and pedagogical issues as well as the professional and personal rivalries between two of its leaders, Jacques Lacan and Sacha Nacht. Since then, French psychoanalysis has been influenced by the linguistically oriented theories of Lacan, Gilles Deleuze, and Félix Guattari, and the feminist, semiotic theories of Julia Kristeva and Luce Irigaray, among others (Turkle 1992).

5. See Nye (1993a, 5 and ch. 4), and Rosario (1992).

6. This was Pierre Janet's opinion expressed at the 1913 International Congress of Medicine in London (see Ellenberger 1970, 344).

7. See Freud's letters to Fliess (1985, 74, 222). These and subsequent citations from Freud's 1887–1904 correspondence to Fliess are from Jeffrey Masson's complete translation of the letters (Freud 1985). In *Studies on Hysteria,* for example, Freud did not reject hereditary etiology. Quite to the contrary, he doubted that hysteria without a preexisting disposition could even exist (Freud & Breuer 1895, 122).

8. Sulloway (1983, ch. 4) carefully analyzes the "Project." Pribram and Gill (1976) have even tried to show that the work prefigures later findings in the neurosciences.

9. Freud's logic on the neurotoxicity of "disturbed sexual discharge" is a convoluted one. In letters to Fliess on migraines, Freud agreed on the etiological contribution of certain olfactory substances such as flower aromas, which they believed were breakdown products of sexual metabolism (1985, 161). Freud went a step further to suggest that similar "human toxic emanations" produced during "menstruation or other sexual processes" may also impinge upon the nervous system at the level of the *corpora cavernosa* of the genitals. "Thus the nose would, as it were, receive information about *internal* olfactory stimuli by means of the *corpora cavernosa,* just as it does about external stimuli by Schneider's membrane [in the nose]: one would come to grief from one's own body" (1985, 161). Basically, the genitals acted as an internal nose sniffing for sexual activity. According to Freud, this would explain the frequency of migraines in menstruating women and "people with disturbed sexual discharge (neurasthenia, coitus interruptus)" (1985, 143).

10. On the onanistic etiology of melancholia see Freud (1985, 94); of neurasthenia see Freud (1985, 40–41); of nose disorders see Freud (1985, 48n.).

11. Sulloway (1983, 184–86) has also highlighted Freud's and Fliess's dated views on onanism.

12. See Ellenberger's excellent review of Janet's life and work (1970), specifically Janet's coining of the word *subconscious* (357n.82) and his priority disputes with Freud (344). Copley (1989, 148) discusses Janet's discomfort with the prominence of eroticism in psychoanalysis.

13. Freud, in fact, miscites Binet's article as 1888 rather than 1887. While Freud initially explained the choice of the fetish object in associationist terms, he later elaborated a radically different notion based on Oedipal castration anxiety. In an article on fetishism, he explained that "the fetish is a substitute for the woman's (the mother's) penis that the little boy once believed in" (1927a, 152). It helps a man abide female castration and the horror provoked by female incompleteness. Thus the fetish "saves the fetishist from becoming a homosexual, by endowing women with the characteristic that makes them tolerable as sexual objects," namely, a (fantasy) penis (154).

14. This would change, such that contemporary French sexological works apply the term *sexual perversion* to conditions they otherwise label as "normal," such as homosexuality and pedophilia (see Bonnet 1993, 113; Rosario 1992, 269).

15. Davidson (1988) has also pointed this out, but I cannot accept his further suggestion that Freud wished to normalize the perversities. Freud's was an ambivalent apologia at best, as can be seen in his "Letter to an American Mother" (1935). Freud refused to label homosexuality an illness, but always viewed it as a defective sexuality, or an "arrest of sexual development." Freud's highly teleological view of psychosexual development culminates in mature, "normal," reproductive heterosexuality.

16. Also see Janet's theories of "inferior forms" of mentation, including the passions (1889).

17. See Marcus (1962, xxv).

18. The essay appeared as volume four of *Die Medizin der Gegenwart in Selbstdarstellungen* (Leipzig: Meiner, 1925) intended as a professional history of contemporary medicine through a series of self-portraits of its leaders.

19. See Strachey's Translator's Note to the 1952 W. W. Norton edition of the work (p. 7). I am grateful to David Halperin for suggesting this etymology.

20. Anzieu (1959, 154–55) states the commonly held belief that, "[a]s if in spite of himself, almost all the other scientific hypotheses [of psychoanalysis] would be discussed in [Freud's] auto-analysis." Ellenberger (1970, 447–50) mythologized this period by describing it as a shamanistic interval after which Freud emerged "internally transformed," elated by a greater truth, and cured of his neurosis; he also "outgrew his dependency on Fliess" who had acted as Freud's "shaman master." Also see Buxbaum (1951) and Jones (1953).

21. From M. Masud R. Khan's Preface to Laplanche and Pontalis (1973).

22. Freud's abandonment of the seduction theory has been a matter of great contention. Masson (1992) argues that Freud had sufficient evidence to believe in the veracity of his female patients' reports of sexual molestation, but Masson then blames the psychoanalytic profession, not Freud, for a cover-up of child sexual abuse.

23. See Freud's *The Psychopathology of Everyday Life* (1901), *Jokes and Their Relation to the Unconscious* (1905), "Obsessive actions and religious practices" (1907), and *The Future of an Illusion* (1927).

24. Freud (1925, 71). I have taken the liberty of restoring the present tense of the original: "Die 'Selbstdarstellung' zeigt, wie die Psychoanalyse meine Lebensinhalt wird" (1940–1952, 16:31).

25. Of his experience in 1885–1886 with Charcot at the Salpêtrière, Freud wrote, "No doubt the whole of what Charcot taught us at that time does not hold good today" (1925, 13). He also noted that during this period, "Janet's name was not so much as mentioned" (13). Later Freud came to realize that "the work [on electrotherapy] of the greatest name in German neuropathology [W. Erb] had no more relation to reality than some 'Egyptian' dream-book, such as is sold in cheap bookshops . . . what I had taken for an epitome of exact observations was merely the construction of phantasy" (16). He accused Breuer of withholding the critical sexual component of Anna O.'s case (21). Their work on hysteria was therefore largely descriptive and theoretically poor (21). It was only in 1902, he claimed, that he started having disciples (the Wednesday Psychological Society) and that psychoanalysis began to be taken seriously. It was only at this point that it began to have an "external history," as Freud puts it, that is, a life separate from his own person (48).

26. In addition to addressing Fliess as his "dearest in truth" (1985, 73), Freud also importuned his regular correspondent, "Daimonie, why don't you write?" (134). The letters betray an intense affection and emotional dependence. Koestenbaum (1989, ch. 1) further discusses the eroticism of Freud's collaborations.

# BIBLIOGRAPHY

## Abbreviations

| | |
|---|---|
| *Arch. anth. crim.* | *Archives d'anthropologie criminelle, de criminologie et de psychologie normale et pathologique* |
| *Arch. neur.* | *Archives de neurologie* |
| *Ann. méd.-psy.* | *Annales médico-psychologiques* |
| *Ann. hyg. publ.* | *Annales d'hygiène publique et de médecine légale* |
| *Arch. Psy. Nerv.* | *Archiv für Psychiatrie und Nervenkrankheiten* |
| *Bull. Soc. anth.* | *Bulletins de la Société d'anthropologie de Paris* |
| *Rev. phil.* | *Revue philosophique* |

## Primary Sources

Allen, Louis, ed. 1966. "Letters of Huysmans and Zola to Raffalovich." *Forum for Modern Languages* 2(3): 214–21.

*American Journal of Insanity.* 1893. Review of *Psychopathia Sexualis* by Richard von Krafft-Ebing. Translated by Charles G. Chaddock. 50: 91–95.

American Psychiatric Association (APA). 1987. *Diagnostic and Statistical Manual of Mental Disorders.* 3d rev. ed. Washington, D.C.: APA.

———. 1994. *Diagnostic and Statistical Manual of Mental Disorders.* 4th ed. Washington, D.C.: APA.

*Annales d'hygiène publique et de médecine légale.* 1829. Prospectus. 1:v–xxxix.

———. 1887. Review of "On the Etiology and Diagnosis (Considered from the Medico-Legal Point of View) of Certain Cases of Nymphomania in Which Women Are Driven To Accuse Their Doctor of Criminal Attempts on Their Person" by C. H. F. Routh in *British Medical Journal.* 3d ser., 18: 493–95.

Aristotle (pseudo-). 1927. *Problemata.* Translated by W. D. Ross. Oxford: Clarendon Press.

Augustine. [397–401] 1982. *Confessions.* Translated by Louis de Mondadon. Paris: Seuil.

Auzouy. 1858. "Du délire des affections ou de l'altération des sentiments affectifs dans les diverses formes de l'aliénation mentale." *Ann. méd.-psy.,* 3d ser., 4: 53–57.

Baillarger, Jules. 1845. "Erotomanie, illusions et hallucinations chez une jeune fille chlorotique." *Ann. méd.-psy.,* 1st ser., 5: 147–50.

Ball, Benjamin. 1887. "La folie érotique." *L'Encéphale* 7: 188–97, 257–69, 403–15.

———. 1888. *La folie érotique.* Paris: Baillière.

Balzac, Honoré de. [1829] 1940. *Physiologie du mariage.* Edited by Maurice Bardèche. Paris: Droz.

Baudelaire, Charles. [1857] 1961. "*Madame Bovary* par Gustave Flaubert." In *Œuvres complètes.* Paris: Pléiade.

———. [1857] 1958. *Les Fleurs du mal.* Paris: Garnier.

Baudin, R. P. 1884. *Fétichisme et féticheurs.* Lyon: Séminaire des missions africaines.

Bayard, Henri-Louis. 1837. "La nymphomanie peut-elle être une cause d'interdiction, ou les faits qui tendraient a l'établir sont-ils pertinens?" *Ann. hyg. publ.,* 1st ser., 18: 416–47.

———. 1843. *Manuel pratique de médecine légale.* Paris: G. Baillière.

Beard, George M. [1869] 1880. *A Practical Treatise on Nervous Exhaustion (Neurasthenia).* 2d ed. New York: W. Wood.

———. 1881. *American Nervousness: Its Causes and Consequences.* New York: Putnam.

Bernard, Leopold. 1889. *Les Odeurs dans les romans de Zola* [Odors in the novels of Zola]. Conférence faite au Cercle artistique. Montpellier: G. Firmin.

Bienville, J. D. T. de. [1771] 1784. *La nymphomanie, ou Traité de la fureur utérine* [Nymphomania, or Treatise on uterine fury]. New edition. Amsterdam: [Marc-Michel Rey].

Binet, Alfred. 1886. *La Psychologie du raisonnement.* Paris: F. Alcan.

———. 1887a. "Le fétichisme dans l'amour." *Rev. phil.* 24: 143–67, 252–74.

———. 1887b. "La vie psychique des micro-organismes." *Rev. phil.* 24: 449–89, 582–611.

———. 1892. *Les altérations de la personnalité.* Paris: F. Alcan.

Boerhaave, Hermann. [1708] 1742. *Academic Lectures on the Theory of Physic.* 5 vols. London: W. Innys.

Bonnemaison, [Julien]. 1875. "Sur un cas d'hystérie chez l'homme." *Archives générales de médecine,* 6th ser., 25: 664–79.

Boorde, Andrew. 1552. *The Breviary of Health, for all manners of sickness and diseases which may be in man or woman.* 2 vols. in 1. London: W. Powell.

Bourget, Paul. [1902] 1929. *Physiologie de l'amour moderne.* Paris: Plon.

Brierre de Boismont, Alexandre-Jacques-François. 1849. "Remarques médico-légales sur la perversion de l'instinct génésique." *Gazette médicale de Paris,* 3d ser., 4: 555–64.

Brillat-Savarin, Jean Anthelme. [1825] 1982. *Physiologie du goût, ou Méditation de gastronomie transcendante* [The physiology of taste, or Meditation on transcendental gastronomy]. Introduction by Jean-François Revel. Paris: Flammarion.

Briquet, Pierre. 1859. *Traité clinique et thérapeutique de l'hystérie.* Paris: Baillière.

———. 1881. "De la prédisposition à l'hystérie." *Gazette médicale de Paris*, 6th ser., 3(39): 551.

Brosses, Charles de. 1760. *Du culte des dieux fétiches, ou Parallèle de l'ancienne religion de l'Egypte avec la religion actuelle de Nigritie* [On the cult of fetish gods, or parallels between the ancient religion of Egypt and the present religion of Nigeria]. Paris.

Broca, Paul. 1869. "L'ordre des primates. Parallèle anatomique de l'homme et des singes." *Bull. Soc. anth.*, 2d ser., 4: 228–401.

———. 1870. "Sur le transformisme." *Bull. Soc. anth.*, 2d ser., 5: 168–242.

———. 1871. *Mémoires d'anthropologie.* Paris: C. Reinwald.

———. 1877. "Sur la circonvolution limbique et la scissure limbique." *Bull. Soc. anth.*, 2d ser., 12: 646–57.

———. 1878. "Le grand lobe limbique et la scissure limbique dans la série des mammifères." *Revue d'anthropologie* 2d ser., 1: 385–498.

———. 1879a. "Anatomie du lobe olfactif." *Bull. Soc. anth.*, 4th ser., 4: 596–98.

———. 1879b. "Recherches sur les centres olfactifs." *Revue d'anthropologie*, 2d ser., 2: 385–455.

*Bulletin générale de thérapeutique médicale et chirurgicale.* 1837. "Cas extraordinaire de mutilation et d'introduction d'un os dans la vessie par suite de l'insensibilité amenée dans les organes génitaux par la masturbation." 13: 320–24.

Burton, Richard. [1620] 1932. *The Anatomy of Melancholy.* London: J. M. Dent.

Cabanès, Augustin (Dr. Jacobus X . . . , pseud.) 1901. *Le Marquis de Sade et son oeuvre devant la science médicale et la littérature moderne.* Paris: Charles Carrington.

Cabanis, Pierre Jean Georges. [1802] 1805. *Rapports du physique et du morale de l'homme.* 2d ed. Paris: Crapart, Caille at Ravier.

Carrière, Édouard. 1849. "La question de l'autorité en médecine. A Monsieur le docteur Amédée Latour." *Union médicale* 3: 385–86, 389–90, 442–44, 445–46.

Carter, Robert Brudenell. 1853. *On the Pathology and Therapy of Hysteria.* London: J. Churchill.

Casper, Johann Ludwig. 1852. "Über Nothzucht und Päderastie und deren Ermittelung Seitens des Gerichtsarztes." *Vierteljahrsschrift für gerichtliche und öffentliche Medicin* 1: 21–78.

Charcot, Jean-Martin. 1885. "Spiritisme et hystérie." *Le Progrès médicale*, 2d ser., 13(4): 63–65.

Charcot, Jean-Martin, and Valentin Magnan. 1882. "Inversion du sens genital." *Arch. Neur.* 3: 53–60, 296–322.

Charcot, Jean-Martin, and Paul Richer. 1887. *Les Démoniaques dans l'art.* Paris: Adrien Delahaye et Emile Lecrosnier.

Chevalier, Julien. 1885. *De l'inversion de l'instinct sexuel au point de vue médico-légale* [Inversion from the medicolegal point of view]. Paris: Octave Doin.

———. 1893. *Une maladie de la personalité. L'inversion sexuelle.* Preface by Dr. A. Lacassagne. Lyon: A. Storck.

Chopart, François. 1792. *Traité des maladies des voies urinaires.* Paris: Croullebois.

Clérambault, G. Gatian de. 1908. "Passion érotique des étoffes chez la femme." *Arch. anth. crim.* 23: 439–70.

———. 1910. "Passion érotique des étoffes chez la femme." *Arch. anth. crim.* 25: 583–89.

———. 1942. *Œuvre psychiatrique.* Edited by Jean Fretet. Paris: Presses Universitaires de France.

Cloquet, Hippolyte. 1821. *Osphrésiologie, ou Traité des odeurs, du sens et des organes de l'olfation, avec l'histoire détaillée des maladies du nez et des fosses nasales et des opérations qui leur conviennent* [Osphresiology, or a treatise on odors, of the sense and organ of olfaction]. 2d ed. Paris: Méquignon-Marvis.

Codet, Henri. 1921. *Essai sur le collectionisme.* Paris: Jouve.

Collet, Frédéric Justin. 1904. *L'Odorat et ses troubles.* Paris: J. B. Baillière.

Comte, Auguste. [1830–1842] 1864. *Cours de philosophie positive* [Course on positive philosophy]. 6 vols. 2d ed. Paris: J. B. Baillière.

Condillac, Étienne Bonnot de. [1746] 1795. *Essai sur l'origine des connoissances humaines* [Essay on the origin of human understanding]. In *Œuvres philosophiques,* vol. 1. Paris: Dufart.

———. [1754] 1984. *Traité des sensations. Traité des animaux.* Paris: Fayard.

Danville, Gaston. 1893. "L'amour est-il un état pathologique?" *Rev. phil.* 35: 261–83.

———. 1894. *La psychologie de l'amour.* Paris: Alcan.

Debourge. 1852. "De la mastupratiomanie." *Journal de médecine, de chirurgie et de pharmacologie* (Brussels) 10(15): 314–22, 404–12.

Delbœuf, J. 1891. "Pourquoi mourons-nous?" *Rev. phil.* 31: 225–57, 408–27.

Demeaux, J. B. D. 1856. *Mémoire sur l'onanisme et des moyens d'en prévenir ou d'en réprimer les abus dans les établissements consacrés à l'instruction publique.* Paris: Wulder.

———. 1857. "Note sur l'onanisme et sur les moyens d'en prévenir ou d'en réprimer les abus dans les établissements consacrés à l'instruction publique." *Le Moniteur des hôpitaux, Revue médico-chirurgicale de Paris,* 1st ser., 5: 929–35.

———. 1861. "Quelques réflexions sur l'onanisme; ses effets sur l'économie; mesures propres à en prévenir les abus dans les établissements destinés à l'instruction publique." *Le Moniteur des sciences médicales et pharmaceutiques,* 2d ser., 3: 17–19, 28–29, 36–38, 42–43.

Deslandes, Léopolde. 1834. "Masturbation." *Dictionnaire de médecine et de chirurgie pratiques* 11:368-78. Paris: J. B. Baillière.

———. 1835. *De l'onanisme et des autres abus vénériens considérés dans leurs rapports avec la santé.* Paris: Lalarge.

Desruelles, Henri Marie Joseph. 1822. "Notice et observations sur les effets de la masturbation, accompagnés de réflexions physiologiques sur la puberté." *Journal générale de médecine de chirurgie et de pharmacie* 79: 31–61.

Dessoir, Max. 1894. "Zur Psychologie der Vita sexualis." *Allgemeine Zeitschrift für Psychiatrie* 50: 941–75.

Diderot, Dénis. [1748] 1951. *Les Bijoux indiscrets* [The indiscreet jewels]. In *Œuvres.* Paris: Pléiade.

———. [1796] 1951. *Supplément ou voyage de Bougainville.* In *Œuvres.* Paris: Pléiade.

———. [1830] 1951. "Suite de l'entretien entre d'Alembert et Diderot." In *Œuvres.* Paris: Pléiade.

Dubarry, Armand. 1896a. *Le Fétichiste.* Paris: Chamuel.

———. 1896b. *Les Invertis (Le vice allemand)*. Paris: Chamuel.

———. 1897a. *L'Hermaphrodite*. Paris: Chamuel.

———. 1897b. *L'Hystérique*. Paris: Chamuel.

———. 1898a. *Les Flagellants*. Paris: Chamuel.

———. 1898b. *Le Couper de nattes*. Paris: Chamuel.

———. 1898c. *Le vieux et l'amour.* Paris: Chamuel.

———. 1899. *Les femmes eunuques*. Paris: Chamuel.

———. 1901. *Le plaisir sanglant*. Paris: Chamuel.

———. 1902a. *L'Abbé écornifleur (l'inceste)*. Paris: Chamuel.

———. 1902b. *Mlle. Calyphige*. Paris: Chamuel.

Dubuisson, Paul. 1902. *Les Voleuses de grands magasins*. Paris: Storck.

Dufour, Théophile, ed. 1930. *Correspondence de Jean-Jacques Rousseau*. Paris: Armand Colin.

Dumesnil, René. 1905. *Flaubert, son hérédité, son milieu, sa méthode*. Paris: Société française d'imprimerie et de librairie.

Dupouy, Roger. 1905. "De la kleptomanie." *Journal de psychologique normale et pathologique* 2: 404–26.

Dupré, Ernest. 1905. "Paul Garnier (1848-1905)". In *Paul Garnier,* 29–43. Clermont-Ferand: Daix.

Duvergier, J. B. 1825. *Collection complète des lois, décrets, ordonnances, règlements et avis du Conseil-d'état*. Paris: Guyot.

Ellis, Havelock. 1895. "Sexual Inversion in Women." *Alienist and Neurologist* 16: 141–58.

———. 1896. [With J. A. Symonds.] *Konträre Geschlechtsgefühl*. Translated by Hans G. Kurella. Leipzig: G. H. Wiegands, Verlag. [Translation of Ellis (1897)].

———. [1897] 1936. *Sexual Inversion*. In *Studies in the Psychology of Sex*, vol. 2. New York: Random House.

———. [1905] 1936. *Sexual Selection in Man*. In *Studies in the Psychology of Sex*, vol. 2. New York: Random House.

———. [1931] 1969. Introduction to *Against the Grain* by J. K. Huysmans, v-xxxii. New York: Dover.

*Encyclopédie ou Dictionnaire raisonné des sciences, des arts et des métiers*. [1751–1772] 1778–1781. Edited by Dénis Diderot and Jean D'Alembert. Lausanne: Société Typographique.

Epaulard, Alexis. 1901. *Nécrophilie, nécrosadisme, nécrophagie*. Lyon: A. Storck.

Esquirol, Jean Étienne Dominique. 1815. "Erotomanie." *Dictionnaire des sciences médicales* 13: 186–92. Paris: Panckoucke.

———. 1838. *Des maladies mentales*. Paris: Baillière.

Fabre, Paul. 1875. "De l'hystérie chez l'homme." *Ann. méd.-psy.*, 5th ser., 13: 354–73.

———. 1881. "De l'hystérie chez l'homme." *Gazette médicale de Paris*, 6th ser., 3 (19 November): 654–57, 687–88, 734–35.

Ferrand, Jacques. [1610] 1623. *De la maladie d'amour, ou Mélancholie érotique* [On love-sickness, or erotic melancholy]. Paris: Moreau.

———. 1640. *Erotomania, or a treatise discoursing of the essence, causes, symptoms, prognostics, and cure of Love, or erotique melancholy*. Translated by Edward Chilmead. Oxford: L. Lichfield.

Flaubert, Gustave. [1856] 1951. *Madame Bovary.* In *Œuvres*, vol. 1. Paris: Pléiade.
———. [1877] 1952. Un cœur simple. *Trois contes.* In *Œuvres*, vol. 2. Paris: Pléiade.
———. 1926–1954. *Correspondance.* New ed. 13 vols. Paris: Louis Conard.
———. 1980–1991. *Correspondance. 3* vols. In *Œuvres complètes*, ed. Jean Bruneau. Paris: Pléiade.
Fournier and Béguin. 1819. "Masturbation." *Dictionnaire des sciences médicales* 31: 100–35. Paris: Panckoucke.
Fournier-Pescay, François. 1821. "Sodomie." *Dictionnaire des sciences médicales* 51: 441–48. Paris: Panckoucke.
Fréron, Elie-Catherine. [1782] 1966. Review of *Les Confessions* by Jean-Jacques Rousseau. *L'anné littéraire* vol.4, letter 8: 145–75. Paris: Mérigot. Reprint. Geneva: Slatkine Reprints.
Freud, Sigmund. 1953–1974. *Standard Edition of the Complete Psychological Works of Sigmund Freud.* 24 vols. Edited by James Strachey. London: Hogarth Press. [Cited below as *S.E.*]
———. [1900]. *The Interpretation of Dreams. S.E.* 4–5.
———. [1901]. *The Psychopathology of Everyday Life. S.E.* 6.
———. [1905a]. *Three Essays on a Theory of Sexuality. S.E.* 7: 123–243.
———. [1905b]. *Jokes and Their Relation to the Unconscious. S.E.* 8.
———. [1907a]. "Delusions and Dreams in Jensen's *Gravida*," and "Postscript" to the 2d ed. (1912). *S.E.* 9: 3–95.
———. [1907b]. "Obsessive Actions and Religious Practices." *S.E.* 9: 116–27.
———. [1912]. "Contributions to a Discussion on Masturbation." *S.E.* 12: 241–54.
———. [1913]. Preface to *Scatological Rites of all Nations* [1891] by John G. Bourke. *S.E.* 12: 333–37.
———. [1925]. *An Autobiographical Study.* And "Postscript" (1935). *S.E.* 20: 3–74. [Translation of *Selbstdarstellung*, Die Medizin der Gegenwart in Selbstdarstellungen, vol. 4, 1–52. Leipzig: Meiner, 1925].
———. [1927a]. Fetishism. *S.E.* 21: 149–57.
———. [1927b]. *The Future of an Illusion. S.E.* 21: 3–56.
———. [1930]. *Civilization and its Discontents. S.E.* 21.
———. 1940–1952. *Gesammelte Werke.* 17 vols. Edited by Anna Freud et al. London: Imago.
———. [1950]. "Project for a Scientific Psychology." *S.E.* 1: 281–397.
———. 1985. *The Complete Letters of Sigmund Freud to Wilhelm Fliess, 1887–1904.* Edited by Jeffrey Masson. Cambridge, Mass.: Harvard University Press.
Freud, Sigmund, and Joseph Breuer. [1895]. *Studies on Hysteria. S.E.* 2.
Galen, Claude. 1625. *De Locis affectis.* In *Opera*, vol. 4, bk. 6. Venice: Iuntas.
Garnier, Paul-Émile. 1883. *La stérilité humaine et l'hermaphroditisme.* Paris: Garnier Frères.
———. 1887. "Rapport sur l'état mental d'un individu inculpé de vol." *Ann. hyg. publ.*, 3d ser., 18: 268–78.
———. 1889. *Anomalies sexuelles apparentes et cachées. Avec 230 observations* [Apparent and hidden sexual anomalies]. Paris: Garnier Frères.

———. 1893. "Un cas de perversion du sens génésique. Obsession appétitive et amoureuse du toucher de la soie avec phénomènes d'orgasme génital à ce contact." *Ann. hyg. publ.,* 3d ser., 29: 457–65.

———. 1895. "Pervertis et invertis sexuels. Les fétichistes. Observations médico-légales." *Ann. hyg. publ.,* 3d ser., 33: 349–69, 385–408.

———. 1897. *Impuissance physique et morale chez l'homme et la femme.* New edition. Paris: Garnier.

———. 1900a. "Le sadi-fétichisme." *Ann. hyg. publ,.* 3d ser., 43: 97–121, 210–47.

———. 1900b. *La génération universelle; lois, secrets et mystères chez l'homme et chez la femme.* 9th ed. Paris: Garnier.

*Gazette des Tribunaux.* 1849. Violation nocturnes de sépultures. . . . Affaire du sergent Bertrand. 11 July.

Georget, Étienne-Jean. 1820. "Hystérie." *Dictionnaire des sciences médicales,* 11: 526–51. Paris: Panckoucke.

———. 1840. "Onanisme." *Dictionnaire de médecine ou répertoire générale des sciences médicales,* 22: 77–80. Paris: Béchet Jeune.

Gide, André. 1925. *Corydon.* Paris: Gallimard.

Gley, Eugène. 1884. "Les Aberrations de l'instinct sexuel." *Rev. phil.* 17: 66–92.

Gock, H. 1875. "Beitrag zur Kenntniss der conträren Sexualempfindung." *Arch. Psy. Nerv.* 5: 564–74.

Gorry, Th. 1879. "Des aliénés voleurs, non existence de la kleptomanie et des monomanies en général comme entités morbides." Medical thesis, Faculty of Medicine of Paris.

Gray, H. A. C. 1875. "Sneezing." *Lancet* (16 January): 110.

Griesinger, Wilhelm. 1868–1869. "Über einen wenig bekannten psychopathischen Zustand." *Arch. Psy. Nerv.* 1: 626–35.

Gschwender. 1869. "Observation d'anésthesie hystérique chez un homme." *Ann. méd.-psy.,* 5th ser., 2: 114–15.

Guérin, Jules. 1849a. "Enseignement libre." *Gazette médical de Paris* 4 (25 August): 649–50.

———. 1849b. "Organisation de l'enseignement supérieur. Nomination de deux commissions, l'une dite de l'enseignement supérieur, l'autre de la médecine." *Gazette médical de Paris* 4 (21 July): 572–73.

Guislain, Joseph. 1881. *Leçons orales sur les phrenopathies, ou Traité théorique et pratique des maladies mentales.* Ghent: E. Vanderhæghen.

Haeckel, Ernst. [1891] 1974. *Anthropogenie, oder Entwickelungsgeschichte des Menschen.* Leipzig: W. Englemann.

Hamilton, Allan McLane. 1896. "The civil responsibility of perverts." *American Journal of Insanity* 50: 503–11.

Dr. Hospital. 1875. "Observation d'érotisme, Lesions du cervelet." *Ann. méd.-psy.,* 5th ser., 14: 252–53.

Huysmans, Joris-Karl. [1884] 1978. *A Rebours.* Paris: Garnier-Flammarion.

———. [1891] 1985. *Là-Bas.* Paris: Gallimard.

———. 1989. *The Road from Decadence. Selected Letters of J. K. Huysmans.* Edited by Barbara Beaumont. London: Athlone.

———. [1931] 1969. *Against the Grain.* Translation by John Howard of *A Rebours.* Introduction by Havelock Ellis. New York: Dover.

Ignotus. 1881. "Les grands bazars." *Le Figaro* (23 March): 1.

[Invert]. 1894–1895. [Letters to Emile Zola published anonymously as] "Le roman d'un inverti." Edited by Dr. Laupts. *Archives d'anthropologie criminelle* 9 (1894): 212–15, 367–73, 729–37; 10 (1895): 131–38, 228–41, 320–25.

Jacquot, Félix. 1849. "Des aberrations de l'appétit génésique." *Gazette médicale de Paris,* 3d ser., 4: 575–78.

Janet, Pierre. [1889] 1973. *L'automatisme psychologique.* Reprint of the 4th ed. Paris: Société Pierre Janet.

*Journal des gens du monde.* 1782. "Sur les *Confessions* de Jean-Jacques Rousseau." 1(2): 102–12.

Kann, Heinrich. 1844. *Psychopathia Sexualis.* Leipzig: Voss.

Klein, August. 1880. *De l'hystérie chez l'homme* [Hysteria in men] Paris: Octave Doin.

Kraepelin, Emil. 1921. *Manic-Depressive Insanity and Paranoia.* Translated by R. M. Barclay. Edited by G. M. Robertson. Edinburgh: E.&S. Livingston.

Krafft-Ebing, Richard von. 1877. "Über gewisse Anomalien des Geschlechtstriebs und die klinisch-forensische Verwertung derselben als eines wahrscheinlich functionellen Degenerationszeichens des zentralen Nerven-Systems. *Arch. Psy. Nerv.* 7: 291–312.

———. 1886. *Psychopathia Sexualis. Eine klinische-forensische Studie.* 1st ed. Stuttgart: Ferdinand Enke.

———. 1890. *Neue Forschungen auf dem Gebiet der Psychopathia Sexualis.* Stuttgart: Ferdinand Enke.

———. 1891. "Über Fetischismus eroticus." *Wiener medizinischer Blatt* 14: 400, 432.

———. 1894. *Der Conträrsexuale vor dem Strafrichter. De sodomia ratione sexus punienda. De lege lata et de lege ferenda. Eine Denkschrift.* Leipzig: Franz Deutiche.

———. 1895. *Psychopathia Sexualis.* Translated into French by Emile Laurent and Sigismond Csapo from the 8th German ed. (1893). Paris: George Carré.

———. 1931. *Psychopathia Sexualis.* Translated into French by René Lobstein from the 16th and 17th German eds. reedited by Albert Moll (1924). Preface by Pierre Janet. Paris: Payot.

Krueg, Julius. 1882. "Perverted sexual instincts." *Brain, A Journal of Neurology* 4: 368–76.

Lacassagne, Alexandre. 1896. "Les vols à l'étalage et dans les grands magasins." *Revue de l'hypnotisme et de la psychologie physiologique* 11: 76–82.

Lallemand, Claude François. 1836–1842. *Des pertes séminales involontaires.* 3 vols. Paris: Béchet Jeune.

Lancereaux, Étienne. 1884. "Hystérie chez l'homme, contractures, hypnotisation." *Gazette des hôpitaux* 57: 731–32.

Larguier de Bancels, J. 1912. "L'œuvre d'Alfred Binet." *L'Année psychologique* 18: 15–32.

Lasègue, Ernest. 1877. "Les exhibitionnistes." *Union médicale,* 3d ser., 23(50)(1 May): 709–14.

———. 1881. "Les hystériques, léur perversité, leurs mensonges." *Ann. méd.-psy.*, 6th ser., 6: 111–18.

Latour, Amédée. 1849a. "L'enseignement libre de la médecine dévoilé." *Union médicale* 3: 409–10.

———. 1849b. "L'enseignement libre des sciences médicales." *Union médicale* 3: 369.

———. 1849c. "De l'autorité en médecine." *Union médicale* 3: 386–87, 389–90, 397–98, 445–46.

Dr. Laupts [Georges Saint-Paul]. 1894–1895. "Enquête sur l'inversion sexuelle (Réponses)," and editorial remarks to "Le roman d'un inverti." *Arch. anth. crim.* 9 (1894): 105–8, 211–15, 367–73, 729–37; 10 (1895): 131–38, 228–41, 320–25.

———. 1896. *Tares et poisons. Perversions et perversités sexuelles. Une enquête sur l'inversion. Notes et documents. Le roman d'un inverti né. Le procès Wilde. La guérison et la prophylaxie de l'inversion* [Taints and poisons: Sexual perversions and perversities]. Preface by Emile Zola. Paris: George Carré.

———. 1907. "A la mémoire d'Emile Zola." *Arch. anth. crim.* 22: 825–41.

———. 1908a. "Réponse à M. Næcke." *Arch. anth. crim.* 23: 313–16.

———. 1908b. "Dégénérescence ou pléthore?" *Arch. anth. crim.* 23: 731–49.

———. 1909. "Lettre au Professeur Lacassagne en réponse au lettre de M. Raffalovich." *Arch. anth. crim.* 24: 693–96.

Laurent, Emile. 1891. *L'Amour morbide, étude de psychologie pathologique.* Paris: Société d'éditions scientifiques.

Ledouble (de Tours) [Anatole Félix?]. 1879. "Hystérie essentielle avec hemianesthésie et troubles visuels chez l'homme." *La Tribune médicale* (7 September): 425–27.

Legrand du Saulle, Henri. 1864. "De l'érotisme et de ses conséquences médico-légales." *Ann. méd.-psy.*, 4th ser., 4: 253–60.

———. 1876. "Les signes physiques des folies raisonnantes." *Ann. méd.-psy.*, 5th ser., 15: 433–53.

Leigh, R. A., ed. 1970. *Correspondance complète de J.-J. Rousseau.* Madison: University of Wisconsin Press.

Leroy, Raoul, and P. Juquelier. 1910. "Les amoureuses des prêtres." *Bulletin de la société clinique de médecine mentale* 3: 242-49.

Leuret, François. 1830. "Monomanie érotique méconnue par des personnes étrangères à l'observation des aliénés." *Ann. hyg. publ.*, 1st ser., 3: 198–220.

Levillain, Fernand. 1891. *La neurasthénie. Maladie de Beard.* Preface by Jean-Martin Charcot. Paris: A. Maloine.

Littré, Maximilien Paul Emile. 1873. *Dictionnaire de la langue française.* Paris: Hachette.

Louyer-Villermay, Jean Baptiste. 1819a. "Nymphomanie." *Dictionnaire des sciences médicales.* Paris: Panckoucke 36: 561–96.

———. 1819b. *Traité des maladies nerveuses ou vapeureuses et particulièrement de l'hystérie et de l'hypochondrie.* Paris: J. B. Baillière.

Lucas, Prosper. 1847–1850. *Traité philosophique et physiologique de l'hérédité naturelle.* Paris: Baillière.

Lunier, Joseph. 1849. "Examen médico-légal d'un cas de monomanie instinctive. Affaire du sergent Bertrand." *Ann. méd.-psy.*, 2d ser., 1: 351–79.

———. 1880. "Des vols aux étalages." *Ann. méd.-psy.*, 6th ser., 3: 210–42.

Magnan, Valentin. 1885a. "Des anomalies, des aberrations et des perversions sexuelles." *Ann. méd.-psy.*, 7th ser., 1: 447–74.

———. 1885b. "Des anomalies, des aberrations et des perversions sexuelles." *Progrès médicale*, 2d ser., 13: 49–50, 65–68, 84–86.

———. 1886. "Des signes physiques, intellectuelles et moraux de la folie héréditaire." *Ann. méd.-psy.*, 7th ser., 3: 91–100, 4: 269–84.

———. 1890. "Des exhibitionnistes." *Ann. hyg. publ.*, 3d ser., 24: 152–68.

———. 1899. "Un cas d'exhibitionnisme." *Ann. méd.-psy.*, 8th ser., 10: 276–81.

Mantegazza, Paolo. 1873. *Fisiologia del amore.* Milan.

———. 1885. *Gli amori degli uomini. Saggio di una etnologia dell'amore.* Milan.

Marc, Charles-Chrétien-Henri. 1829. Prospectus and Introduction. *Ann. hyg. publ.*, 1st ser., 1: v–xxxix.

———. 1840. *De la folie considérée dans ses rapports avec les questions médico-judiciaires* [Of madness considered in its relation to medico-judicial questions]. 2 vols. Paris: Baillière.

Martineau, Henri. 1907. *Le roman scientifique d'Emile Zola.—La médecine et les Rougon-Macquart.* Paris: J. B. Baillière.

Marx, Karl. [1867] 1890. *Das Kapital. Kritik der politischen Oekonomie.* Hamburg: Otto Meissner.

Matthey, André. 1816. *Nouvelles recherches sur les maladies de l'esprit.* Paris: Paschoud.

Maugras, Thierry. 1849. "L'autorité et l'association." *Union médicale* 3: 425.

Maury, Louis-Ferdinand-Alfred. 1860. *La Magie et l'astrologie dans l'antiquité et au moyen âge, ou étude sur les superstitions paiennes qui se sont perpetuées jusqu'à nos jours.* Paris: Didier.

Medical Circular No. 1—Revised. 1941. "Minimum psychiatric inspection." Reprinted in the *Journal of the American Medical Association* 116(18): 2059-61.

Michéa, Claude François. 1849. "Des déviations maladives de l'appétit vénérien." *Union médicale* 3: 338–39.

———. 1865a. "De l'épilepsie compliquée de chorée rhythmique ou électrique." *Gazette des hôpitaux* 38(11): 41–42.

———. 1865b. "Cas d'attaques d'hystérie à forme extraordinaire alternant avec de l'ataxie musculaire, complication de somnambulisme naturel." *Gazette des hôpitaux* 38(103): 410–11, 414–15.

Mirbeau, Octave. [1899] 1988. *Le Jardin des supplices.* Paris: Gallimard.

Moll, Albert. 1889. *Der Hypnotismus.* Berlin: Fischer.

———. 1891. *Die conträre Sexualempfindung.* Berlin: Fischer. Translated by Pactet and Romme as *Les perversions de l'instinct génital. Etude sur l'inversion sexuelle* (Paris: Carré, 1893).

Moreau (de Tours), Jacques-Joseph. 1859. *La Psychologie morbide dans ses rapports avec la philosophie de l'histoire ou de l'influence des névropathies sur le dynamisme intellectuelle.* Paris: Masson.

Moreau (de Tours), Paul. [1877] 1880. *Des aberrations du sens génésique.* Paris: J. B. Baillière & Fils.

———. 1882. *De l'homicide commis par les enfants.* Paris: Asselin.

———. 1884. "On The Aberrations of the Genesic Sense." Translated by Joseph Workman. *Alienist and Neurologist* 5: 367–85.

———. 1888. *De la folie chez les enfants.* Paris: J. B. Baillière & Fils.

Morel, Bénédict A. 1851. "Études historiques et physiologiques sur l'aliénation." *Ann. méd.-psy.,* 2d ser., 3: 550–73.

———. 1854. "Rapport médico-légal sur l'état mentale de Dugout Caroline accusée de vol." *Ann. méd.-psy.,* 2d ser., 6: 603–9.

———. 1857. *Traité des dégénérescences physiques, intellectuelles et morales de l'espèce humaine et des causes qui produisent ces variétés maladives* [Treatise on degenerations]. Paris: Baillière.

Mouchet. 1848. "Note sur un cas d'hystérie chez l'homme." *Gazette médicale de Paris,* 3d ser., 3 (26 February): 167–68.

Mourette. 1869. "Hystérie chez l'homme." *Bulletin médicale de l'Aisne.* Reported in *Ann. méd.-psy.,* 5th ser., 1: 501–2.

Müller, Friedrich Max. [1878a] 1879. *Sur l'origine et le development des religions.* Translated by J. Darmesteter. Paris: Reinwald.

———. [1878b] 1898. *Lecture on the Origins and Growth of Religion.* Lecture delivered 1878. In *Collected Works,* vol. 9. London: Green.

Näcke, Paul Adolf. 1905. "Le monde homosexuel de Paris." *Arch. anth. crim.* 20: 182–85, 411–14.

———. 1907. "Ein Besuch bei den Homosexuellen in Berlin." *Archiv für Kriminal-anthropologie und Kriminalistik* 15: 244–63.

———. 1908. "Einteilung der Homosexuellen." *Allgemeine Zeitschrift für Psychiatrie* 65: 109–28.

Nordau, Max Simon. [1893] 1894–1895. *Dégénérescence.* 2 vols. Translated by Auguste Dietrich. Paris: Félix Alcan. Appeared originally as *Entartung* (Berlin: Carl Dunder, 1893).

*Onania.* [1710?] 1723. *Onania; or, the Heinous Sin of Self-Pollution, and All its Frightful Consequences, in both Sexes, Considered, with Spiritual and Physical Advice to those, who have already injur'd themselves by this abominable Practice.* 8th ed. London: Elizabeth Rumball for Thomas Crouch.

Parent-Duchâtelet, Alexandre-Jean-Baptiste. 1832. "Penchants vicieux et criminels observés chez une petite fille." *Ann. hyg. publ.,* 1st ser., 7: 173–94.

———. 1836. *De la prostitution dans la ville de Paris, considerée sous le rapport de l'hygiène publique, de la morale et de l'administration* [Prostitution in the city of Paris]. Paris: Baillière.

*Les Physiologies parisiennes.* 1850. 20 parts in 1 volume. Paris: Aubert.

Pinel, Philippe. 1801. *Traité médico-philosophique sur l'aliénation mentale ou la manie.* Paris: Richard, Gaille & Ranvier.

Pinel, Scipion. 1844. *Traité de pathologie cérébrale ou des maladies du cerveau.* Paris: Librairie Médicale de Just Rouvier.

Plater, Felix. 1664. *Histories and observations of all the afflictions of the functions of the body and soul*. London: Peter Cole. English translation of *Observationum, in hominis affectibus plerisque, corpori et animo, functionum læsione, dolore, aliave molestia et vitio insensis*. (Bassel: Ludovic Konig, 1641).

Plato. 1986. *Phædrus*. Translated by C. J. Rowe. Wiltshire: Aris & Phillips.

Raffalovich, Marc André. 1894a. "Quelques observations sur l'inversion." *Arch. anth. crim.* 9: 216–18.

———. 1894b. "L'éducation des invertis." *Arch. anth. crim.* 9: 738–40.

———. 1895a. "L'Uranisme. Inversion sexuelle congénitale." *Arch. anth. crim.* 10: 99–127.

———. 1895b. "A propos du roman d'un inverti et de quelques travaux récents sur l'inversion sexuelle." *Arch. anth. crim.* 10: 333–36.

———. 1895c. "L'Affair Oscar Wilde." *Arch. anth. crim.* 10: 445–77.

———. 1896a. *Uranisme et unisexualité. Étude sur différentes manifestations de l'instinct sexuel* [Uranism and unisexuality: A study of different manifestations of the sexual instinct]. Paris: Masson.

———. 1896b. "Unisexualité anglaise." *Arch. anth. crim.* 11: 429–31.

———. 1897a. "Annales de l'unisexualité." *Arch. anth. crim.* 12: 87–102, 185–224.

———. 1897b. Review of *Les Hors nature* by Rachilde. *Arch. anth. crim.* 12: 321–24.

———. 1903. "A propos de l'affaire Shakespeare-Bacon." *Arch. anth. crim.* 18: 662–65.

———. 1904. "Les groupes d'uranistes à Paris et à Berlin." *Arch. anth. crim.* 19: 926–36.

———. 1905. "A propos du syndicat des uranistes." *Arch. anth. crim.* 20: 283–86.

Raimond, Jean. 1849. "Feuilleton." *Union médicale* 3: 365–66.

Régis, E. 1899. "Un cas de perversion sexuelle à forme sadique." *Arch. anth. crim.* 14: 399–419.

Reignier, Lagardelle, and Legrand du Saulle. 1877. "Sodomie et assassinat." *Ann. méd.-psy.*, 5th ser., 17: 190–202.

Restif de La Bretonne. [1779] 1983. *Le Pornographe, ou Idées d'un honnête homme sur un projet de règlement pour les prostituées: propre à prevenir les malheurs qu'occasionnent le publicisme des femmes*. Paris: Editions d'Aujourd'hui.

Reveillé-Parise, Joseph Henri. 1828. Review of *Traité d'hygiène appliqué à l'éducation de la jeunesse* by Simon de Metz. *Revue médicale* 2: 87–96.

Reydellet. 1819. Pédérastie. *Dictionnaire des sciences médicales* 40: 37–45.

Ribot, Theodule. 1885. *Les maldies de la personnalité*. Paris: F. Alcan.

———. 1887. "Sur la nature du plaisir." *Rev. phil.* 24: 180–92.

Rochet. 1875. "L'Hystérie chez l'homme." *Gazette médicale de Paris* 4: 609–11.

Rodamel. 1806. "Sur une nymphomanie, accompagnée de délire périodique, rédigée en forme de Mémoire à consulter." *Mémoires de la Société médicale d'émulation* 6: 150–64.

Rolet, J. 1907. Review of *Le roman scientifique d'Emile Zola.—La médecine et les Rougon-Macquart* by Henri Martineau. *Arch. Neur.*, 3d ser., 1: 513.

Rony-Duprest. IX (1801). "Histoire d'un cas particulier de satyriasis." *Mémoires de la Société médicale d'émulation* 4: 438–40.

Rousseau, Jean-Jacques. [1750] 1964. *Discours sur les sciences et les arts* [Discourse on the sciences and arts]. In *Œuvres complètes* 3: 1–30. Paris: Pléiade.

———. [1752] 1964. *Narcisse, ou l'amant de lui même* [Narcisse or the lover of himself]. In *Œuvres complètes* 2: 957–1018. Paris: Pléiade.

———. [1755] 1964. *Discours sur l'origine et les fondements de l'inégalité parmi les hommes.* In *Œuvres complètes,* 3: 111–223. Paris: Pléiade.

———. [1762] 1969. *Émile, ou De l'éducation* [Emile, or on education]. In *Œuvres complètes* 4: 239–868. Paris: Pléiade.

———. [1782–1789] 1959. *Les Confessions* and "Ébauches des Confessions." In *Œuvres complètes* 1: 1–656, 1148–64. Paris: Pléiade.

Dr. Rozier. 1830. *Des habitudes secrètes ou des maladies produites par l'onanisme chez les femmes.* 3d ed. Paris: Audin.

Sacher-Masoch, Leopold. [1870] 1989. *Venus in Furs* [*Venus im Pelz*]. New York: Zone.

Sade, Donatien Alphonse François marquis de. [1795] 1976. *La Philosophie dans le boudoir.* Paris: Gallimard.

———?. [1800] 1910? *Zoloë et ses deux acolytes; ou, Quelques decades de la vie de trois jolies femmes.* Paris: Bibliothèque des curieux.

Sainte-Claire Deville, Henri. 1880. "Les odeurs de Paris." *Ann. hyg. publ.,* 3d ser., 4: 361–64.

Saint-Paul, Georges. (Also see Laupts.)

———. 1892. *Essais sur le langage intérieur.* Lyon: Storck.

———. 1902. "L'Instinct sexuel (A propos d'un ouvrage de M. Havelock Ellis)." *Arch. anth. crim.* 17: 213–25.

———. 1904. *Le langage intérieur et les paraphrases. La fonction endophasique.* Paris: Félix Alcan.

———. 1907. *Plus fort que le mal. Essai sur le mal innomable. Pièce en quatre actes.* Published under the pseudonym G. Espé de Metz. Paris: A. Maloine.

———. 1930. *Invertis et homosexuels.* Thèmes psychologiques. Paris: Vigot.

Santenoise. 1900. "Religion et folie." *Rev. phil.* 50: 142–64.

Schminke. 1872. "Ein Fall von conträrer Sexualempfindung." *Arch. Psy. Nerv.* 3: 225–26.

Scholz. 1873. "Bekenntnisse eines an perverser Geschlechtsrichtung Leidenden." *Vierteljahrsschrift für gerichtliche Medicin und öffentliches Sanitätswesen* 19: 321–28.

Sérieux, Paul. 1888. *Recherches cliniques sur les anomalies de l'instinct sexuel.* Paris: Levasseur & Babé.

———. 1921. *Valentin Magnan. Sa vie et son œuvre (1835–1916).* Paris: Masson.

Serrurier. 1820. "Pollution." *Dictionnaire des sciences médicales.* 44: 92–141. Paris: Panckoucke.

Servæs, F. 1876. "Zur Kenntniss von der conträren Sexualempfindung." *Arch. Psy. Nerv.* 6: 484–95.

Shaw, C. J., and G. N. Ferris. 1883. "Perverted sexual instinct." *Journal of Nervous and Mental Disease* 10: 185–204.

*Le Siècle.* 1849. "Affaire du sergent Bertrand." Tribunaux. (11 July): 4–5.

Simon, Théodore. 1912. "Alfred Binet." *L'Année psychologique* 18: 1–14.

Soubourou, Pierre Henri René. 1904. "La Psychologie des voleuses dans les grands magasins." Medical thesis, Faculté de Médecine de Bordeaux.

Soupault, Maurice. 1896. Review of *De l'exhibitionisme chez les épileptiques* by Pribat. *Arch. anth. crim.* 11: 338–39.

Stark. 1877. "Über conträre Sexualempfindung." *Allgemeine Zeitschrift für Psychiatrie und psychisch-gerichtliche Medicin* 33: 209–16.

Stefanowsky, Dimitry. 1892a. "Le Passivisme." *Arch. anth. crim.* 7: 294–98.

———. 1892b. "Passivism—A variety of sexual perversion." *Alienist and Neurologist* 13: 650–57.

———. 1894. "Sur la symptomatologie de l'inversion sexuelle." *Arch. anth. crim.* 9: 741–44.

Stekel, Wilhelm. 1924. *Peculiarities of Behavior: Wandering Mania, Dipsomania, Cleptomania, Pyromania, and Allied Impulsive Acts.* 2 vols. English translation of *Impulshandlungen* (1922) by J. S. Van Teslaar. New York: Liveright.

Tamassia, Arrigo. 1878. "Sull'inversione dell'istinto sessuale." *Rivista sperimentale di freniatria e di medicina legale* 4: 97–117, 285–91.

Tarde, Gabriel. 1891. "L'Amour morbide." *Archives de l'anthropologie criminelle et des sciences pénales* 5: 585–95.

Tardieu, Ambroise Auguste. [1857] 1878. *Etude médico-légale sur les attentats aux mœurs* [Medicolegal study of assaults on decency]. 7th ed. Paris: J.-B. Baillière.

Theophrastos. 1919. *Enquiry into Plants and Minor Works on Odours and Weather Signs.* Translated by Arthur Hort. Loeb Classical Library. London: Heinmann.

Tissot, Samuel-Auguste-André-David. 1758. *Tentamen de Morbis ex Manustruptione.* Lausanne: M. M. Bosquet.

———. [1760] 1781. *L'Onanisme, ou Dissertation physique sur les maladies produites par la masturbation.* 7th ed. Lausanne: Grasset. Reprint ed., Paris: Editions de la Différance, 1991.

———. [1761] 1795. *Avis au peuple sur sa santé.* 7th ed. Blois: Masson & Durie.

———. [1766] 1826. *De la santé des gens de lettres.* New ed. Introduction and edition by F.-G. Boisseau. Paris: J.-B. Baillière.

———. 1770. *Essai sur les maladies des gens du monde.* Lausanne: François Grasset.

Toulouse, Edouard. 1896. *Emile Zola.* Paris: Société des éditions scientifiques.

Tournier, César. 1897. "Le livre de M. Raffalovich sur l'uranisme et l'unisexualité." *Arch. anth. crim.* 12: 326–32, 709–14.

*Trésor de la langue française.* 1988. Centre National de Recherches Scientifiques. Paris: Gallimard.

Ulrichs, Karl Heinrich. [1864–1879] 1994. *Forschungen über das Räthsel der mannmännlichen Liebe.* 4 vols. Edited by Hubert Kennedy. Berlin: Verlag rosa Winkel.

Veuillot, Louis. 1867. *Les Odeurs de Paris* [The odors of Paris]. Paris: Palmé.

Virey, Julien Joseph. [1828] 1831. *Hygiène philosophique appliquée à la politique et à la morale.* New edition. Paris: Crochard.

Voisin, Auguste Félix. 1826. *Des causes morales et physiques des maladies mentales et de quelques autres affections nerveuses telles que l'hystérie, la nymphomanie et le satyriasis.* Paris: J. B. Baillière.

Voisin, A.-F., J. Socquet, and A. Motet. 1890. "État mental de P. . . . Poursuivi pour avoir coupé les nattes de plusieurs jeunes filles." *Ann. hyg. publ.*, 3d ser., 23: 331–40.

Voltaire. [1764] 1879. "Sentiment des citoyens." In *Œuvres complètes*, 25: 309–14. Paris: Garnier.

Westphal, Karl. 1869. "Die conträre Sexualempfindung: Symptom eines neuropathischen (psychopathischen) Zustandes." *Arch. Psy. Nerv.* 2: 73–108.

———. 1876. "Zur conträre Sexualempfindung." *Arch. Psy. Nerv.* 6: 620–621.

Wilhelm, Eugène. [Dr. Numa Prætorius, pseud.]. 1909. "A propos de l'article du Dr. Laupts sur l'homosexualité." *Arch. anth. crim.* 24: 198–207.

———. 1912. "Publications allemandes sur les questions sexuelles." *Arch. anth. crim.* 27: 301–9.

Willis, Thomas. 1670. *De anima brutorum, qui hominis vitalis ac sensitiva est.* In *Opera Omnia*. Geneva: Samuel de Tournes.

Woodward, Samuel B. 1839. "Deslande's essay." [letter to the editor]. *Boston Medical and Surgical Journal* 19: 348–49.

Zacchia, Paolo. 1651. *Quæstiones medico-legales.* 3d ed. Amsterdam: Johannis Baeu.

Zola, Emile. [1871] 1960. *La Curée.* In *Les Rougon-Macquart*, vol. 1. Paris: Pléiade.

———. [1873]. "Le Ventre de Paris." Preparatory dossier, unpublished ms. Bibliothèque Nationale, Nouvelles Acquisitions Françaises 10277.

———. [1873] 1960. *Le Ventre de Paris.* In *Les Rougon-Macquart*, vol. 1. Paris: Pléiade.

———. [1880] 1968. "Le Roman expérimental." In *Œuvres complètes*, ed. H. Mitterand, 10: 1145–1203. Lausanne: Cercle du livre précieux.

———. [1882]. "Au Bonheur des Dames." Preparatory dossier, unpublished ms. Bibliothèque Nationale, Nouvelles Acquisitions Françaises 10338.

———. [1883] 1964. *Au Bonheur des Dames.* In *Les Rougon-Macquart*, vol. 3. Paris: Pléiade.

———. [1889] 1966. *La Bête humaine.* In *Les Rougon-Macquart*, vol. 4. Paris: Pléiade.

———. [1893] 1967. *Le Docteur Pascal.* In *Les Rougon-Macquart*, vol. 5. Paris: Pléiade.

———. 1896. Preface to *Tares et poisons. Perversions et perversités sexuelles* by Dr. Laupts [Georges Saint-Paul]. Paris: George Carré.

## Secondary Sources

Abelove, Henry. 1993. "Freud, Male Homosexuality, and the Americans." In *The Lesbian and Gay Studies Reader,* ed. H. Abelove, M. A. Barale, D. M. Halperin, 381–93. New York: Routledge.

Ackerknecht, Erwin. 1948. "Hygiene in France, 1815–1848." *Bulletin of the History of Medicine* 22: 117–55.

———. 1967. *Medicine at the Paris Hospital, 1794–1848.* Baltimore: Johns Hopkins University Press.

Adam, Antoine. 1968. Preface to *Les Bijoux indiscrets* by Denis Diderot [1748]. Paris: Garnier Flammarion.

Albert, Nicole. 1993. "Sappho Mythified, Sappho Mystified, or The Metamorphoses of Sappho in Fin-de-Siècle France. In *Gay Studies from the French Cultures,* ed. R. Mendès-Leite and P.-O. de Busscher, 87–104. New York: Haworth.

Alexander, Franz G., and Sheldon T. Selesnick. 1966. *The History of Psychiatry: An Evaluation of Psychiatric Thought and Practice from Prehistoric Times to the Present.* New York: Harper & Row.

Alexandrian, Sarane. 1989. *Histoire de la littérature érotique.* Paris: Seghers.

Antheaume, André. 1925. *Le roman d'une épidémie parisienne. La Kleptomanie?* Paris: Gaston Doin.

Anzieu, Didier. 1959. *L'auto-analyse. Son rôle dans la découverte de la psychanalyse par Freud. Sa fonction en psychanalyse.* Paris: Presses Universitaires de France.

Apter, Emily. 1991. *Feminizing the Fetish. Psychoanalysis and Narrative Obsession in Turn-of-the-Century France.* Ithaca, N.Y.: Cornell University Press.

Ariès, Philippe. 1960. *L'enfant et la vie familiale sous l'Ancien Régime.* Paris: Plon.

Aron, Jean-Paul, and Roger Kempf. 1979. "Triumphs and Tribulations of the Homosexual Discourse." In *Homosexualities and French Literature,* ed. G. Stambolian and E. Marks, 141–57. Ithaca, N.Y.: Cornell University Press.

———. 1984. *La Bourgeoisie, le sexe, et l'honneur.* Paris: Editions Complexe.

Augé, Marc. 1988. *Le Dieu objet.* Paris: Flammarion.

Azar, Amine A. 1975. "Le sadisme et le masochisme innominés. Étude historique et épistémologique de la brèche de 1890." Doctoral diss., University of Paris.

———. 1986. "La psychopathia sexualis de Krafft-Ebing, ou l'invraisemblable célébration d'un centenaire." *Psychanalyse à l'université* 11(44): 709–13.

Baecque, Antoine de. 1991. "The 'Livres remplis d'horreur': Pornographic Literature and Politics at the Beginning of the French Revolution." In *Erotica and the Enlightenment,* ed. P. Wagner, 123–65. Frankfurt: Verlag Peter Lang.

Baldick, Robert. 1955. *The Life of Joris-Karl Huysmans.* Oxford: Clarendon Press.

Barker-Benfield, Graham John. 1972. The Spermatic Economy: A Nineteenth-Century View of Sexuality. *Feminist Studies* 1: 45–74.

———. 1976. *The Horrors of the Half-Known Life: Male Attitudes Towards Women and Sexuality in America.* New York: Harper & Row.

Bataille, Georges. 1972. *Le procès de Gilles de Rais.* Paris: J.-J. Pauvert.

Baudrillard, Jean. 1972. *Pour une critique de l'économie politique du signe.* Paris: Gallimard.

———. 1979. *La société de consommation.* Paris: Denoël.

Bayer, Ronald. 1987. *Homosexuality and American Psychiatry: The Politics of Diagnosis.* Princeton, N.J.: Princeton University Press.

Beecher, Donald A. 1992. "Quattrocento Views on the Eroticization of the Imagination." In *Eros and Anteros: The Medical Traditions of Love in the Renaissance,* ed. D. Beecher and M. Ciavolella, 49–65. Ottawa: Dovehouse Editions.

Benstock, Shari. 1989. "Paris Lesbianism and the Politics of Reaction, 1900–1940." In *Hidden from History: Reclaiming the Gay and Lesbian Past,* ed. M. B. Duberman, M. Vicinus, and G. Chauncey, 332–46. New York: New American Library.

Bérubé, Allan. 1990. *Coming Out Under Fire.* New York: Free Press.

Birkett, Jennifer. 1986. *The Sins of the Fathers: Decadence in France 1870–1914.* London: Quartet Books.

Bleys, Rudi C. 1995. *The Geography of Perversion: Male-to-Male Sexual Behavior Outside the West and the Ethnographic Imagination, 1750–1918.* New York: New York University Press.

Bloch, Jean. 1974. "Rousseau's Reputation as an Authority on Childcare and Physical Education in France before the Revolution." *Pædagogica Historica* 14: 5–33.

Blum, Carol. 1986. *Rousseau and the Republic of Virtue. The Language of Politics in the French Revolution.* Ithaca: Cornell University Press.

Bonnet, Gérard. 1993. *Les Perversions sexuelles.* 2d ed. Paris: Presses Universitaires de France.

Boswell, John. 1980. *Christianity, Social Tolerance, and Homosexuality: Gay People from the Beginning of the Christian era to the Fourteenth Century.* Chicago: University of Chicago Press.

Brumberg, Joan J. 1984. "Chlorotic Girls, 1870–1920: A Historical Perspective on Female Adolescence." In *Women and Health in America,* ed. J. W. Leavitt, 186–195. Madison: University of Wisconsin Press.

Buican, Denis. 1984. *Histoire de la génétique et de l'évolutionisme en France.* Paris: Presses Universitaires de France.

Bullough, Vern L., and Martha Voght. 1976. "Homosexuality and Its Confusion with the 'Secret Sin' in pre-Freudian America." In *Sex, Society and History,* ed. Vern L. Bullough, 112–24. New York: Science History Publications.

Butler, Judith. 1990. "Gender Trouble, Feminist Theory and Psychoanalytic Discourse." In *Feminism/Postmodernism,* ed. L. Nicholson, 324–40. New York: Routledge.

Buxbaum, Edith. 1951. "Freud's Dream Interpretation in the Light of his Letters to Fliess." *Bulletin of the Menninger Clinic* 15: 197–212.

Canadé Sautman, Francesca. 1996. "Invisible Women: Lesbian Working-class Culture in France, 1880–1930." In *Homosexuality in Modern France,* ed. J. Merrick and B. T. Ragan, Jr., 177–201. New York: Oxford University Press.

Canguilhem, Georges. [1966] 1989. *The Normal and the Pathological.* Translated by Carolyn Fawcett. New York: Zone.

———. 1983. "Histoires de religions et histoires des sciences dans la théorie du fétichisme chez Auguste Comte." In *Etudes d'histoire et de philosophie des sciences,* 5th ed. Paris: J. Vrin.

Cardon, Patrick. 1993. "A Homosexual Militant at the Beginning of the Century: Marc André Raffalovich." In *Gay Studies from the French Cultures,* ed. R. Mendès-Leite and P.-O. de Busscher, 183–91. New York: Haworth.

Castel, Robert. 1976. *L'Ordre psychiatrique: L'âge d'or de l'aliénisme.* Paris: Minuit.

Chauncey, George. 1982–1983. "From Sexual Inversion to Homosexuality: Medicine and the Changing Conceptualization of Female Deviance." *Salmagundi* 58: 114–46.

Classen, Constance, David Howes, and Anthony Synnott. 1994. *Aroma: The Cultural History of Smell.* London: Routledge.

Coleman, William. 1982. *Death is a Social Disease. Public Health and Political Economy in Industrial France.* Madison: University of Wisconsin Press.

Colwill, Elizabeth. 1996. "Pass as a Woman, Act as a Man: Marie-Antoinette as Tribade in the Pornography of the French Revolution." In *Homosexuality in Modern France,* ed. J. Merrick and B. T. Ragan, Jr., 54–79. New York: Oxford University Press.

Copley, Antony. 1989. *Sexual Moralities in France, 1780–1980: New Ideas on the Family, Divorce, and Homosexuality.* London: Routledge.

Corbin, Alain. 1982. *Le miasme et la jonquille, l'odorat et l'imaginaire social, 18è–19è.* Paris: Aubier Montaigne.

Dansel, Michel. 1991. *Le Sergent Bertrand. Portrait d'un nécrophile heureux.* Paris: Albin Michel.

Darnton, Robert. 1991. *Edition et sédition: l'univers de la littérature clandestine au XVIIIè siècle.* Paris: Gallimard.

Davidson, Arnold. 1987. "Sex and the Emergence of Sexuality." *Critical Inquiry* 14: 16–48.

———. 1988. "How to Do the History of Psychoanalysis: A Reading of Freud's *Three Essays on Sexuality.*" In *The Trial(s) of Psychoanalysis,* ed. F. Meltzer, 39–64. Chicago: University of Chicago Press.

———. 1990. "Closing Up the Corpses: Diseases of Sexuality and the Emergence of the Psychiatric Style of Reasoning." In *Meaning and Method: Essays in Honor of Hilary Putnam,* ed. G. Boolos, 295–325. Cambridge: Cambridge University Press.

Dawson, Robert L. 1987. "The *Mélange de poésies diverses* (1781) and the Diffusion of Manuscript Pornography in Eighteenth-Century France." In *'Tis Nature's Fault: Unauthorized Sexuality during the Enlightenment,* ed. R. P. Maccubbin, 229–43. Cambridge: Cambridge University Press.

de Lauretis, Teresa. 1984. *Alice Doesn't: Feminism, Semiotics, Cinema.* Bloomington: Indiana University Press.

Deleuze, Gilles. 1967. Introduction to *La Bête humaine* by Emile Zola. *Œuvres complètes,* 6: 13–21. Paris: Cercle du livre précieux.

Derrida, Jacques. 1967. *De la grammatologie.* Paris: Minuit.

———. 1972. *La Dissémination.* Paris: Seuil.

Dowbiggin, Ian. 1991. *Inheriting Madness: Professionalization and Psychiatric Knowledge in Nineteenth-Century France.* Berkeley: University of California Press.

Duffy, John. 1963. "Masturbation and Clitoridectomy: A Nineteenth-Century View." *Journal of the American Medical Association* 186: 166–68.

Duggan, Lisa. 1993. "The Trials of Alice Mitchell: Sensationalism, Sexology, and the Lesbian Subject in Turn-of-the-Century America." *Signs* 18: 791–814.

Dumesnil, René. 1928. *La publication de Madame Bovary,* 3d ed. Amiens: Editions Edgar Malfère.

Ellenberger, Henri F. 1970. *The Discovery of the Unconscious.* New York: Basic Books.

Ellis, Peter, and Graham Mellsop. 1985. "De Clérambault's Syndrome—A Nosological Entity?" *British Journal of Psychiatry* 146: 90–95.

Ellman, Richard. 1988. *Oscar Wilde.* New York: Knopf.

Elosu, Suzanne. 1929. "La maladie de Jean-Jacques Rousseau." *Bulletin de la Société française de l'histoire de la médecine* 23: 349–56.

Emch-Deriaz, Anoinette S. 1984. "Towards a Social Conception of Health in the Second Half of the Eighteenth Century: Tissot (1728–1797) and the New Preoccupation with Health and Well-Being." Ph.D. diss., University of Rochester, Rochester, N.Y.

Engelhardt, H. Tristram. 1985. "The Disease of Masturbation." In *Sickness and Health in America,* ed. J. Leavitt and R. Numbers, 13–21. Madison: University Wisconsin Press.

Enoch, David, W. H. Trethowan, and J. C. Barker. 1967. *Some Uncommon Psychiatric Syndromes.* Bristol, Eng.: John Wright & Sons.

Epstein, Julia. 1995. *Altered Conditions: Disease, Medicine, and Storytelling.* New York: Routledge.

Evans, Martha Noel. 1991. *Fits and Starts: A Genealogy of Hysteria in Modern France.* Ithaca, N.Y.: Cornell.

Fairchild, Hoaxie N. 1961. *The Noble Savage: A Study in Romantic Naturalism.* New York: Russell & Russell.

Féray, Jean-Claude. 1981. "Une histoire critique du mot homosexualité." *Arcadie* 28(325–28): 11–21, 115–24, 171–81, 246–58.

Figlio, Karl. 1978. "Chlorosis and Chronic Disease in Nineteenth-Century Britain." *International Journal of Health Services* 8: 589–617.

Fogel, Maurice. 1991. "Perversity and the Perverse." In *Perversions and Near-Perversions in Clinical Practice,* ed. G. Fogel and W. A. Myers, 1–16. New Haven, Conn.: Yale University Press.

Foucault, Michel. 1963. *Naissance de la clinique: Une archéologie du regard médical.* Paris: Presses Universitaires de France.

———. 1966. *Les mots et les choses.* Paris: Gallimard.

———. 1972. *Histoire de la folie à l'âge classique.* Paris: Gallimard.

———. 1973. *Moi, Pierre Rivière ayant égorgé ma mère, ma soeur, et mon frère.* Paris: Gallimard.

———. 1976. *Histoire de la sexualité.* Vol. 1: *La volonté de savoir.* Paris: Gallimard.

———. 1978. *Herculine Barbin dite Alexina B.* Paris: Gallimard.

———. 1980. *Power/Knowledge. Selected Interviews and Other Writings, 1972–1977.* Edited by Colin Gordon. New York: Pantheon.

Friedlander, Ruth. 1973. "Bénédict-Augustin Morel and the Development of the Theory of Degenerescence (The Introduction of Anthropology into Psychiatry)." Ph.D. diss., University of California, San Francisco.

Frye, Northrop. 1957. *The Anatomy of Criticism.* Princeton, N.J.: Princeton University Press.

Gagné, Pierre, and Lucie Desparois. 1995. "L'érotomanie mâle: Un type de harcèlement sexuel dangereux." *Canadian Journal of Psychiatry* 40: 136–41.

Garber, Marjorie. 1992. *Vested-Interests: Cross-Dressing and Cultural Anxiety.* New York: Routledge.

Geras, Norman. 1971. "Essence and Appearance: Aspects of Fetishism in Marx's Capital." *New Left Review* 65: 69–85.

Gerlach, Wolfgang. 1938. "Das Problem des 'weiblichen Samens' in der antiken und mittelaltlichen Medizin." *Sudhoffs Archiv* 30(4–5): 177–93.

Gilbert, Arthur N. 1975. "Doctor, Patient, and Onanist Diseases in the Nineteenth Century." *Journal of the History of Medicine* 30: 217–34.

Gilman, Sander. 1993. "The Image of the Hysteric." In *Hysteria Beyond Freud,* S. Gilman et al., 345–452. Berkeley: University of California Press.

Godfrey, Sima. 1984. "Mummy dearest: Cryptic codes in Gautier's 'Pied de momie.'" *Romantic Review* 75: 302–11.

Goldberg, Jonathan. 1992. *Sodometries: Renaissance Texts, Modern Sexualities.* Stanford, Calif.: Stanford University Press.

Goldstein, Jan. 1987. *Console and Classify: The French Psychiatric Profession in the Nineteenth Century.* New York: Cambridge University Press.

———. 1991. "The Uses of Male Hysteria: Medical and Literary Discourse in Nineteenth-Century France." *Representations* 34: 134–65.

Goleman, Daniel. 1991. "New View of Fantasy: Much Is Found Perverse." *New York Times,* 7 May, C1, C12.

Gould, Steven J. 1981. *The Mismeasure of Man.* New York: W. W. Norton.

Goulemot, Jean Marie. 1980. "'Prêtons la main a la nature.' II. Fureurs utérines." *Dix-huitième siècle* 12: 97–111.

———. 1991. *Ces livres qu'on ne lit que d'une main. Lecture et lecteurs de livres pornographiques au XVIIIe siècle.* Aix-en-Provence: Alinea.

Greenberg, David F. 1988. *The Construction of Homosexuality.* Chicago: University of Chicago Press.

Grimm, Robert. 1995. "The Dawn of Contrary Sexual Sensitivity." Unpublished ms.

Grosskurth, Phyllis. 1980. *Havelock Ellis.* London: Allen Lane.

Guicciardi, Jean-Pierre. 1987. "Between the Licit and the Illicit: The Sexuality of the King." In *'Tis Nature's Fault: Unauthorized Sexuality during the Enlightenment.* ed. R. P. Maccubin, 88–97. Cambridge: Cambridge University Press.

Halperin, David. 1990. *One Hundred Years of Homosexuality.* New York: Routledge.

Hansen, Bert. 1989. "American Physicians' Earliest Writings about Homosexuality, 1880–1900." *Milbank Quarterly* 67, suppl. 1: 92–108.

Hare, E. H. 1962. "Masturbatory Insanity: The History of an Idea." *Journal of the Mental Sciences* 108: 1–25.

Harrington, Anne. 1988. "Hysteria, Hypnosis, and the Lure of the Invisible: The Rise of Neo-Mesmerism in *Fin-de-siècle* French Psychiatry". In *The Anatomy of Madness,* vol. 3, ed. W. F. Bynum, R. Porter, M. Shepherd, 226–46. London: Routledge.

Harrington, Anne, and Vernon Rosario. 1992. "Olfaction and the Primitive: Nineteenth-Century Thinking on Olfaction." In *Olfaction and the Central Nervous System,* ed. M. Serby and K. Chobor, 3–27. New York: Springer Verlag.

Harris, Ruth. 1989a. "Melodrama, Hysteria and Feminine Crimes of Passion in the Fin-de-Siècle. *History Workshop Journal* 25: 31–63.

———. 1989b. *Murders and Madness: Medicine, Law and Society in the Fin-de-Siècle.* Oxford: Oxford University Press.

Hekma, Gert. 1994. "'A Female Soul in a Male Body': Sexual Inversion as Gender Inversion in Nineteenth-Century Sexology." In *Third Sex, Third Gender: Beyond Sexual Dimorphism in Culture and History,* ed. Gilbert Herdt, 213–39. New York: Zone.

Hemmings, F. W. J. 1982. *Baudelaire: The Damned.* London: Hamish Hamilton.

Herdt, Gilbert. 1989. "Introduction: Gay and Lesbian Youth, Emergent Identities, and Cultural Scenes at Home and Abroad." In *Gay and Lesbian Youth,* ed. G. Herdt, 1–42. New York: Haworth.

Héritier-Auger, Françoise. 1989. "Semen and Blood: Some Ancient Theories Concerning Their Genesis and Relationship." In *Fragments for a History of the Human Body,* pt. 3, ed. M. Feher, 280–99. New York: Zone.

Herrn, Rainer. 1995. "On the History of Biological Theories of Homosexuality." In *Sex, Cells, and Same-Sex Desire: The Biology of Sexual Preference,* ed. J. P. De Cecco, D. A. Parker, 31–56. New York: Haworth.

Hesnard, Angelo. 1928. *La Psychanalyse. Théorie sexuelle de Freud.* Paris: Stock.

Hudson, Robert. 1977. "The Biography of Disease: Lessons from Chlorosis." *Bulletin of the History of Medicine* 51(3): 448–63.

Hunt, Lynn. 1991. "The Many Bodies of Marie-Antoinette: Political Pornography and the Problem of the Feminine in the French Revolution." In *Erotism and the Body Politic,* ed. L. Hunt, 108–30. Baltimore: Johns Hopkins University Press.

___, ed. 1993. *The Invention of Pornography: Obscenity and the Origins of Modernity, 1500–1800.* New York: Zone.

Hunter, Kathryn M. 1991. *Doctors' Stories: The Narrative Structure of Medical Knowledge.* Princeton, N.J.: Princeton University Press.

Iacono, Alfonso M. 1992. *Le Fétichisme. Histoire d'un concept.* Paris: Presses Universitaires de France.

Jacquart, Danielle. 1983. "La réflexion médicale médiévale et l'apport arabe." In *Nouvelle histoire de la psychiatrie,* ed. J. Postel and C. Quetel, 43–53. Toulouse: Privat.

Jones, Ernest. 1953. *The Life and Work of Sigmund Freud. Vol. 1: 1856–1900.* New York: Basic Books.

Jordanova, Ludmilla. 1987. "The Popularization of Medicine: Tissot on Onanism." *Textual Practice* 1: 68–80.

Jury, Paul. 1947. "La fessé de Jean-Jacques Rousseau." *Psyché. Revue internationale de psychanalyse et des sciences de l'homme* 4 (February): 159–82.

Kaplan, Louise. 1991a. *Female Perversions: The Temptations of Emma Bovary.* New York: Doubleday.

———. 1991b. "Women masquerading as women." In *Perversions and Near-Perversions in Clinical Practice,* ed. G. Fogel and W. A. Myers, 127–52. New Haven, Conn.: Yale University Press.

Kendricks, Walter. 1988. *The Secret Museum. Pornography in Modern Culture.* Hammondsworth, Eng.: Penguin.

Kennedy, Hubert. 1988. *Ulrichs: The Life and Work of Karl Heinrich Ulrichs, Pioneer of the Modern Gay Movement.* Boston: Alyson.

———. 1997. "Karl Heinrich Ulrichs: First Theorist of (Homo)Sexuality." In *Science and Homosexualities,* ed. Vernon Rosario, 26–45. New York: Routledge.

King, Helen. 1993. "Once upon a Text: Hysteria from Hippocrates." In *Hysteria Beyond Freud,* Sander Gilman et al., 3–90. Berkeley: University of California Press.

Kirk, Marshall, and Hunter Madsen. 1989. *After the Ball: How America Will Conquer its Fear and Hatred of Gays in the 90s.* New York: Penguin.

Kleinman, Arthur. 1988. *The Illness Narratives: Suffering, Healing, and the Human Condition.* New York: Basic Books.

Koestenbaum, Wayne. 1989. *Double Talk: The Erotics of Male Literary Collaboration.* New York: Routledge.

Kofman, Sarah. 1982. *Le respect des femmes: Kant et Rousseau.* Paris: Galilée.

Landes, Joan B. 1988. *Women and the Public Sphere in the Age of the French Revolution.* Ithaca, N.Y.: Cornell University Press.

Lanteri-Laura, Georges. 1979. *Lecture des perversions. Histoire de leur appropriation médicale.* Paris: Masson.

Laplanche, Jean, and J.-B. Pontalis. 1973. *The Language of Psycho-Analysis.* Translated by D. Nicholson-Smith. New York: W. W. Norton.

Laqueur, Thomas. 1989. "The Solitary Evil, the Solitary Vice and Pouring Tea." In *Fragments for a History of the Human Body,* pt. 3, ed. M. Feher, 335–42. New York: Zone.

———. 1990. *Making Sex: Body and Gender from the Greeks to Freud.* Cambridge, Mass.: Harvard University Press.

———. 1992. "Credits, Novels, Masturbation." Unpublished ms. presented at the Choreographic History Conference, February 16, University of California, Riverside.

Latour, Bruno. 1985. *Pasteur: Bataille contre les microbes.* Paris: Nathan.

Lejeune, Philippe. 1975. *Le Pacte autobiographique.* Paris: Seuil.

Lever, Maurice. 1985. *Les bûchers de Sodom.* Paris: Fayard.

———. 1991. *Donatien Alphonse François, marquis de Sade.* Paris: Fayard.

Lottman, Herbert. 1989. *Flaubert, a Biography.* Boston: Little, Brown.

Lucey, Michael. 1995. *Gide's Bent: Sexuality, Politics, Writing.* New York: Oxford University Press.

McCormack, Jerusha H. 1991. *John Gray: Poet, Dandy, and Priest.* Hanover, N.H.: Brandeis University Press.

MacDonald, Robert. 1967. "The Frightful Consequences of Onanism: Notes on the History of a Delusion." *Journal of the History of Ideas* 28: 423–31.

Marcus, Steven. 1962. Introduction to *Three Essays on the Theory of Sexuality,* by Sigmund Freud. New York: Basic Books.

Marks, Elain. 1979. "Lesbian Intertextuality." In *Homosexualities and French Literature,* ed. G. Stambolian and E. Marks, 353–77. Ithaca, N.Y.: Cornell University Press.

Marry, Bernard. 1979. *Les Grands magasins.* Paris: Picard.

Masson, Jeffrey Moussaieff. 1986. *A Dark Science: Women, Sexuality, and Psychiatry in the Nineteenth Century.* New York: Farrar, Straus, & Giroux.

———. 1992. *The Assault on Truth: Freud's Suppression of the Seduction Theory.* New York: Harper Collins.

Mauss, Marcel. 1968–1969. *Œuvres.* 2 vols. Edited by Victor Karady. Paris: Minuit.

Maza, Sarah. 1991. "The Diamond Necklace Affair Revisited (1785–1786): The Case of the Missing Queen." *Eroticism and the Body Politic,* ed. L. Hunt, 63–89. Baltimore: Johns Hopkins University Press.

Merrick, Jeffrey. 1996. "The Marquis de Villette and Mademoiselle de Roucourt: Representations of Male and Female Sexual Deviance in Late Eighteenth-Century France." In *Homosexuality in Modern France,* ed. J. Merrick and B. T. Ragan, Jr., 30–53. New York: Oxford University Press.

Micale, Mark S. 1990. "Charcot and the Idea of Hysteria in the Male: Gender and Mental Science, and Medical Diagnosis in Late Nineteenth-Century France." *Medical History* 34: 363–411.

———. 1995. *Approaching Hysteria: Disease and Its Interpretations.* Princeton, N.J.: Princeton University Press.

Miller, Michael B. 1981. *The Bon Marché: Bourgeois Culture and the Department Store, 1869–1920.* Princeton, N.J.: Princeton University Press.

Misch, Georg. [1907] 1950. *A History of Autobiography. Vol. 1: Antiquity.* Translated by E. W. Dickes. London: Routledge & Kegan Paul.

Mosse, George L. 1968. "Max Nordau and his Degeneration," introduction to *Degeneration* by Max Nordau. Lincoln: University of Nebraska Press.

———. 1985. *Nationalism and Sexuality: Respectability and Abnormal Sexuality in Modern Europe.* New York: Fertig.

Moulin, Patricia. 1982. "Extenuating Circumstances." In *I, Pierre Rivière, having slaughtered my mother, my sister, and my brother. . . . A case of parricide in the 19th century,* ed. Michel Foucault, trans. F. Jellinek, 212–218. Lincoln: University of Nebraska Press.

Mumford, Kevin J. 1992. "'Lost Manhood' Found: Male Sexual Impotence and Victorian Culture in the United States." *Journal of the History of Sexuality* 3: 33–57.

Neuman, Robert P. 1975. "Masturbation, Madness, and the Modern Concept of Childhood and Adolescence." *Journal of Social History* 8: 1–22.

Newton, Esther. 1972. *Mother Camp: Female Impersonators in America.* Englewood Cliffs, N.J.: Prentice Hall.

Nye, Robert A. 1975. *The Origins of Crowd Psychology. Gustave Le Bon and the Crisis of Mass Democracy in the Third Republic.* London: Sage.

———. 1984. *Crime, Madness and Politics in Modern France. The Medical Concept of National Decline.* Princeton, N.J.: Princeton University Press.

———. 1989. "Sex Difference and Male Homosexuality in French Medical Discourse, 1800–1930." *Bulletin of the History of Medicine* 63: 32–51.

———. 1993a. *Masculinity and Male Codes of Honor in Modern France.* New York: Oxford University Press.

———. 1993b. "The Medical Origins of Sexual Fetishism." In *Fetishism as Cultural Discourse,* ed. E. Apter and W. Pietz, 13–30. Ithaca, N.Y.: Cornell University Press.

O'Brien, Patricia. 1983. "The Kleptomania Diagnosis: Bourgeois Women and Theft in Late Nineteenth-Century France." *Journal of Social History* 17: 65–77.

Okin, Susan Moller. 1979. *Women in Western Political Thought.* Princeton, N.J.: Princeton University Press.

Oosterhuis, Harry. 1991. "Homosexual Emancipation in Germany Before 1933: Two Traditions." In *Homosexuality and Male Bonding in Pre-Nazi Germany: Original Transcripts from* Der Eigene, ed. H. Oosterhuis, 1–28. New York: Haworth.

————. 1997. "Richard von Krafft-Ebing's 'Step-Children of Nature': Psychiatry and the Making of Modern Sexual Identity." In *Science and Homosexualities,* ed. Vernon Rosario, 67–88. New York: Routledge.

Outram, Dorinda. 1989. *The Body and the French Revolution.* New Haven, Conn.: Yale University Press.

Papetti, Yolande, et al. 1980. *La Passion des étoffes chez un neuropsychiatre, G. G. de Clérambault.* Paris: Solin.

Park, Katherine. 1997. "The Rediscovery of the Clitoris: French Medicine and the *Tribade,* 1570–1630. In *The Body in Parts: Discourses and Anatomies in Early Modern Europe,* ed. Carla Mazzio and David Hillman. New York: Routledge. Forthcoming.

Pauvert, Jean-Jacques. 1994. *Nouveaux (et moins nonveaux) visages de la censure* and *L'affaire Sade.* Paris: Belles Lettres.

Perron, Roger. 1988. *Histoire de la psychanalyse.* Paris: Presses Universitaires de France.

Pick, Daniel. 1989. *Faces of Degeneration, A European Disorder, c.1848–c.1918.* Cambridge: Cambridge University Press.

Pietropaolo, Domenico. 1992. "Love, Sex, and Eugenics in the *City of the Sun.*" In *Eros and Anteros: The Medical Traditions of Love in the Renaissance,* ed. D. Beecher and M. Ciavolella, 134–45. Ottawa: Dovehouse Editions.

Pietz, William. 1985. "The Problem of the Fetish I." *Res* 9: 5–17.

————. 1987. "The Problem of the Fetish II: The Origin of the Fetish." *Res* 13: 23–45.

————. 1988. "The Problem of the Fetish IIIa: Bosman's Guinea and the Enlightenment Theory of Fetishism." *Res* 16: 105–23.

————. 1993. "Fetishism and Materialism: The Limits of Theory in Marx." In *Fetishism as Cultural Discourse,* ed. E. Apter and W. Pietz, 119–51. Ithaca, N.Y.: Cornell University Press.

Pigeaud, Jackie. 1992. "Reflections on Love-Melancholy in Robert Burton." In *Eros and Anteros: The Medical Traditions of Love in the Renaissance,* ed. D. Beecher and M. Ciavolella, 211–31. Ottawa: Dovehouse Editions.

Pollard, Patrick. 1991. *André Gide: Homosexual Moralist.* New Haven, Conn.: Yale University Press.

Porter, Roy. 1995. "Forbidden Pleasures." In *Solitary Pleasures: The Historical, Literary and Artistic Discourses of Auto-Eroticism,* ed. P. Bennett and V. Rosario, 75–98. New York: Routledge.

Portmann, Marie-Louise. 1980. "Relations d'Auguste Tissot (1728–1797) médecin à Lausanne, avec le patriciat bernois." *Gesnerus* 37: 21–27.

Pribram, Karl, and Merton Gill. 1976. *Freud's "Project" Reassessed: Preface to Contemporary Cognitive Theory and Neuropsychology.* New York: Basic Books.

Ragan, Bryant T., Jr. 1996. "The Enlightenment Confronts Homosexuality." In *Homosexuality in Modern France,* ed. J. Merrick and B. T. Ragan, Jr., 8–29. New York: Oxford University Press.

Regis, Emmanuel, and Angelo Hesnard. 1914. *La Psychanalyse des nevroses et des psychoses.* Paris: F. Alcan.

Rey, Michel. 1987. "Parisian Homosexuals Create a Lifestyle, 1700–1750: The Police Archives." In *'Tis Nature's Fault: Unauthorized Sexuality during the Enlightenment,* ed. R. P. Maccubbin, 179–91. Cambridge: Cambridge University Press.

———. 1989. "Police and Sodomy in Eighteenth-Century Paris: From Sin to Disorder." In *The Pursuit of Sodomy: Male Homosexuality in Renaissance and Enlightenment Europe,* ed. K. Gerard and G. Heckma, 129–46. New York: Haworth.

Rosario, Vernon. 1992. "Sexual Liberalism and Compulsory Heterosexuality." *Contemporary French Civilization* 16(2): 262–79.

Roudinesco, Elisabeth. 1982. *La Bataille de cent ans: histoire de la psychanalyse en France. Vol. 1: 1885–1939.* Paris: Ramsay.

Rousseau, George S. 1982. "Nymphomania, Bienville and the Rise of Erotic Sensibility." In *Sexuality in Eighteenth-Century Britain,* ed. P.-G. Boucé, 95–119. Totowa, N.J.: Manchester University Press.

Russett, Cynthia E. 1989. *Sexual Science: The Victorian Construction of Womanhood.* Cambridge, Mass.: Harvard University Press.

Schiebinger, Londa. 1989. *The Mind Has No Sex? Women in the Origins of Modern Science.* Cambridge, Mass.: Harvard University Press.

Schiller, Francis. 1979. *Paul Broca. Founder of French Anthropology, Explorer of the Brain.* Berkeley: University of California Press.

Schwarz, Gerhart S. 1973. "Devices to prevent masturbation." *Medical Aspects of Human Sexuality* 6(May): 141–53.

Schwartz, Joel. 1984. *The Sexual Politics of Jean-Jacques Rousseau.* Chicago: University of Chicago Press.

Sedgwick, Eve Kosofsky. 1988. "Privilege of Unknowing." *Genders* 1: 102–24.

Segal, Jonathan. H. 1989. "Erotomania Revisited: From Kraepelin to *DSM-III-R.*" *American Journal of Psychiatry* 146: 1261–66.

Seguier, Hubert. 1966. "Revue historique de la notion de kleptomanie." *L'Encéphale* 55: 336–69, 452–66.

Setz, Wolfram, ed. 1991. *Der Roman eines Konträrsexuellen.* Berlin: Verlag rosa Winkel.

Sewell, Brocard. 1963. *Two Friends: John Gray and André Raffalovich.* Aylesford, Eng.: Saint Albert's Press.

———. 1968. *Footnote to the Nineties: A Memoir of John Gray and André Raffalovich.* London: Cecil & Amelia Woolf.

Showalter, Elaine. 1985. *The Female Malady: Women, Madness and English Culture, 1830–1980.* New York: Pantheon.

———. 1993. "Hysteria, Feminism, and Gender." In *Hysteria Beyond Freud,* Sander Gilman et al., 286–344. Berkeley: University of California Press.

Shuttleworth, Sally. 1990. "Female Circulation: Medical Discourse and Popular Advertising in the Mid-Victorian Era." In *Body/Politics: Women and the Discourses of Science,* ed. M. Jacobus, E. Fox Keller, and S. Shuttleworth, 47–68. New York: Routledge.

Sibalis, Michael. 1996. "The Regulation of Male Homosexuality in Revolutionary and Napoleonic France, 1789–1715." In *Homosexuality in Modern France,* ed. J. Merrick and B. T. Ragan, Jr., 80–101. New York: Oxford University Press.

Sicherman, Barbara. 1977. "The Uses of a Diagnosis: Doctors, Patients and Neuras-thenia." *Journal of the History of Medicine* 32: 33–54.

Siddall, A. Clair. 1982. "Chlorosis—Etiology Reconsidered." *Bulletin of the History of Medicine* 56: 254–60.

Signer, Stephen. 1991. "De Clérambault's Concept of Erotomania and Its Place in His Thought." *History of Psychiatry* 2: 409–17.

Silverman, Debora. 1989. *Art Nouveau in Fin-de-Siècle France.* Berkeley: University of California Press.

Sissa, Giulia. 1989. "Subtle Bodies." In *Fragments for a History of the Human Body,* pt. 3, ed. M. Feher, 132–56. New York: Zone.

Smith-Rosenberg, Carroll. 1986. *Disorderly Conduct: Visions of Gender in Victorian America.* New York: Oxford University Press.

Smith-Rosenberg, Carroll, and Charles Rosenberg. 1973. "The Female Animal: Medical and Biological Views of Woman and Her Role in Nineteenth-Century America." *Journal of American History* 60: 332–56.

Spitz, René. 1953. "Authority and Masturbation, Some Remarks on a Bibliographical Investigation." *Yearbook of Psychoanalysis* 9: 113–45.

Starobinski, Jean. 1957. *Jean-Jacques Rousseau: La transparence et l'obstacle.* Paris: Gallimard.

Staum, Martin S. 1980. *Cabanis: Enlightenment and Medical Philosophy in the French Revolution.* Princeton, N.J.: Princeton University Press.

Steakley, James D. 1975. *The Homosexual Emancipation Movement in Germany.* New York: Arno Press.

———. 1997. "*Per scientiam ad justitiam:* Magnus Hirschfeld and the Politics of Innate Homosexuality." In *Science and Homosexualities,* ed. V. Rosario, 133–54. New York: Routledge.

Stengers, Jean, and Anne Van Neck. 1984. *Histoire d'une grande peur: La masturbation.* Brussels: Editions de l'Université de Bruxelles.

Stocking, George, Jr. 1968. *Race, Culture and Evolution.* New York: Free Press.

Stoller, Robert. 1985. *Observing the Erotic Imagination.* New Haven, Conn.: Yale University Press.

Sullivan, Andrew. 1995. *Virtually Normal: An Argument about Homosexuality.* New York: Alfred A. Knopf.

Sulloway, Frank. 1983. *Freud, Biologist of the Mind.* New York: Basic Books.

Szasz, Thomas S. 1970. *Ideology and Insanity.* Garden City, N.Y.: Doubleday.

Tarczylo, Théodore. 1983. *Sexe et liberté au siècle des Lumières.* Paris: Presses de la Renaissance.

Taublin, Amy. 1991. "Days of Our Lives: TV and the Thomas Hearings." *Village Voice,* 29 October, 27.

Taylor, Pamela, B. Mahendra, and John Gunn. 1983. "Erotomania in Males." *Psychological Medicine* 13: 645–50.

Thomasset, Claude, and Danielle Jacquart. 1985. *Sexualité et savoir médicale au Moyen Age.* Paris: Presses Universitaires de France.

Todorov, Tzvetan. 1970. *Introduction à la littérature fantastique.* Paris: Seuil.

Trumbach, Randolph. 1987. "Sodomitical Subcultures, Sodomitical Roles, and the Gender Revolution of the Eighteenth Century: The Recent Historiography." In *'Tis Nature's Fault: Unauthorized Sexuality during the Enlightenment.* ed. R. P. Maccubin, 108–21. Cambridge: Cambridge University Press.

———. 1989. "The Birth of the Queen: Sodomy and the Emergence of Gender Equality in Modern Culture, 1660–1750." In *Hidden from History: Reclaiming the Gay and Lesbian Past,* ed. M. B. Duberman, M. Vicinus, and G. Chauncey, Jr., 129–40. New York: New American Library.

Turkle, Sherry. 1992. *Psychoanalytic Politics: Jacques Lacan and Freud's French Revolution.* 2d ed. New York: Basic Books.

Veith, Ilza. 1965. *Hysteria: History of a Disease.* Chicago: Chicago University Press.

Vircondelet, Alain. 1990. *Joris Karl Huysmans.* Paris: Plon.

Voisin, Marcel. 1981. *Le Soleil et la nuit. L'imaginaire dans l'œuvre de Théophile Gautier.* Brussels: Éditions de l'Université de Bruxelles.

Wack, Mary F. 1990. *Lovesickness in the Middle Ages: The Viaticum and Its Commentaries.* Philadelphia: University of Pennsylvania Press.

Wagner, Peter. 1991. "Anticatholic Erotica in Eighteenth-Century England." In *Erotica and the Enlightenment,* ed. P. Wagner, 166–209. Frankfurt: Verlag Peter Lang.

Walkowitz, Judith R. 1982. "Jack the Ripper and the Myth of Male Violence." *Feminist Studies* 8(3): 543–74.

Weber, Eugen. 1986. *France: Fin-de-Siècle.* Cambridge, Mass.: Harvard University Press.

Weeks, Jeffrey. 1976. "'Sins and Diseases': Some Notes on Homosexuality in the Nineteenth Century." *History Workshop* 1: 211–19.

———. 1977. *Coming Out: Homosexual Politics in Britain from the Nineteenth Century to the Present.* London: Quartet Books.

Weiner, Dora. 1970. "Le droit de l'homme à la santé. Une Belle idée devant l'Assemblée Constituante: 1790–1791." *Clio Medica* 5: 209–23.

———. 1974. "Public Health under Napoleon, the Conseil de Salubrité de Paris, 1802–1815." *Clio Medica* 9: 271–84.

———. 1993. *The Citizen-Patient in Revolutionary and Imperial Paris.* Baltimore: Johns Hopkins University Press.

Williams, Elizabeth A. 1994. *The Physical and the Moral: Anthropology, Physiology, and Philosophical Medicine in France, 1750–1850.* Cambridge: Cambridge University Press.

Williams, Huntington. 1983. *Rousseau and Romantic Autobiography.* Oxford: Oxford University Press.

Williams, Rosalind H. 1982. *Dream Worlds: Mass Consumption in Late Nineteenth-Century France.* Berkeley: University of California Press.

Wolf, Theta H. 1973. *Alfred Binet.* Chicago: University of Chicago Press.

Wolff, Charlotte. 1986. *Magnus Hirschfeld: A Portrait of a Pioneer in Sexology.* London: Quartet Books.

Zilboorg, Gregory. 1941. *History of Medical Psychology.* New York: W. W. Norton.

Zerilli, Linda M. G. 1994. *Signifying Woman: Culture and Chaos in Rousseau, Burke, and Mill.* Ithaca, N.Y.: Cornell University Press.

# INDEX

All laws are grouped under the entry for "Laws"
Medical cases with abbreviated names are grouped
under the entry for "Cases"